Shakespeare and the

Comedy of Forgiveness

Shakespeare
and the
Comedy of Forgiveness

ROBERT GRAMS HUNTER

Columbia University Press
New York and London, 1965

Robert Grams Hunter is Associate Professor of English at
Dartmouth College.

This study, prepared under the Graduate Faculties of Columbia University,
was selected by a committee of those Faculties to receive one of the Clarke
F. Ansley awards given annually by Columbia University Press.

Acknowledgments

This book owes a great deal to those members of the Department of English at Columbia who read it when it was submitted to them as a Ph.D. dissertation. My greatest debt is to my adviser, Professor S. F. Johnson, and I hope this study is in some degree worthy of the example of his scholarship. Professors W. W. Appleton and Robert Brustein were extremely helpful and encouraging. Friends who read and criticized portions of the manuscript include Richard Gregg, Philip Handler, Chauncey Loomis, Darrell Mansell, Thomas Vance, and Brian Wilkie. Dartmouth College helped me by giving me a term free from teaching duties and by providing me with funds for clerical assistance. Finally, I am grateful to Lois Sloane for her help in preparing the manuscript for the publisher.

ROBERT GRAMS HUNTER

Dartmouth College
July, 1964

Contents

Shakespeare and the
Comedy of Forgiveness

Introduction

"In the workshop," "in the world," "out of the depths," "on the heights." [1] Edward Dowden created a "life" for Shakespeare that is itself almost an allegorical drama, a Playwright's Progress. By assuming that Shakespeare was sad when he wrote sad plays and merry when he wrote merry ones, Dowden convinced himself and a great many others that the emotional and spiritual biography of Shakespeare was available to us. His biographical theories are now largely discredited as naïvely assuming far too direct a connection between the spiritual, emotional, and intellectual condition of an artist and the kind of work he turns out. It is, after all, perfectly possible that Shakespeare was in the depths when he wrote *The Merry Wives of Windsor* and on the heights as he completed the last scene of *King Lear*. And yet the pattern which emerged for Dowden from the canon of Shakespeare's plays, as opposed to the deductions he made about the writer's life, still seems to be generally accepted, tacitly or otherwise, as valid. Fundamentally this is because Dowden's pattern *is* valid—and useful—and yet in some cases it has, I think, prevented students of Shakespeare from seeing the connections that exist between works from the different periods of Dowden's handy scheme. This is particularly true of the "depths" and the "heights" comedies. All too often we are told by the more impressionistic critics (those gourmets of culture) that *Measure for Measure* and *All's Well That Ends Well* are cold, bitter, and dark, while *Cymbeline, The Winter's Tale,* and *The Tempest* are warm, sweet, and glowing. Recently this particular oversimplification has come in for questioning. We are beginning to discover that "there is a strong case for avoiding the traditional separation of 'problem plays' from 'romances' and considering as a group the 'later comedies.' " [2]

This study will be an attempt at such a consideration, or rather, more modestly, it will be an attempt to investigate one feature—the denouement in forgiveness—which is common to five of the later comedies (*All's Well That Ends Well, Measure for Measure, Cymbeline, The Winter's Tale,* and *The Tempest*) together with one of the earlier comedies, *Much Ado About Nothing.* I am in some doubt, however, as to whether the common feature which I see as uniting these plays may properly be regarded as thematic or structural, or both —if, indeed, the two can be separated, for perhaps theme and structure are mutually interdependent in the drama. In any case, the term "structure" is itself a rather bothersome one. What precisely does a play's structure consist of?

Because a drama is an event in time, it has to have a beginning, a middle, and an end. When the story which a play tells is rationally constructed, these three parts are found, on the authority of the Alexandrian grammarians, to do three essential narrative jobs. In the beginning (the protasis) "the characters are introduced and the subject entered on"; in the middle (the epitasis) "the plot thickens"; at the end (the catastrophe) comes "the change or revolution which produces the conclusion or final event of a dramatic piece." [3] All this is admirably straightforward, unarguably objective, and perhaps even a bit obvious.

When, however, we stop talking about narrative or dramatic "structure" in general and begin to narrow our discussion to the structure of what Northrop Frye has called a "narrative category" [4] within the dramatic genre, something rather disturbing occurs. We discover that in comedy "the catastrophe is the conversion of affairs into a happy ending." [5] "Happy" is an intrusively subjective qualification here and prompts the question, "Happy for whom?" For the characters in the play? Certainly not—or at least, not necessarily. The catastrophe of *L'École des Femmes,* for example, is not in the least happy for its leading character, Arnolphe (whom we last see "S'en allant tout transporté et ne pouvant parler"). Clearly the ending of a comedy is happy because it pleases the characters of whom we, the members of the audience, approve.

The larger structural parts of comedy, in addition to establishing certain narrative facts, depict events which are designed to arouse certain emotional responses in the spectator. In romantic comedy, the protasis arouses desire, the epitasis frustrates that desire, and the catastrophe satisfies it. The audience at a romantic comedy is first presented with a situation which it wants to see brought to a certain outcome. That desire is then frustrated by the creation of barriers to the wished-for solution. Finally, desire is satisfied by the overcoming of those barriers and the achievement of the outcome which the audience has wanted. Let us consider a clear example of this sequence in action.

Structurally, Plautus' *Stichus* must be one of the simplest comedies ever written. In it two sisters are happily married to two brothers. The men have left town on an extended business trip. The women miss them dreadfully. The men return eager to make love to their wives, and they do so, off-stage, while on-stage their slaves eat, drink, and make merry. That is all and it is enough. The play communicates its emotional movement from frustration to happiness and as a result the *Stichus* is a satisfactory comic experience.

The desire which is aroused in the protasis and frustrated in the epitasis of this play is sexual. That is, the wives at the beginning of the play express their desire for their husbands and we, the members of the audience, desire that their desires should be satisfied. The frustrating force is lack of proximity. The men and women who desire one another are not in the same place. Now this may appear to be unquestionably the archetypal sexual frustration—the Ur-frustration, so to speak—but, in fact, in comedy and perhaps in life, the satisfaction of desire is usually prevented by something more complex than the fact that it takes a certain amount of time to traverse a certain amount of space. This simplicity in the frustrating force explains the simplicity of the *Stichus* as a whole. In comedy the major action (the epitasis) of the drama usually grows out of whatever it is that prevents the happy ending from taking place in Act One. For example, the frustrating force in most New Comedy is basically poverty. The young man is without the cash necessary to pay for the slave girl or prostitute he desires, and the main action of the play develops from the clever slave's attempts to get the money for his master. The frustrating forces must be dramatized and so the aspects of the young man's poverty are personified, usually as a rich but stingy father, representing the difficulty of supply, and an avaricious *leno* (pimp slave-dealer) standing for the exigency of demand.

Personification of the frustrating force raises a problem for the comic dramatist. Since, in comedy, frustrating forces have to be defeated, the characters who personify such forces must share in that defeat, but the spectacle of human beings suffering defeat cannot be allowed to interfere with the happiness that an audience expects at the conclusion of comedy. In order to make sure that such interference does not occur, the dramatist may do one of two things. He may engineer a change of mind which will make it possible for the frustrator to participate in the happy ending. Or he may make the frustrating agent so repulsive in character that the audience's pleasure will be increased by the spectacle of his degradation and rejection. In terms of the New Comedy plot outlined above, he may reconcile the father and reject the *leno*.

The sort of comedy we have so far been considering assumes a concluding happiness desired by the protagonists, the sort of comedy in which boy wants girl, girl wants boy, and external forces act to keep them from getting what they want. Shakespearean comedy is, however, very often not of this kind. Boy may begin by wanting girl, but change his mind halfway through the play, as happens with Claudio in *Much Ado About Nothing*. Or he may reject the girl immediately and decisively when she is first offered to him, as Bertram rejects Helena in *All's Well That Ends Well*. This typically Shakespearean variation on the basic romantic comedy situation is one which raises certain problems. Instead of mutual desire frustrated by a third force, we have a situation in which desire is frustrated by the object of desire, in which the functions of the comic hero and the comic villain are to some degree combined.

Such a combination is awkward in terms of audience response. The first job of the comic dramatist is to make us want the happy ending toward which his play is moving, as Shakespeare makes us want the happiness of Helena in the first scene of *All's Well*. Helena wants to marry Bertram and be loved by him, while the audience wants to enjoy the spectacle of Helena marrying Bertram and being loved by him. The audience, when its desire is frustrated, dislikes the frustrator of it. But the frustrator, Bertram, remains the object of the heroine's desire, the *sine qua non* of the play's happy ending. Shakespeare is now faced with a paradox. He must give his play a happy ending by granting felicity to a character whom his audience dislikes. Fortunately this paradox is emotional rather than logical and any drama is a playing with the emotions of an audience. Shakespeare must now set about the job of reconciling our hearts to Bertram. Bertram has offended us and Shakespeare must coax us into forgiving him. Within the play, Bertram has offended Helena. The strength of her love for him makes her forgiveness of him a foregone conclusion. Bertram has also offended the world of his play, the society of which he is a member. This society, represented by his king and his mother, must also forgive him and it does. If the play is to succeed fully as a work of art, however, the audience must acquiesce in these forgivenesses. We, too, must forgive Bertram. Whether or not this, in fact, happens, and why it does or does not, have been the subjects of a great deal of speculation—speculation which will be considered, and added to, in the course of this discussion.

All's Well That Ends Well is by no means the only Shakespearean comedy which depends upon forgiveness for its comic denouement. I have already mentioned *Much Ado About Nothing*, with its painful scene of the rejection of the heroine and its subsequent presentation of Claudio's guilt, remorse, and final forgiveness. Posthumus in *Cymbeline* offends, as Claudio had offended, by allowing himself to believe the lies of a villain. His remorse, unlike Claudio's, precedes rather than follows his discovery of the heroine's innocence. Though he still thinks she is guilty, he comes to the conclusion that the sin of which Imogen is accused is venial by comparison with the vengeance which Posthumus thinks he has exacted for it. In *The Winter's Tale,* it is the offense rather than the remorse that is self-generated. Leontes does not need the sevices of a Don John or a Iachimo to convince him of Hermione's infidelity and only the intervention of heaven disabuses him of his delusions. The pain of his remorse is proportionately the more intense, therefore.

The crimes which Claudio, Bertram, Posthumus, and Leontes commit are crimes against love. Romantic comedy demands that its heroes embody an ideal of romantic love. These Shakespearean heroes fall short of that ideal and must be forgiven for doing so. The sins which require forgiveness in *Measure for Measure* and *The Tempest* are of another order. Angelo offends first by trying to impose an impossibly strict sexual ethic on the citizens of Vienna, and then by trying to use his authority to force Isabella to sleep with him. The main concern in *Measure for Measure* is with problems of authority, morality, and religion—with the effects of Angelo's action on Isabella's ideal of sexual purity and the duke's ideal of human justice. In *The Tempest,* Shakespeare has varied the structure of his romantic comedy by using two plots: the romantic love story of Ferdinand and Miranda, and the forgiveness story with Alonso at its center. The happy outcomes of these plots are interdependent. The happiness of Ferdinand and Miranda depends upon the reconciliation of their fathers through Alonso's remorse and Prospero's forgiveness of him. The love of the children, in turn, ratifies the reconciliation of the fathers. In these two plays, then, the offenses to be forgiven are not primarily against the ideal of romantic love, but the forgiveness of the offenders is necessary if the plays are to end in the moment of love and reconciliation appropriate to the tone and action of these comedies.

Whatever the nature of the offenses committed in these six plays, the audience must be brought to acquiesce in the forgiveness of the

offenders. This has not always happened. *All's Well* is the clearest example of a play which has frequently failed to communicate its final
forgiveness of the hero. "I cannot reconcile my heart to Bertram,"
says Dr. Johnson. "A man noble without generosity and young without truth; who marries *Helen* as a coward, and leaves her as a profli-
gate: when she is dead by his unkindness, sneaks home to a second
marriage, is accused by a woman he has wronged, defends himself by
falshood, and is dismissed to happiness." [6] Clearly the forgiveness of
Bertram was not shared by Dr. Johnson. His attack is one which, if
admitted to be valid, certainly pulverizes the play subjected to it. That
validity has, of course, been denied, but the denial has taken a form
that is ultimately more damaging to the play than Dr. Johnson's strictures, for to maintain, as Coleridge does, that Bertram is really a very
good fellow, "a young nobleman in feudal times, just bursting into
manhood, with all the feelings of pride of birth and appetite for pleasure and liberty natural to such a character," is to make it necessary to
regard the king as a tyrant. As for Helena, if Bertram is in the right,
then, inevitably, "it must be confessed that her character is not very
delicate" [7]—and we are no longer discussing Shakespeare's play.
Dr. Johnson is right in insisting that Bertram behaves badly—very,
very badly. The point is that we are asked to forgive him all the same.
This is to some degree true of Claudio in *Much Ado*, of Posthumus,
of Leontes, of Alonso (though his bad behavior takes place before the
play begins). It is supremely true of Angelo. Even Coleridge cannot
see Angelo as merely high-spirited, and the results of his being unable
to do so are instructive. He attacks the play more savagely than Dr.
Johnson had attacked *All's Well* and he does so, what is more, on the
same grounds. "The pardon and marriage of Angelo . . . baffles the
strong indignant claims of justice (for cruelty, with lust and damnable baseness, cannot be forgiven, because we cannot conceive of
them as being *morally* repented of)." [8]

The necessity for pardon has not proved so much of a stumbling
block to the success of Shakespeare's four other comedies of forgiveness. In *Much Ado* Shakespeare has been at some pains to provide his

hero with excuses for his conduct, and in any case the charm of Beatrice, Benedick, and Dogberry effectively diverts the audience from most of the uneasiness they might feel about what is ostensibly the play's main plot. In the late romances, the emphasis falls very heavily upon the remorse which precedes the offender's forgiveness, and, as a result, the moment of forgiveness, when it comes, has been more fully prepared for than it is in the earlier comedies. Though the difficulty of the interpretive problems raised by the pardoning of the offenders varies from play to play, these six comedies nevertheless form a group whose members are similar in structure and concerned with analogous themes and emotions. Consideration of them as a group ought to illuminate each of them as a single work of art.

I should like to begin that consideration by studying the literary tradition to which these plays belong. The moment of forgiveness common to all six is, of course, a crucial point in terms of audience response. The reactions of Johnson and Coleridge to two of these plays demonstrate that clearly enough. Those reactions do not provide evidence, however, for believing either that these two very great critics were insensitive readers, or that Shakespeare was an incompetent playwright. They demonstrate, rather, that in these plays Shakespeare was working in a dramatic tradition that was outmoded before Johnson's time. That tradition was originally medieval and didactically Christian. In the course of the sixteenth century it became secularized, along with the rest of the drama. Nonetheless, the resemblance of Shakespeare's comedies of forgiveness to their medieval prototypes is strong, and it helps to define the nature of the later plays.

In tracing the tradition to which Shakespeare's comedies of forgiveness belong, I shall not confine myself exclusively to dramatic literature. Drama and narrative have always existed in a symbiotic relationship, nourishing one another, and the continuity between medieval and Renaissance drama is, in part, a result of the fact that the playwrights of both periods were dramatizing the same kind of story. They were also drawing on the shared beliefs and attitudes of their audiences, as all dramatists must, and the beliefs and attitudes that surrounded the concept of forgiveness were, in the Middle Ages and Renaissance, Christian. To illustrate the nature of these beliefs, I shall make some use of the theologians, particularly Aquinas and Luther, and my main source for the Shakespearean era will be that great repository of orthodox Elizabethan attitudes, *The Book of Homilies.* Finally, however, I shall not be primarily interested in defining what the plays I consider have to say about the Christian doctrine of the forgiveness of sins.[9] Instead, I shall try first to show how that doctrine inspired the development of a literary form, and then to demonstrate the importance of a sympathetic understanding of that doctrine for the success of certain individual works of art.

Forgiveness of Sins in the
Medieval Drama

The forgiveness of sins is necessarily a central concern in the religious drama of the Middle Ages. For all three of the medieval theatrical genres—mystery, morality, and miracle—the paramount question is that of God's forgiveness of sinful humanity. The mystery cycles concern themselves with the fall, salvation, and final judgment of man and the fundamental lesson of Christianity is repeated endlessly in these plays. God's mercy is freely extended to all mankind, without exception. In order to profit by this mercy, sinful man must accept it. He must acknowledge Christ's sacrifice as the cause of his salvation. The power of faith is not, however, the finally decisive force in assuring man's salvation according to the mystery cycles. In the great climactic scenes of God's Judgment upon the latter day, the saved are invariably seen as differentiated from the damned by the quality of their works. To be sure, those who will be saved are far from feeling any pharisaical complacency about their chances. They consider themselves miserable sinners. They doubt their righteousness and even the efficacy of their sufferings in purgatory, and they beg for mercy:

> When I in earth was at my will,
> this world me blent, bothe lowd and still,
> but thy Commandement to fulfill
> I was full negligent.
>
> But purgyd it is with paynes ill,
> in Purgatory that sore can grill;

> Yet thy grace I hope to come till,
> after my great Torment.
>
> And yet, lord, I must dreed thee
> for my great sinnes, when I thee se,
> for thou art most in maiesty;
> for mercy now I call.   (65–76)[1]

So says the "Papa Salvatus" of the Chester *Last Judgment*. It is, however, what he *did* on earth that saves him and his lucky fellows from
the torments that await the "Papa damnatus" and his companions.

The text on which the Last Judgments of the mysteries are based is
Matthew 25:31–46, and indeed they are so close to that description
of the latter day as hardly to deserve the term expansion. In the York
Cycle,[2] for example, Christ, addressing the blessed children on his
right hand, says:

> Whenne I was hungry ye me fedde,
> To slake my thirste youre harte was free,
> Whenne I was clothles ye me cledde,
> Ye wolde no sorowe uppon me see.   (285–88)

Which makes the good souls wonder:

> Whanne hadde we, lorde, that all has wroght,
> Meete and drinke the with to feede?
> Sen we in erthe hadde neuere noght
> But thurgh the grace of thy godhede.   (301–4)

And they receive the reply:

> Mi blissid childir, I schall you saye,
> What tyme this dede was to me done,
> When any that nede hadde, nyght or day,
> Askid you helpe and hadde it sone.   (309–12)

The good ascend to their reward where "joie and blisse schall ever
be." The wicked, who failed to realize that charity shown to their

fellow man is shown to God, are turned over to "Satanas the fende."

The final effect of the mysteries, therefore, is to give their audiences a picture of God's justice as a meting out of deserved rewards and punishments. Their didactic purpose was to persuade men to act righteously, and their method was that of the hell-fire sermon dramatized. The horrible fate that awaits the unforgiven sinner is the final image of these dramas.

One should remember, in considering the medieval and sixteenth-century attitudes toward the problems of mercy and forgiveness, that, for the men of these periods, the virtue of justice was not notable for any admixture of benignity. Deeds of what seem to us abominable cruelty were regarded as praiseworthy when they were performed in justice's name. King Cambises was a cruel tyrant who had one of his councilors flayed alive, but he was not considered cruel and tyrannical for that reason. His flaying alive of Sisamnes was "his one good deede of execution," [3] a sterling example of even-handed justice at work. The print entitled *Justitia* in Breughel's series of engravings of the Virtues[4] strikes the modern sensibility as the daydream of a sadist —so much so that we suspect, probably quite unjustifiably, that the title is meant as the bitterest irony. Justice implied the horrible but deserved sufferings of the guilty and God's justice implied them in the highest degree. The hair-raising visions of the Last Judgment by the Northern painters of the fifteenth century were meant to hang in the courtroom as well as in the chapel, and to serve as a reminder that the process in which judge, jury, and accused were there engaged was only a type of the final moment of justice which they would all one day face.[5] The example of heavenly justice would presumably inspire its earthly ministers to emulate its perfect impartiality and also discourage them from a leniency that might encourage in the criminal further sin and eventual damnation and an eternal suffering far more painful than anything mere man could inflict. Since God's justice was sure and terrible, and since all men are sinners, the prospect of which the final scene of the mystery cycles reminded their audiences cannot have been entirely pleasing.

Fortunately for the sanity of our ancestors, however, the relationship of God to man has many aspects and the terror of his justice is only one of them. His mercy also plays its role in determining man's fate and the Last Judgment is not the only moment in the history of mankind at which the medieval dramatist pictures God as considering, in a quasi-judicial way, the alternatives of punishment and salvation for his erring creatures. Another such moment comes when God is conceived of as deciding to allow Christ to offer himself as a scapegoat for the sins of humanity. The most famous literary representation of this decision comes in Book III of *Paradise Lost*, but the scene had been depicted again and again since at least the early twelfth century. The form that it took in the Middle Ages is generally known as the debate of the Four Daughters of God.[6]

This debate is an allegorical dramatization of the dialectic of divine mercy. Its ultimate origin is in one verse of Psalm 85: "Mercy and truth are met together; righteousness and peace have kissed each other." These lines and the Jewish commentary upon them in the Midrach appealed strongly to the allegorizing mystics of the twelfth century. Both St. Bernard of Clairvaux and Hugo of Tours developed this image into allegory. St. Bernard's version, which was to have the larger influence, tells the following story: After the fall of Adam, the four virtues presented to God their opinions of what should constitute man's fate. To Justice and Truth it is quite clear that man must suffer punishment for his crime. Anything else would constitute a mockery of what Justice and Truth are. Mercy opposes their counsels and points out that the punishment of man would mean the overthrow of Mercy. Peace deplores the altercation. God considers the dilemma and solves it. He proposes that if a being, "himself guiltless, should die out of love for man, Death could not hold him, for Love, being stronger than Death, would enter Death's home and bind him, and so free the dead."[7] Truth and Mercy search heaven and earth for an acceptable candidate for this sacrifice until Christ takes the burden upon himself. At this point the reconciliation described by the Psalm takes place.

St. Bernard's sermon provides a welcome solution for the writer who feels called upon to dramatize the motives for God's sacrifice of his only son. Since a great many writers did feel called upon to do precisely that, St. Bernard's scene is frequently repeated in the various literatures of Europe. Nontheatrical versions in English occur in Langland's *Piers Plowman* and in Giles Fletcher's *Christ's Victory and Triumph in Heaven and Earth over and after Death,* published in Shakespeare's lifetime (1610). In the drama, the scene occurs with great frequency in what remains of the French theatre of the Middle Ages. Two English dramatic versions of the scene have survived from the fifteenth century.

In the *Ludus Coventriae,*[8] Trewth (Veritas), Mercy (Misericordia), Ryghtwysnes (Justicia), and Acorde (Pax) debate the merits of man's case before the throne of God. The episode has been moved up in time to just before Christ's descent to earth and the "pageant" ends with the Salutation and Annunciation. The arguments of Veritas and Justicia are pre-eminently true and just and rationally unanswerable. Trewth points out that to forgive man now would be to violate consistency:

> Whan Adam had synnyd thou seydest thore
> that he xulde deye and go to helle
> And now to blysse hym to resstore
> twey contraryes mow not to-gedyr dwelle.   (61–64)

Furthermore man's crime deserves all the punishment that can be visited upon him:

> that wretche that was to the so unkende
> he may not have to meche wo.   (67–68)

Mercy emphasizes man's repentance:

> hym grevyth fful gretly his transgressyon   (77)

But Justicia is not impressed:

> Xulde he be savyd. nay nay nay. (96)

and she makes the important point:

> that the ryghtwysnes of god hath no diffynicion. (100)

That is to say, God's justice (his sense of right) is boundless, without limits. Justice demands the punishment of the guilty. Man is guilty. Since God's justice cannot be circumscribed, man must be punished. Mercy is appalled:

> Systyr Ryghtwysnes ye Are to vengeabyl
>
> .   .   .   .   .
>
> Above all hese werkys god is mercyabyl. (105-7)

Pax intervenes at this point. She tactfully grants the strength of the arguments on both sides, though her nature inclines her to favor Mercy's contention:

> thow trewth and ryght sey grett reson
> Yett mercy seyth best to my pleson
> ffor yf mannys sowle xulde abyde in helle
> be-twen God and man evyr xulde be dyvysyon
> And than myght not I pes dwelle. (116-20)

She suggests that the decision be left to God and to this all four sisters agree. Christ proposes the sacrifice, no man or angel capable of it can be found, and after a "counsel of the trinite," Christ is sent to save man and the virtues are reconciled. In the words of Misericordia:

> Now is the loveday mad of us fowre fynialy
> now may we leve in pes . as we were wonte

Misericordia et veritas obviauerunt sibi
Justicia et pax. osculate sunt. (185–88)

Because the mystery plays present the history of mankind's relationship to God, the various parts of the cycle can emphasize the various aspects of God in that relationship. God's mercy can be demonstrated in the decision to allow humanity a chance of salvation through Christ's sacrifice. His justice can be shown upon the Judgment Day in the reward or punishment of each member of humanity according to the quality of his works. In the judgment scene of the mysteries, the accused are plural. Mankind is represented by men and women, good and bad. Some deserve salvation, some deserve everlasting torment, each receives his just deserts, and the member of the audience who takes warning from the punishment of the damned is able to identify himself with the saved and to leave the play determined to emulate the latter.

In the moralities, the situation is quite different. There the accused is singular, one man representative of all men. This change results in a narrative structure distinctly related to that of the comedy of forgiveness. In theme, the mystery and morality are frequently similar. Both seek to show man the nature of his relationship to God and the means by which the sinner can attain salvation. The methods of the two kinds of play are very different, however. The mystery defines the relationship of God to man by presenting its history from Creation to Last Judgment. The morality works by example. It creates a single character whose relationship to God serves to define every man's relationship to God. The process by which this representative soul attains salvation must constitute a valid example to all men of how salvation can be attained. Everyman, Mankind—whatever he is called, he must be representative of all the race. He must be a sinner, for we are all miserable sinners. He will attain salvation because God will forgive him for the offense he has committed. The morality is, therefore, a play which ends necessarily with the forgiveness of an erring hero.

The earliest of the surviving English moralities is *The Castle of Perseverance*[9] (c. 1425) and it can stand as representative of the form, at least as it was practiced in the period before the Reformation. Its hero, Mankind, sins extensively and thoroughly. By far the longer portion of this extremely long play is devoted, naturally enough, to the hero's misdeeds, the defeat of the Virtues, and the consequent ascendancy in the hero's mind and actions of Lechery, Covetousness, Pride, Sloth, and the rest. All this provides the audience with a good deal of entertainment, none of it, unfortunately, germane to our purpose. After almost three thousand lines of psychomachia, Death enters to claim Mankind, who is deserted by all the illusory pleasures of this world. On his deathbed, in the terror and suffering of his last moments, Mankind turns to God:

> I bolne & bleyke in blody ble,
> & as a flour, fadyth my face.
> to helle I schal bothe fare & fle,
> but God me graunte of his grace.
> I deye certeynly:
> now my lyfe I haue lore;
> myn hert brekyth; I syhe sore;
> a word may I speke no more;
> I putte me in Godys mercy. (3000–8)

He dies, and out from under the deathbed pops Anima, Mankind's soul. It is with his fate that the rest of the play is concerned. Because of the sinfulness of Mankind's life, his soul is in grave danger of eternal damnation. He calls repeatedly upon Mercy but there is no reply, and his bad angel is carrying him off to Hell when the Four Daughters of God enter to consider his case. What follows is roughly the same debate that takes place in the *Ludus Coventriae*. There are, however, important differences.

The four heavenly virtues ordinarily argue out the question of the appropriate fate for mankind after Adam's fall from innocence but before Christ's expiatory sacrifice. Here the case has altered.

Christ has suffered his crucifixion. The question at issue is the fate of a single, though representative, human soul. Again, the arguments of Justice and Truth are logically impeccable. Mankind deserves eternal damnation for the sins that he has committed. His last-minute repentance, if admitted as valid, will serve as a bad example to others, and to sin in the expectation of eventual forgiveness is especially damnable:

> late repentaunce, if man saue scholde,
>   wheyther he wrouth wel or wyckednesse;
> thanne euery man wolde be bolde
>   to trespas, in trost of Foryevenesse;
> For synne in hope is dampnyd, I holde;
>   For-gevyn is neuere hys trespase.   (3276–281)

Furthermore, he has failed to do the good works which might serve to counterbalance his wickedness:

> For he wolde neuere the hungry
>   neyther clothe nor fede,
> Ner drynke gyf to the thrysty,
>   nyn pore men helpe at nede.   (3473–476)

This, of course, is precisely that failure of charity which we have seen sending the damned howling to hell in the last scene of the mysteries. It does not have that effect here, however. Mercy appeals to Christ's sacrifice, which is sufficient to atone for any and all of the sins of humanity:

> Lord, thou that man hathe don more mysse thanne good,
>   if he dey in very contricioun,
> Lord, the lest drope of thi blod,
>   For hys synne makyth satisfaccioun.
> as thou deydyst, Lord, on the Rode,
>   graunt me my peticioun!

lete me, Mercy, be hys Fode,
    & graunte hym thi saluacion.   (3367–374)

But his penance has not been sufficient to merit salvation, says
Justice:

    Ouyr late he callyd confescion;
    ouer lyt was his contricion;
    he made neuere satisfaccion;
        dampne hym to helle be-lyve!   (3428–431)

In the end, however, Justice and Truth are won over by the arguments of their sisters and God decrees that, Mankind having repented at the last, he shall be judged with mercy rather than according to his deserts.

    Fayre falle thee, Pes, my dowter dere!
        on thee I thynke, & on Mercy.
    Syn ye a-cordyd beth all in fere,
        my Jugement I wyl yeue you by,
    not aftyr deseruynge, to do reddere,
        to dampne Mankynde to turmentry,
    but brynge hym to my blysse ful clere,
        In heuene to dwelle endelesly.   (3562–569)

He sends his four daughters to take Mankind from the Devil, and
the play ends with Mankind sitting on the right hand of God.

    The Debate of the Four Daughters of God, originally intended
to explain God's sacrifice of Christ, is here adapted to the dramatization of the doctrine of forgiveness of sins as it is set forth in the
Summa Theologica.[10] For St. Thomas Aquinas, the forgiveness of
sins depended upon the penance of the sinner and, with his customary care and clarity, St. Thomas defines precisely the nature of that
supremely important act. Full penance consists of three parts: contrition, confession, and satisfaction.[11] (See the speech of Justice
quoted above, lines 3428ff.) Of these, the essential is the first, con-

trition, the "voluntary sorrow for sin whereby man punishes in himself that which he grieves to have done." [12] Contrition, whether as a part of the formal sacrament of Penance, or nonsacramentally as a virtue, "is the cause of the forgiveness of sin." [13] But its nature as a cause must be carefully defined. "God alone is the principal efficient cause of the forgiveness of sin." [14] Contrition is the "dispositive cause," a material cause in the sense that it "disposes matter to receive something." [15]

Salvation comes from God's grace and his love for mankind as manifested in Christ's sacrifice. Without that grace, the forgiveness of sins is impossible. With it, forgiveness becomes dependent upon the will of the sinner. To benefit by Christ's atonement, the sinner must experience contrition, "the will to atone." [16] Contrition makes God's mercy available to men, and it is thus at the center of the answer of medieval Christianity (and consequently of medieval religious drama) to the supreme question, "What shall a man do to be saved?" Luther challenged that answer by his insistence that "the forgiveness of the guilt does not rest on the contrition of the sinner nor on the office or power of the priest. Rather it rests on faith which clings to the Word of Christ." [17] This insistence is at the heart of Luther's break with Catholicism. Though the English reformation drew its first intellectual and spiritual inspiration from Luther's revolt, it did not finally accept the *"sola fides"* as its basic doctrine regarding the forgiveness of sins. As we shall see later, the orthodoxy in which Shakespeare and his contemporaries were expected to believe (whether they did or not is another question) was very close to the *Summa Theologica* when it came to the forgiveness of sins.

A pattern of sin, contrition, and forgiveness is the basic pattern of the medieval morality. It is also, and this is important, presented by these plays as hopefully the basic pattern of the lives of each member of the audience. By precept and experience, medieval man knew himself to be a sinner—one who deserved damnation at God's hands. The morality showed him that through contrition he could avoid his deserts and win forgiveness. The morality pattern of sin, repentance, and forgiveness, and the lesson which that pattern was intended to convey are essentially shared by the third, and frequently neglected, medieval dramatic "genre," the miracle play.

The "genres" of the religious drama of the fourteenth and fifteenth centuries would seem to be clearly identifiable. It is possible to make neat distinctions between morality, mystery and miracle and it is perhaps inevitable, therefore, that scholars of the medieval drama should have insisted that two of the three forms be confused.[18] There does seem to be general agreement on the nature of the morality play, and anyone who has read an example of the form knows perfectly well what a morality is. Mystery and miracle, however, when applied to drama, are often taken to be synonymous terms. In this discussion I make the following distinction between them: the mystery is a play (or series of plays) concerned with the story of the creation, fall, redemption, and Last Judgment of man, and based primarily on incidents selected from the Old and New Testaments. The miracle, on the other hand, I take to be a nonallegorical drama, based on nonscriptural narrative, but didactically religious in purpose.

All three of these forms are obviously important in the shaping of Shakespeare's dramatic tradition. Tradition in art is what survives of the lessons learned by the artists of the past. Their solutions to the problems they encountered are available to the artists who succeed them and those successors may react to tradition either by following it or by rejecting it in favor of what seem to be better solutions. The mystery cycles and moralities taught the writers of drama a great deal about how to make plays. It is possible, however, that the miracles taught them considerably more.

The most obvious limitation of the usefulness of the cycle plays in forming a dramatic tradition is their restriction in subject matter to scriptural texts. To be sure, a great diversity exists within those limits and the writer who has successfully dramatized the murder of Abel, the episode of the woman taken in adultery, and the crucifixion of Christ has learned how to achieve a variety of dramatic effects. Once this dramatization has been done, however, the writer

of cycle plays can do little more than revise the work of his predecessors, and though such "revision" sometimes results in great drama—
witness the work of the Wakefield Master—in the end the art of the
mystery cycle necessarily becomes a kind of machine for polishing
itself. Its writers seem to have denied themselves even the originality
of dramatizing different scriptural incidents, for the selection of epi-
sodes was governed by the demands of theology rather than by those
of art. As A. P. Rossiter puts it, "a principle of selection is at work,
which takes Abraham and Isaac (because the Father's sacrifice 'pre-
figures' the Crucifixion), takes Moses (for the Commandments), but
quite rejects all the wealth of histrionic fable centring in Elijah. The
vast plot had no more use for Samuel and David than for those very
dramatic personages Jezebel and Joab. It was controlled by a logic
which was theologic." [19] The logic which controlled Shakespeare
was quite different. It was dramatic, theatrical logic, and for all
their didacticism (and often their didacticism is barely noticeable)
this is also the logic that controlled the writers of the miracle plays.

Since the subject matter of the mysteries, the incidents portrayed,
were by and large always the same, the general manner of their
presentation was bound to fall into a kind of iconographical pattern.
The dramatizer of nonscriptural materials, of *exemplum* or saint's
life, had more to think out for himself in deciding how to present any
single incident on stage. To make an analogy with another art, let us
imagine that a fifteenth-century painter is given a commission for
an Annunciation. The problem of how to convey the occurrence of
so esoteric an event is in reality very simple because the symbolism
for it has been standardized for centuries. Even the painter's compositional choices have been made for him: angel right, Virgin left,
dove above. Our artist can busy himself with deciding to dress the
Virgin in red velvet and to put the lilies on the window sill this time.
Now let us further imagine that the same painter is commissioned to
do a "St. Zenobius raising from the dead a boy who has been killed
in a fall from a horse." To complicate matters the patron insists that
within the same frame the resurrected boy be shown lovingly greeting

his uncle, the cardinal. It would be a nice compliment to the present cardinal if his features were used for those of his honored predecessor. And so on. Obviously, our painter has a far more taxing compositional problem here. Does he put the resurrection scene in the center and subordinate the cardinal, or should both incidents be given equal prominence? Where does he fit in the horse? Problems analogous to these face the dramatist who chooses or is chosen for the job of turning into a play the life of St. Fiacre or the *exemplum* of the incestuous daughter. Such narrative material is strikingly like the romances and *novelle* from which the Elizabethan writers of comedy draw their plots, and the problems involved in turning story into play invite similar solutions.

It is not, however, my purpose to present a detailed argument in favor of what seems to me the strong probability that the Elizabethan drama developed in large part from the medieval miracle play. It is true that the standard modern historians of the medieval English drama—Chambers, Rossiter, and Craig—ignore the idea or treat it very sketchily. The case for the theory has been clearly put by J. M. Manly and it seems best to refer the reader to his argument and content myself with quoting his conclusions:

> My contention is simply that the miracle play did not differ in any essential from the romantic comedy and tragedy which formed so large a part of the repertory of the companies which, under the patronage of noblemen and wealthy commoners, swarmed through England in the period immediately preceding the advent of Marlowe and Shakespeare, and consequently that it was probably in the miracle play, rather than in the better-known Scripture play and morality, that the technique and the themes of the stage of Shakespeare were developed.[20]

Let us accept Manly's contention as a working hypothesis and then proceed to investigate it by asking what effect, if any, the miracle play may have had in forming the tradition from which our six comedies emerged. To do that it is necessary first to establish precisely what the characteristics of the miracle play were. Unfortunately, that is not an easy task. Although there is abundant evidence that the miracle play "flourished in every part of England from the time of its earliest introduction, about the year 1100, down to the time of Queen Elizabeth," [21] the entire corpus of the surviving medieval miracle drama in English consists of three plays.[22] This is a meager basis for even the most ingenious speculation. Fortunately, however, the medieval drama was not confined to England. The miracle play flourished elsewhere, and in France it left behind extensive remains. From these remains a very clear idea of the nature of the genre can be gained.

In general the miracle play teaches (for like all medieval religious drama it has a didactic *raison d'etre*) by means of example. It is possible to differentiate among the three medieval dramatic genres by considering them as three distinct methods of teaching.[23] The preacher and the medieval dramatist shared the problem of making the abstract truths of the Christian religion less abstract, and they arrived at similar solutions. They used the Scriptures themselves. The doctrines of Christianity are the outgrowth of the events of the Old and New Testaments and by relating and commenting on those events, one may make vivid the doctrines which they inspired. This is the method of the mystery play. Or they make the abstract less abstract by means of metaphor. "The mind of man is a battlefield for the Virtues and Vices." Extend the metaphor and you have allegory—the *Psychomachia* of Prudentius, or *The Castle of Perseverance*. Finally, they illustrate doctrine by example, as Christ himself so brilliantly illustrated his with the Parables. This is the method of the miracle play.

There are two kinds of example from which one can learn—good example and bad. The method of good example is the method of those miracle plays which present us with the lives of the saints and are designed to impress us with the courage and strength of the faith of holy men and women in adversity.[24] Indeed, the intensity of the saints' sufferings seems to have become the main attraction of this kind of miracle play. According to Eugene Lintilhac, "La thème ordinaire des *Vies* et *Miracles* des Saints . . . c'est le martyre du héros. Sans doute l'imagination spéciale des auteurs orne ce thème fondamental de détails abondants et variés, qui répondaient évidemment à un goût particulier de leur public: mais ils rebutent vite le nôtre." [25] Both Lintilhac and Grace Frank cite, as an example of this deplorable but not exclusively medieval taste for the spectacle of human suffering, the fate of the unfortunate Ste. Barbe as it is presented in the play of which she is the heroine: "Bound to a stake, naked, she is beaten, burned, and her breasts are torn off; at the instigation of her own father she is rolled in a barrel studded with nails and dragged by the hair over a mountain before finally being decapitated." [26]

The miracle plays of the saints follow Horatian precept by instructing us through examples of Christian fortitude and, presumably, delighting us by appealing to some of the nastier impulses of our nature. But this is not the only method by which the miracle play works. It also employs the technique of the bad example. The great sinners held up to us as examples in the French miracles may well outnumber the saints who fill that role in these plays. An exemplary drama based on the life of a sinner suggests to modern expectation the story of a bad man who comes to a bad end. "Take warning by my fall" is usually the didactic message of such works of art, and examples of this type do occur in the miracle plays. The mother of *Le Roy Thierry*[27] makes trouble for her son's wife by substituting a litter of puppies for the three lovely boys to which the poor girl has given birth, and we take pleasure and warning from the fact that after setting her daughter-in-law adrift in a small boat, the old woman drops dead and her corpse turns quite black. Such is the well-deserved end of the unrepentant sinner, but most of the sinners of the miracles are not exemplary in this *Struwwelpeter* sense. Though their sins are every bit as heinous, they instruct us not by their deserved punishment, but by their repentance and forgiveness. As a result, the plays in which they appear constitute, I believe, the medieval originals of the form that evolved into the Shakespearean comedy of forgiveness.

Whether by accident of survival or because such plays were commonly written to praise the mercy and intercessive power of the Virgin Mary, these early plays of forgiveness are commonly found among the type known as the *Miracles de Notre Dame*. Forty such miracles have survived in a pair of manuscripts (the Cangé Ms.) "plausibly dated in the latter half of the fourteenth century." [28] They represent, presumably, the repertory of an organization devoted to the glorifying of the Virgin through the presentation of plays honoring her. As evidence of the medieval narrative drama they are invaluable and they have been most unwisely neglected by the historians of the English theater. Because only a small fraction of the dramatic art of the fourteenth and fifteenth centuries has come down to us, it is essential that the study of that drama should not confine itself to the plays which have survived in one language and from one country. If we are to understand the English drama of this period, we must do so on the basis of what we know of the drama of the rest of Europe, and particularly of the dramatic activity that was going on directly across the Channel in the Low Countries and France. To make the tacit assumption that only what has survived in English ever existed in English is to guarantee a distorted view of the medieval drama. Let us make the opposite assumption: that what existed in French probably had its approximate equivalent in English and that something like the *Miracles de Notre Dame* contributed to the tradition which produced the Elizabethan drama.

It is extremely difficult to characterize within a short space a group of plays as diverse as the fourteenth-century dramas contained in the Cangé Ms. A majority of them are concerned with the careers of sinners who repent, often rather perfunctorily, of their misdeeds and appeal to the Virgin for aid in the troubles which their crimes bring upon them. The intercession of the Virgin assures their salvation in the life to come and their immunity from punishment in this world as well. The fascinating diversity of the sins dramatized makes it difficult to select any one play to represent the group, but *Le Miracle de Saint Jehan le Paulu, Hermite*,[29] a dramatic version of a favorite medieval story, that of the Hairy Anchorite, will serve our purposes as well as any.

The play opens, as many of them do, with a sermon on the glories of the Virgin. One of the listeners, Jehan, is thereby strengthened in his determination to live the life of a holy hermit. Unfortunately, his good intentions are endangered when he is persuaded to entertain as his servant l'Ennemi, a devil who has assumed human form in order to lead Jehan into sin and entrap his soul for Satan. Jehan is completely taken in by the devil's attractive exterior:

> Tu as biau corps et doulx visage
> Et de bon lieu me sembles estre.   (97–98)

L'Ennemi settles down to await his chance. This soon comes in the form of a beautiful princess who has accompanied her father out hunting and managed to become separated from the rest of the party. Night is falling when she arrives at the hermit's cell and asks for shelter. This is soon granted though unfortunately the cottage contains only one bed. The princess retires and Jehan confesses to his servant that the situation makes him a bit uneasy:

> Il ne me vient point a plaisir
> Que je voise en mon lit jesir,
> Car se j'y vois en verité
> J'ay grant doubte d'estre tempté
> Et que pechié ne me surprengne,
> Laquelle chose ja n'aviengne!   (572–77)

He is terribly sleepy, but afraid to go to bed:

> Le someil m'abat: que feray?
> En mon lit dormir pas n'yray
>   Puis qu'i a femme.   (582–84)

L'Ennemi soothes him with hypocritical reassurances:

> Si vous couchiez d'elle au plus loing
> Que pourrez, et clinez les yex
> Et vous endormez: c'est le miex
> Que puissez faire. (591–94)

Jehan allows himself to be convinced and thus L'Ennemi manages to lead the hermit into temptation. Unfortunately, Jehan's original misgivings turn out to have been justified. He lacks the strength to resist the temptation of the princess's beauty and he robs her of her virginity. Even worse, when l'Ennemi assures him that, since it is the king's daughter he has deflowered, he will undoubtedly suffer death for his crime, Jehan panics completely and allows his diabolical servant to talk him into murdering the girl and tossing her body into a pit. Once the sin is committed, l'Ennemi is not slow to triumph over his unfortunate master:

> Or vous tien je pris en mes laz,
> Murtrier, mauvais, non pas hermittes,
> Mais luxurieux ypocrites:
> Joyeux m'en vois. (665–68)

Jehan is horrified by what he has done and prays to the Virgin for forgiveness and help. To demonstrate the sincerity of his repentance, he burns his house and clothes, and vows to go naked on all fours and never to speak to another human.

He keeps his vow for seven years until once more a royal hunting party arrives on the scene. Some huntsmen catch a glimpse of Jehan and taking him for a wild beast (he is covered with hair; *paulu* = *poilu*) track him to his lair, capture him, and bring him before the king. Throughout his seven years of penance, heaven has kept a benevolent eye on Jehan. God has been impressed with the intensity of his contrition and the Virgin, accompanied by angels, has appeared to him. Now God has decided that Jehan has suffered long enough. As the king and his huntsmen, with Jehan on a leash, are proceeding to the palace they meet a christening party on its way to the cathedral. Suddenly the newborn babe, who is being carried by the midwife, tells Jehan to stand up, for God has forgiven him and wants him to officiate at the baptism:

> Saches ta grant contriccion
> T'a fait pardonner les pechiez
> Dont tu estoies entechiez,
> Et t'a fait trouver en Dieu grace. (1134–137)

The king is not slow to grasp the significance of this extraordinary event:

> Par ce poons nous estre apris,
> N'avons pas une beste pris,
> Mais un saint homme penancier. (1145–147)

He, too, urges Jehan to rise and tell his story, which the hermit does, admitting in the course of it that he is the murderer of the king's child. The king's reaction to this confession is interesting:

> Biau preudons, or entendez. Toute
> La demerite vous pardoin.
> Puis que Dieu, qui voit près et loing,
> Le vous pardonne franchement,
> Aussi fas je certainement. (1248–251)

What God has forgiven, man must forgive. The courtiers approve their sovereign's mercy and Jehan leads them all to the pit into which he threw the princess's body. There God appears to him and tells him that he will be granted any request he chooses to make. Jehan asks that his victim be restored to life. His wish is granted and the girl is discovered alive. The play ends with the joyous reunion of father and daughter and the king's decision to make Jehan a bishop.

The play of *Jehan le Paulu* is constructed on the same pattern of sin, repentance, and forgiveness that was also to serve as the foundation of the medieval morality play. In this, *Jehan le Paulu* is like the majority of the *Miracles de Notre Dame*. It is unusual chiefly for the prolongation and intensity of the sinner's penance. Ordinarily the evidence of a sinner's contrition is considerably less spectacular. The heroine of *La Femme du Roy de Portigal*,[30] for instance, commits murder twice. First, she decapitates a man who, by pretending, in the dark, to be her fiancé, has robbed her of her virginity. She is then faced with the problem of making her bridegroom, the King of Portugal, believe that she is a virgin on their wedding night. This she does, like Beatrice-Joanna in *The Changeling*, by getting a virgin (her cousin in this case) to agree to take her place. Unfortunately, the cousin refuses to leave the bed when her presence is no longer required and says that since the king has had her virginity, she will be queen. The usurper then makes the mistake of going back to sleep, whereupon the girl gags her, ties her to the bed, sets it afire, and hurries her husband (a sound sleeper) from the room before he can suspect the presence of a third party. The girl's crimes are not discovered until she does what, as a good Christian, she has intended to do all along—she confesses her crimes to a priest and asks for absolution. Her confessor, the king's chaplain, betrays the secrets of the confessional and writes a letter to the king which reveals all. The king orders that his wife be burnt at the stake. Throughout her career of crime, however, the girl has remained loyally devoted to the Virgin, to whom she has appealed for guidance in moments of pre-homicidal indecision. Now she appeals once more, and her prayers are heard. The Virgin appears to a holy hermit and tells him to order the king to forgive his wife and put to death the priest who has betrayed her. This is done and the play ends with the royal couple vowing to devote their lives to the service of the Blessed Virgin.

The King of Portugal's wife suffers very little as a result of her crimes and does not, in fact, seem even to feel particularly sorry that she has committed them. It is hard for a modern reader not to feel that the heroine of this play has got off lightly because the Virgin is on her side. We should try to remember, however, that in addition to serving as demonstrations of the potent intercessive powers of the Mother of God, these plays are designed to show an audience of sinners that any sins, including their own, will be forgiven if the sinner repents and asks God's forgiveness. The outward evidence of contrition is far less important than the inner, spiritual fact, and the visible signs of repentance in the miracle plays vary from the intense, self-imposed suffering of Jehan le Paulu to the seeming insouciance of the King of Portugal's wife.

By no means all of the miracles of the Virgin are examples of the sin, repentance, forgiveness pattern, however. A very interesting group is concerned with the vicissitudes of persecuted and calumniated heroines—*La fille du roy de Hongrie, Berthe, Femme du roy Pepin, Le Roi Ostes,* the already cited *Roy Thierry,* and others. These are medieval religious versions of the kind of narrative that Shakespeare dramatized in his late romances. As such they illuminate, by analogy, those complex and elusive masterpieces and we shall consider them when we come to a discussion of our last three plays. Meanwhile, let us concentrate on the evidence for the existence in English of equivalents to the *Miracles de Nôtre Dame.*

Such evidence does exist. It is extremely scanty, but it suffices to establish the fact that nonscriptural, nonallegorical plays as well as mystery cycles and moralities were written and acted in four-teenth- and fifteenth-century England. We already knew that, of course, from references to the titles of such plays, but in the fragment called *Duk Moraud* and in the *Croxton Play of the Sacrament* we have examples of what such plays were like. They are very much like the *Miracles de Notre Dame* (though in neither is the Virgin the miracle-working figure) and they are both constructed on the pattern of sin, repentance, and forgiveness.

The fragment called *Duk Moraud* [31] was not recognized to be a document in the history of the drama until early in this century. It is "an actor's 'part', preserved in a fourteenth-century hand on the margin of an assize roll," [32] but until its examination by the German scholar W. Heuser, the experts who had seen it took it for a group of lyric poems. Heuser recognized it for what it was and published it, along with an excellent commentary, in 1907. The action of the play is clearly discernible from the fragment which remains.

Duk Moraud enters, identifies himself, and boasts of his worldly happiness, his high position, and his sterling qualities. He prays Christ to save him from "wykyt thowtes," says good-bye to his wife, who is going on a trip, and proceeds to seduce his daughter. His wife returns and, afraid that she will discover the incestuous relationship, Moraud talks his daughter into matricide. Their incest results in a child and, again prompted by her father, the girl destroys this evidence of their guilt. Up to this point in the play, the duke has not been visited by pangs of remorse. He has felt uneasiness at the possibility of being found out, but otherwise his actions have not dimmed in the slightest that sense of superiority he expressed in his opening speech. At this juncture, however, he goes to church and there is suddenly filled with a conviction of his sinfulness. He confesses to a priest and is told to stop sinning and do penance. He is determined to reform, but when he announces his intention to his daughter, she is infuriated and kills him. He dies asking Christ to forgive her:

> Now my lyf wyl pase
> Fro me this ilk stonde,
> I am smetyn in the fas
> With carful strokes & rownde.
> Iesu ful of gras
> For-geue the this trespas
>   that thou ast don to me,
> & geue the gras to blyn
> Of that wykyd syn
> Quylk thou ast don so fre. (253–62)

The fragment necessarily comes to an end at this point. There is evidence to indicate, however, that the play went on to dramatize

Christ's answer to the duke's prayer. Our play is entitled *Duk Moraud* because these words appear at the top of the manuscript as an identification of the part it contains, but it does not necessarily follow that the play was originally so titled or that Duk Moraud was even thought of as the drama's leading character. If only one actor's role from a given Shakespearean tragedy had survived, we might assume that Shakespeare had written a play called *Claudius, King of Denmark,* or *Ophelia, the Councilor's Daughter,* but we would be wrong.

The story which the Duk Moraud fragment dramatizes was well known in the Middle Ages. The tale of the incestuous daughter, as it is usually called, has survived in three English nondramatic versions. One of these is in verse;[33] the others are prose *exempla,* one from the *Gesta Romanorum,* the other from the *Alphabet of Tales.*[34] In all three, the father's death takes place about two thirds of the way through the story, which goes on to relate the further adventures of the daughter. She leaves home after murdering her father and goes to a large city where she lives "with grete dauncynge & pride," willing to sleep with any man who will have her:

> She ne forsoke preste ne clerke,
> Ne none that weryd breche ne serke,
> That with hire wold dele. (178–80)

One day she finds herself forsaken by her usual companions in favor of a preacher ("Sent Austyne" according to the metrical version). Her curiosity is aroused and she, too, attends the sermon, which affects her so deeply that she interrupts the preacher to confess and beg for forgiveness. She wants to be shriven immediately, but the preacher asks her to wait until the sermon is over. When he finishes, however, the good man is horrified to discover that the woman has died before he could give her absolution. At this point an angel appears on the scene and announces (according to the *Gesta Romanorum* version) that:

Be the grete mercy of Iesu Criste, and prayere of hys blessyd modre, and the grete sorrowe that she had for here synnes, she is right wele, and sittes full hye in heuyn blisse, and is as white as lille floure, and as bryght as any golde in goddis sight; therfore pray not for here, but pray here to pray for the, and for all that bene in dedly synne, that ye mow be all in blisse that she is in.[35]

If the sinner experiences contrition, God will forgive. Incest, matricide, infanticide, and patricide are not enough to require even the expiatory sufferings of purgatory if the sinful creature whole-heartedly desires God's forgiveness. The overwhelming importance of the virtue of contrition as the single essential ingredient in merit-ing the forgiveness of sins is the lesson of the tale of the incestuous daughter.

Although it is impossible to determine from the *Duk Moraud* frag-ment whether or not the Virgin played a role in the heroine's for-giveness, the play in all essential respects could be an English version of a *Miracle de Notre Dame*. In the *Croxton Play of the Sac-rament*,[36] however, the miracle is worked, not by the Virgin, but by Christ's real presence in the consecrated host. The action of the play is well described by the title given it in the manuscript at the point when the prologue ends and the play proper begins: "Here after foloweth the Play of the Conversion of Ser Jonathas the Jewe by Myracle of the Blessed Sacrament." The appearance of a fifteenth-century ancestor of Barrabas and Shylock is deplorable evidence of the continuity of one English theatrical tradition,[37] but more inter-esting from the point of view of this essay are the deeds and fate of Ser Jonathas. His sin is, to the religious sensibility, even more shock-ing than the crimes of Duk Moraud's daughter, for sacrilege, the attempt directly to insult God, contains the horror of all violations of His Commandments. The spectacular means by which Ser Jonathas is brought to contrition and forgiveness are appropriate to the seriousness of his crime.

The play, after a prologue announcing that it will be produced in Croxton on the following Monday, introduces us to a wealthy

Christian merchant, Aristorius. He receives the equally wealthy Ser Jonathas, who along with four other Jews is interested in getting hold of a consecrated wafer in order to find out if there is really anything extraordinary about it. Ser Jonathas offers Aristorius £20 if he will get a host for him, but the Christian is unable to overcome his scruples until the price reaches £100. The bargain is made and kept, and the Jews gain possession of the host. Then follows a scene of comic horror, one of those bits of medieval grotesquerie that fascinate and puzzle the modern reader. The Jews stab the host. It bleeds. Horrified, the blasphemers decide to destroy the wafer by throwing it into a cauldron of boiling oil. Ser Jonathas picks up the host, but it sticks to his hand like a leech. "He runneth wood" as a result and his fellows tie him up, nail the wafer to a post, and pull on Jonathas' arm. His arm is finally freed, but his hand remains nailed to the post. At this point the Jews retire to take council and the audience is briefly entertained by a comic turn put on by a quack doctor and his servant. The Jews return and toss wafer and hand both into boiling oil, which immediately turns to blood. The host is then placed in a sealed oven, which explodes. The image of Christ emerges and addresses the heathen. His message is not of vengeance, but of forgiveness:

> I shew yow the streytenesse of my greuaunce,
> And all to meue yow to my mercy.   (659–60)

The Jews are so moved. Each in turn asks Christ for forgiveness and He sends them off as a group to report their experiences to the bishop. The Jews are joined by Aristorius the merchant, whom the bishop grants forgiveness for his part in the crime, on condition that he give up trade and do good deeds. The priest from whom the host was stolen is severely scolded for leaving his pyx unlocked, and the five Jews are baptized "with gret solempnyte."

Sin, repentance, forgiveness—the pattern is clearly present in the *Croxton Play*. So, of course, is a great deal else. The audience has received a vivid lesson in the doctrine of the real presence and a strong warning has been issued as to the dangers of sacrilege. It is also likely that the dramatization of blasphemy had the effect of temporarily freeing its spectators from the rigors of their own piety. One of the great powers of the drama is its ability to provide us with a safe release from the necessary, salutary, self-imposed tyrannies that govern our daily lives. Our reason tells us that we must control our sexual desires, that we must not steal, that we must refrain from telling our friends the truth about themselves, that we must not kick the boss in the pants. The drama permits us to do all these things plus those that we dare not consciously even want to do. *Jehan le Paulu* frees us temporarily and safely from the tyranny of sexual morality. *Duk Moraud* releases us from taboos so fundamental that we hardly dare to admit their necessity. The *Croxton Play* frees its audience, however briefly, from one of the greatest of the medieval tyrannies—the tyranny of holy things. By associating the central Christian mystery with scenes of grotesque and violent slapstick, it provides a release analogous to that granted by the religious parodies of the *asinaria festa* and the Boy Bishop, and it must have provoked an emotional response similar to that inspired by the antics of Christ's tormentors in the "Buffeting" scenes of the mystery cycles.[38] Vicarious wickedness is clearly one of the great attractions of the miracle plays, but they should not be dismissed, therefore, as designed solely to titillate an audience. Even less should they be seen as simply equivalent to the sort of melodrama which satisfies superficial morality by having the hero/villain whose crimes we have delightedly shared come to a bad end.

The miracles were written within the framework of a clear and generally accepted vision of the human condition and they were meant to express a serious and important truth about man's relationship to the universe. For the authors and audiences of these plays, each man's life would inevitably be judged according to the perfect justice of God, and each man's fate throughout eternity would be the result of that judgment. Man's duty in this life was to act well, to avoid sin, and to behave with charity toward his fellows. By leading a perfect life man might merit salvation, but unfortunately perfection is not to be attained by human beings. We are sinners by nature, and we can expect only punishment at the hands of justice. Unless God tempers his justice with mercy, we will all spend eternity in hell. God, of course, is merciful. Christ's sacrifice has satisfied the claims of justice and our sins have been forgiven. We must accept that forgiveness, and contrition for our sins is the means of acceptance.

Both morality and miracle show us men in the process of gaining salvation. With these men we are invited to identify ourselves. At the center of every morality or miracle is the figure whom (from the speech headings in the *Castle of Perseverance*) we may call *humanum genus,* and he is ourselves. This is clearly the case in the morality play where the *humanum genus* figure is deliberately generalized through allegory. It is less obvious but equally true of the sinner in the miracles. Whether in miracle or morality, *humanum genus,* like us, is too weak to resist the allurements of sin. Like us, he does what he ought not to have done, and like us, he deserves eternal damnation for his crimes. His contrition saves him from that fate, and because he is like us, we rejoice in his escape. The happy ending of the miracle plays is more than ordinarily happy because it is the ending to which every member of the audience hopefully aspires.

It is essential to an understanding of these plays to grasp the fact that we are expected to identify with these figures and not to sit in judgment on them. The very horror of their sins should not alienate or shock us but should reassure us. If the sins of Jehan le Paulu, the incestuous daughter, or Ser Jonathas can be wiped away by contrition, then what we have been too weak to prevent ourselves from actually doing may meet with mercy on the Latter Day. Surely this is the response these plays are meant to evoke. If we apply to them standards of morality based on the fitting of punishment to crime, the miracles become incomprehensible; or worse, they seem to pander to man's natural desire to be wicked without suffering for it. In discussing the *Miracles de Notre Dame,* Petit de Juleville expresses a modern uneasiness at what appears to be their odd moral tone:

Le rôle fait à la Vierge dans ces drames est parfois bien étrange . . . et il y a là matière à surprise, et presque à scandale pour la foi de nos jours, moins robuste ou plus raisonnable. . . . Le pécheur le plus endurci, le plus abominable criminel, parvenu au moment critique où sa perte allait devenir irrévocable par la mort, pourvu qu'il invoquât, fût-ce même un peu machinalement, le nom de Marie, était sauvé (j'allais dire malgré Dieu) par la toute-puissante intercession de la Vierge.[39]

It is difficult not to share these doubts, but it is essential to remember that these plays are celebrations, not of justice, but of mercy, and as such they are meant to provide antidotes against the despair of a sinning humanity convinced of its inability to merit salvation.

Shakespeare's comedies of forgiveness are in the same tradition as the miracle plays and they must be approached in something of the same spirit. In them, too, we will meet with versions, or descendants, of the *humanum genus* figure—with men like Bertram, Angelo and Leontes. With such figures, as with their ancestors in the miracles and moralities, we are expected to identify ourselves. We are not supposed to sit in judgment upon them, and to look to these comedies for a meting out of deserved rewards and punishments is to miss their point. Dr. Johnson's primary objection to Shakespeare's art is instructive:

His first defect is that to which may be imputed most of the evil in books or in men. He sacrifices virtue to convenience, and is so much more careful to please than to instruct, that he seems to write without any moral purpose. . . . He makes no just distribution of good or evil, nor is always careful to shew in the virtuous a disapprobation of the wicked; he carries his persons indifferently through right and wrong, and at the close dismisses them without further care, and leaves their examples to operate by chance. This fault the barbarity of his age cannot extenuate; for it is always a writer's duty to make the world better, and justice is a virtue independant on time or place.[40]

Here again we must answer that in this group of comedies at least (for, of course, Dr. Johnson was thinking also, and perhaps primarily, of the tragedies) the virtue celebrated is mercy and not justice. Dr. Johnson is completely right and completely wrong. Shakespeare does not, of course, comply with the strict neoclassical demands for poetic justice. He does not show "in the virtuous a disapprobation of the wicked," because his world was not divided into the virtuous and the wicked. It was composed of men who committed both virtuous and wicked actions. To the Johnsonian objection that, for example, Bertram does not deserve to be "dismissed to happiness," the medieval and Shakespearean answer would be the question, "Who does?" And to Coleridge's statement that "the pardon and marriage of Angelo . . . baffles the strong indignant claim of justice (for cruelty, with lust and damnable baseness, cannot be forgiven because we cannot conceive of them as being morally repented of)" [41] the medieval and Shakespearean answer would be a flat, and probably rather shocked, denial. "To say that in this life there is any sin of which one cannot repent, is erroneous, first, because this would destroy free-will, secondly, because this would be derogatory to the power of grace, whereby the heart of any sinner whatsoever can be moved to repent. . . ." [42]

The medieval play of forgiveness developed as a form to meet a didactic and spiritual need. It provided a comforting reassurance to the sinner (and its celebration of God's mercy must have done much to ensure its popularity) while the tabloid pleasures of vicarious wickedness could hardly have detracted from its dramatic power. In the course of the sixteenth century the drama was to change markedly. New forms were developed; classical comedy and tragedy were revived. But the medieval types persisted. The miracle plays, above all, made their contribution to the Elizabethan tradition that emerged from what often seems the aesthetic chaos of the mid-sixteenth century. The greatest alteration undergone by the play of forgiveness in this process was its transformation from a religious to a secular drama.

The nature of that process is complex and cannot be explained in terms of the drama alone. The medieval author of dramatic miracles, like his Renaissance counterpart, did not invent his own plots. In writing a miracle play of forgiveness, he followed one of two procedures. Either he dramatized a narrative—an *exemplum contritionis*[43] like the story of the incestuous daughter—which had already been adapted to the purposes of religious didacticism, or he took a secular story like that told by the French metrical *Roman de la Violette* and, by altering it slightly, turned it into the piously instructive drama of *Ostes, Roi d'Espaigne*.[44] Shakespeare, in constructing his comedies of forgiveness, worked in an analogous manner. He either selected a story in which the sin/contrition/forgiveness pattern was already present (as in *Cymbeline*) or he altered his narrative source so as to create such a pattern (as in *The Winter's Tale*).

The resemblance of the medieval play of forgiveness to the Renaissance comedy of forgiveness appears to have a double explanation. In the first place, the medieval and Renaissance authors of such plays were dramatizing the same kind of narrative. In addition, however, the miracle play of forgiveness was a dramatic form, a pattern of events, a sequence of emotions and expectations aroused and fulfilled which continued to attract later playwrights after the specifically religious *raison d'être* of the sin/contrition/forgiveness pattern had ceased to exist.

The fundamental concern of the medieval play of forgiveness and of medieval drama in general is man's relationship to God. The fundamental concern of Elizabethan romantic comedy is the relationship of man to man—or, more accurately, of man to woman. And yet, given this change, the basic pattern of the comedy of forgiveness is remarkably unaltered: these comedies dramatize an action in which a central figure sins, repents, and is forgiven. Within these plays, as within the nature of God, are forces which demand justice and forces which plead for mercy, and it is the reconciliation in forgiveness of these forces that permits the comedies to end happily. Furthermore, that forgiveness, like God's, is freely given by the offended party and it is merited, as it is in the miracle and morality plays, by contrition. Nor should this be surprising, since a fundamental tenet of the Christian doctrines concerning the relationship of men to one another, a tenet as fervently insisted upon by Luther as by Aquinas, is that in forgiving those who trespass against us, we should emulate the charity of God.

Pre-Shakespearean Comedies of Forgiveness

It was not until the 1570s and eighties that purely secular, non-allegorical comedies of forgiveness began to be written in English. Secular drama of other kinds had, of course, been produced long before that. The morality was adapted to the more or less secular purposes of the schoolmaster and the political propagandist in such plays as Redford's *Wyt & Science* or the pro-Marian *Respublica,* while, as a form of religious drama, it proved to be an excellent vehicle for dramatized theological controversy. In both the religious and secular moralities of the sixteenth century, the medieval pattern of a *humanum genus* figure subjected to temptation and succumbing to it, only to be forgiven and saved, continues to be discernible as the commonest basic structure for these plays. In the nonallegorical drama, the earliest *surviving* secular play is Medwall's *Fulgens and Lucres,* dating from around 1495. Other secular narrative plays written for the amusement and possibly the edification of courtiers and schoolboys dot those pages of Harbage's *Annals* that cover the pre-Elizabethan Tudor period. There is also a handful of surviving narrative dramas written with an at least partially religious purpose. It is among these that, not surprisingly, we find plays which reflect something of the spirit and something of the form of the medieval miracle play of forgiveness, and it is such plays that foreshadow the early Elizabethan comedies of forgiveness with which this chapter will eventually deal.

The stories which contributed plots to the medieval miracle plays were very often not originally religious in nature. The tale of blasphemy which is told by the *Croxton Play* clearly does depend upon religion for its point, but the stories of *Jehan le Paulu,* the Incestuous Daughter, *La Femme du Roy de Portigal,* or *Le Roy Thierry* are religious by adaptation. To the deeply religious mind, to be sure, there is no such thing as a purely secular subject. Any story, any incident, has a religious significance, or can be made to have one. A case in point is the *Interlude of Calisto and Melebea,*[1] an adaptation for the English stage of the *Celestina* of de Rojas.[2] A good example of what might be called the beatification of the secular, *Calisto and Melebea* was printed for John Rastell sometime between 1526 and 1529.[3] Its anonymous author found, when he turned to the *Celestina,* what is certainly one of the masterpieces on the subject of man's relationship to woman. The Spanish work is a tough-minded tragedy of love, unsentimental and remarkably free of moralizing. It considers its lovers strictly in the context of this world and it judges the actions and characters it presents (insofar as it judges them at all) by secular standards. When Sempronio, discussing the bawd Celestina with his fellow servant Parmeno, asks, "I wonder what devil taught her all her knaveries?" he gets the reply, "I will tell you: necessity, poverty and hunger, than which there are no better tutors in the world."

For all its secularity of tone, it is not in the least difficult to imagine how the *Celestina* might be transformed into a piece of standard Christian moral didacticism. Illicit love does come to a series of unfortunate ends in murder, accidental death, and suicide, and a writer of exalted moral sensibilities could easily conclude such a drama by pointing out that he had shown us a spectacle of sin meeting deserved punishment, of lascivious lovers who, forgetting God, had bathed in lawless lust until they were struck down for their crimes. An exemplary tragedy, a warning to fair women, is certainly potentially present in the *Celestina.*

But an exemplary tragedy is precisely what the author of the English *Calisto and Melebea* did not write. Indeed, he discards com-

pletely all the tragic consequences of Calisto's love. His adaptation
stops short at the end of the second act of de Rojas' nontheatrical
drama,[4] just at the point where Celestina has talked Melebea into
paying an ostensibly innocent visit to Calisto. Up to this point the
author has made his adaptation with commendable fidelity to the
original.[5] He has added a few speeches, such as an opening soliloquy
in which Melebea reveals the situation and her state of mind, and he
has eliminated or turned into narrative the scenes which concern
themselves with the love affairs of the two servants, Sempronio and
Parmeno. Several characters who are not strictly necessary to the
main plot (Melebea's mother and some nonessential servants) are
dropped. But the main effect of the first two acts of the *Celestina* is
present in the English version; in particular, the interlude preserves
some of the force of the psychologically brilliant temptation scene in
which the old bawd tricks her way past Melebea's defenses and gets
the girl to agree to visit Calisto. But with this scene, the contribution
of de Rojas to the English play ends abruptly.

What follows is totally foreign to the spirit of the Spanish work.
Celestina has a brief soliloquy of triumph and then departs forever
from the stage. Her place is taken by Danio, Melebea's father. He
has had a disturbing dream, one that has left him worried about his
daughter's safety, and he is relieved to find her "in Joy & prosperite."
Melebea asks him to tell her what he had dreamt, and he obliges with
the following: He found himself walking in a fair orchard which contained, on the one hand, "a hote bath, holesome & pleasyng," and on
the other "a pyt of foule stynkyng water." He sees Melebea walking
toward the wholesome bath when suddenly she is approached by a
dog—"a foule rough bych aprikeryd cur it was"—which, by fawning
upon her, deflects her onto the path which leads to the foul pit. Just
as Melebea has reached the brink and is about to fall in, her father
awakes, quaking with fear. At this point the author tells his actor how
he should convey Melebea's reaction to her father's vision:

> Hic melebea certo tempore nō loquiꝰ sed vultu
> lamentabli respicit.   (981)

When her father asks her what is the matter, she breaks down and confesses that she has sinned:

> Alas dere fader alas what haue I done
> Offendyd god as a wrech unworthy
> D[*anio*]   wherein / dyspayre not god is full of mercy
>   Et genuflectat
> [*Melebea*]   Than on my knees now I fall downe
>   And of god chefely askyng forgyfnes
>   And next of you for in to oblyuyon
>   I haue put your doctryne & lessons dowtles   (991–98)

Melebea then proceeds to interpret her father's dream:

> The prikyeryd cur & the foule bych
> which made her self so smoth & fayre to see
> Betokenyth an old quene a baudy wych
> Callyd celystyne. . . .   (1009–12)

When he understands the nature of her offense, her father bids her once more:

> Humbly to besech god of hys mercy
> For to forgyue you your syn & mysery.
> M[*elebea*]:   O blyssid lord & fader celestiall
>   whose infynite merci no tong can exprese
>   Though I be a sinner wrech of wrechis all
>   yet of thy gret merci graunt me forgifnes
>   Full sore I repent my syn I cõfese
>   Intendying hens forth neuer to offend more
>   Now humbly I besech thy mercy therfore.   (1028–36)

The play ends with a long speech by the father on the proper upbringing of children.

Calisto and Melebea is not an easy play to assign to one of the ordinary categories of the dramatic genre. Gayley sees it as the "first English romantic drama" [6] (this was before the discovery of *Fulgens and Lucres*) while A. W. Reed rather less accurately describes it as "a comedy of romantic intrigue." [7] It is clearly neither. If its author had chosen to add Calisto's conversion to Melebea's and had ended the play with the marriage of the happy couple, then the interlude might deserve Gayley's characterization of it. As it is, both Gayley and Reed make the mistake of seeing the play primarily as a foreshadowing of the Renaissance rather than as a product of the medieval tradition. At times it is both, but it is finally the latter. *Calisto and Melebea* is a kind of miracle play in which Melebea is the *humanum genus* figure and Celestina functions as a female morality-vice who tempts the heroine as l'Ennemi had tempted Jehan le Paulu. By surrendering to temptation, Melebea offends God "as a wrech unworthy," but is saved by his intervention and, we may be sure, forgiven as a result of the sincerity of her contrition. Thus the *Celestina* has been transformed from a realistic story of love in this world to a dramatic *exemplum* whose final concern is the relationship of man to God.

There are, however, obvious differences between this interlude and the miracle plays which we examined in the previous chapter. For one thing, Melebea's offense is far less serious than those committed by the *humanum genus* figures of the earlier plays. Jehan le Paulu raped and murdered a girl. The incestuous daughter slept with and killed her father, killed her mother, and killed her child. Ser Jonathas and his friends insulted the highest mystery of the Christian religion. Melebea merely agrees to visit a young man and she does not even carry out her intention. One wonders why the author contented himself with so anemic a crime. Surely the taste for vicarious sin was as strong in the sixteenth century as it had been earlier or has been since. It is true that by Christian standards Melebea had sinned. Christ himself tells us that those who want to commit adultery have committed adultery in their hearts, and the skill of de Rojas is such that it is perfectly clear that Melebea, in consenting to Celestina's ostensibly innocent proposal, is at least half-consciously aware that she intends to make love to Calisto. Nevertheless, the English adaptor of the play could have waited until adultery had been committed before he tacked on his edifying conclusion. The author of the *Duk Moraud* fragment or of *Jehan le Paulu* would certainly have done so. It is possible that the play was written for an academic audience—the father's closing speech on the education of the young suggests as much —and that the author felt a certain diffidence about presenting too lurid a picture of sexual immorality to a group of schoolboys, though the educators of the Renaissance were not quite so devoted as we are to the notion that children are best prepared for life by having its true nature concealed from them. It is really more likely that other considerations led the author of *Calisto and Melebea* to avoid the dramatization of the serious crimes which occur in the *Celestina*.

One such consideration may well have been religious. The interlude betrays no particular religious bias, but it was written during a period of great sensitivity to questions of doctrine and its ideological neutrality is probably deliberate. We have seen that the doctrine of the forgiveness of sins was one of the points on which Luther concentrated an important portion of his reforming zeal and it may be that the author of our interlude wished to avoid taking any dangerously clear-cut stand on the matter. The difficulty of avoiding such a stand would have been increased by the dramatization of a really heinous crime. If this was indeed one of the author's motives for toning down the sins of the *humanum genus* figure, the play provides a good example of the basic reason for the secularization of the drama. Once religious faith becomes a matter for violent controversy, any religious drama is automatically polemical. The Protestants did not deliberately destroy the religious drama in England any more than the Catholics destroyed it in France. Both parties were eager to use religious drama for polemical purposes, but the attempt seems to have proved too dangerous to civil order to have been countenanced by any intelligent government, and an author who wanted to provide a stimulating but inoffensive pastime for an audience of varying religious beliefs would automatically steer clear of the dramatization of controversial doctrine. As a consequence of such caution, the crime to be forgiven in *Calisto and Melebea* may have been softened so as to avoid too great an emphasis on the theological arguments surrounding the forgiveness of sins.

Another obvious result of this hesitancy to dramatize religious things is the disappearance of God, as a physical presence, from the scene. God's intervention was an automatic feature of the medieval miracle play. Either he or the Virgin descends, surrounded by saints and angels, to prevent the punishment of the sinner on earth or to declare, as spectacularly as possible, the forgiveness of his sins in heaven. In the miracles of forgiveness, this intervention takes place after the crimes of the sinner have been committed, and sometimes, as with the resurrection of the princess in *Jehan le Paulu,* the earthly consequences of the erring creature's misdeeds are canceled by God's special grace. The spectacular quality of the event has been eliminated by the author of *Calisto and Melebea.* God, to be sure, intervenes to save Melebea, but he does so by means of a human agent, her father, and his intervention is timed, as we have seen, to prevent the carrying out in action of the sin which she has committed in intention. As a result, this interlude has developed resemblances to the Shakespearean comedy of forgiveness that are not apparent in the medieval miracle play.

One of the main concerns of the writer of secular comedies of forgiveness is the avoidance of crime, for the crimes which are pardoned in these plays invariably turn out to have been committed only in intention. Hero's death as a result of Claudio's repudiation, Bertram's adultery with Diana, Angelo's judicial murder of Claudio and his violation of Isabella, the murder of Imogen, the death of Hermione, the deaths of Prospero and Miranda—all these are eminently forgivable because they did not happen. The offenders in these plays are pardoned for crimes which they committed only within their minds, but which they think they have committed in action. The author of a secular comedy of forgiveness will either choose a story in which the protagonist sins by intention only, or he will modify the genuine sins in his narrative source so that they do not take effect.

The author of *Calisto and Melebea* does this rather crudely by ending his play before the sins in his source can take place. Melebea sins in intention but, unlike Shakespeare's *humanum genus* figures, she is fully aware that she has not sinned in action.

In the *Interlude of Calisto and Melebea,* a secular love tragedy is altered so that it will assume the basic form of a miracle play of forgiveness—but a miracle which is moving away from the straightforwardly religious, highly colored medieval drama of sin and repentance toward a secularized comedy of human relationships. It has, however, by no means reached its goal, for the finally important relationship in this interlude is that of the heroine to God.

This remains the case with the other semisecularized narrative drama which we shall examine: Thomas Garter's *Commody of the moste vertuous and Godlye Susanna,*[8] which was entered on the Stationer's Register in January, 1569. That a story taken from the Apocrypha should remain basically religious when transferred to the stage is not surprising. What its author did to it in the process of making that transfer is interesting, however. Because he was dealing with a very familiar and almost scriptural narrative, Thomas Garter was not free to change the basic outline of his plot. He was not at liberty to eliminate any essentials, but he was able to add to the bare bones of his story. The plot, of course, is a fine one and its central figure is one of the best known examples of a type that we have seen to be a favorite of the *Miracles de Notre Dame,* the calumniated innocent, a figure who, in Hero, Imogen, and Hermione was to have her Shakespearean incarnations. In romantic comedy, the interest of such a figure lies primarily in her relationship with the man whose love she loses, and in the suffering she experiences when she loses that love, and when she realizes that the man she loves thinks her capable of betraying him. The virtuous and godly Susanna is not the heroine of a romantic comedy. Her husband, Joachim, has a much more important role in Garter's play than in the Apocryphal narrative. Garter promotes him to be ruler of the country and gives him a soliloquy on the cares of government, but when it comes time for us to be presented with his reaction to the accusation that his wife is an adultress, no such reaction occurs. Joachim is simply dismissed from the scene—forgotten about until Susanna's vindication. Nor does Susanna's love for her husband have anything to do with her rejection of the adultery proposed by the wicked elders. She refuses their advances because she will not "attempt my Lord my God with this so vyle a sinne." (772) At her trial, the possibility that her innocence might be vindicated by human means, by an appeal to her husband or to the law, never occurs to her. When the presiding judge urges her to speak on her own behalf, she does not even reply to him, but directs her plea to God, certain that man is powerless to help her and that God will receive her soul.

God, of course, does more than that. He intervenes to save her life. As in *Calisto and Melebea,* he intervenes through a human agent, Daniel, and one wonders just how the actor went about interpreting his author's stage direction: "Here God rayseth the spirit of Daniel." [9] Presumably Garter was depending on his audience's familiarity with the story. It does not, of course, really very much matter whether Daniel conveys his divine inspiration or not, for the bit of lawyer's cleverness by which he saves the situation is no more dependent, for its dramatic effect, upon the fact that it is prompted by God than is the brilliance of Portia, that later and more secular "Daniel come to judgment." The paradox of *Calisto and Melebea* holds true for *Susanna.* The finally important relationship, the only dramatically realized relationship in the play, is that of the heroine to her God, but, even more than in the earlier interlude, the role played directly by God in the "commody" is almost nonexistent.

Against the Susanna main plot, Garter sets its obverse, the story of the calumniators, the corrupt judges Voluptas and Sensualitas. Their story is constructed on the *humanum genus* theme, with the central figure doubled. They are, in their villainy, the unknowing agents of the devil, who sends his creature, the Vice Ill Report, to tempt the judges into tempting Susanna. (It is worth noting that God disappeared from the scene long before Satan did—if, indeed,

Satan ever has.) Ill Report has an easy job of it, for both Voluptas and Sensualitas are hardened sinners. Most interesting from our point of view is the slight but central change that Garter makes in the final fate of the calumniators as it is presented in the Apocrypha. There the wicked elders are quickly gotten rid of: "They came upon the two elders . . . & dealte with them, even lykewyse as they wolde have done with theyr neyghboures: yes they dyd accordyng to the lawe of Moses, and put them to death." [10] After checking Deuteronomy to discover that the Law of Moses prescribes death by stoning as the appropriate punishment for his villains, Garter follows his source, but adds to it. Rather than simply dismissing the wicked to their fates, he gives them final speeches in which to satisfy the traditional requirement for an ending in divine, if not in human, forgiveness. Voluptas calls on God to forgive his sins and to defend him from the fiend, and Sensualitas echoes him with:

> Not iustice Lord, but mercie we doe crave to ease our bandes.
> And by thy mercie both we yeelde our soules into thy hands.
>
> (1247–248)

There is no mention of the specific wrong done to Susanna, and no suggestion that she should pardon them or that they should ask her for pardon.

The process by which the miracle play of forgiveness was secularized into the comedy of forgiveness seems to be one in which the form of the drama remains intact while those of its surface details which most clearly indicate its religious nature disappear. The basic pattern of a sinner who is tempted and falls, who experiences contrition and is forgiven, remains the basic pattern of the comedy of forgiveness long after its *raison d'être* in religious didacticism has disappeared. In *Calisto and Melebea* and in Garter's *Susanna*, the religious connotations of the pattern are insisted upon. The sins committed are still seen primarily as offenses against God. The contrition experienced by the sinner is for having offended God. The forgiver

of the offense is God. Nonetheless, the role of God as an active agent
in these plays has been drastically reduced.

To complete the process of secularization, the plays which we will
next consider have only to change the primarily important dramatic
and moral relationship which they explore. In the plays we have thus
far investigated, that relationship has been of man to God. In the
plays which follow, it will be of man to man, and the sins committed
will be offenses against the offender's fellow humans. The contrition
experienced will be for having offended other men, and the necessary
forgiveness will be granted by men to men. In *The Vertuous and
Godlye Susanna* no mention whatever is made of the possibility that
Susanna might forgive her persecutors nor does it occur to them to
ask her to do so. Far different is the case with the false judge and
his victim in Whetstone's *Promos and Cassandra*,[11] the first of the
fully secularized comedies of forgiveness which we shall consider.

It is unfortunate for a clearer understanding of the history of the
English drama that Shakespeare was inspired by *Promos and Cassandra* to write one of his most difficult and interesting comedies. As
a result, the rare reader of Whetstone's play cannot help but find the
characters haunted by their Shakespearean incarnations. Angelo and
Isabella constantly interrupt their ancestors to state, with tremendous
poetic force, the ideas and emotions which the hippity-hop of Whetstone's fourteeners seems to parody in anticipation. The consequence
is the impossibility of seeing Whetstone's work in its proper and
honorable place in the English tradition. Whetstone was an intellectual, a literary man highly conscious of what he was doing and well
up on the achievements of his continental contemporaries. His Pref-
ace to *Promos and Cassandra* makes it clear that he thought of himself as a reformer of the drama and that he saw his play as a salutary
innovation. Like many other salutary dramatic innovations, it seems
to have failed to get itself performed,[12] but it was printed and, in
time, underwent its glorious apotheosis in the form of *Measure for
Measure.*

As a document of literary history, *Promos and Cassandra* seems to me to stand in approximately the same relationship to Elizabethan comedy that Sackville and Norton's *Gorboduc* holds in the development of Elizabethan tragedy. Whetstone's play, much more than the better known *Gammer Gurton's Needle* or *Ralph Roister-Doister*, predicts the comic achievement of Shakespeare and his contemporaries. The scenes of lowlife are much in the spirit of the satirical comedies of Chapman, Jonson, Dekker, Middleton, and Marston, while the relationship of the main plot to Shakespearean comedy in general is self-evident from Shakespeare's use of the play as a source. I should like, therefore, to forget, for the moment, that *Promos and Cassandra* is the source of one very great comedy and to consider it rather as a significantly early example of the great tradition of Elizabethan comedy as a whole and of the comedy of forgiveness in particular.

The source of *Promos and Cassandra*, like that of so many Elizabethan comedies, was an Italian novella, and though Whetstone was not the first Englishman[13] to tap that remarkable reservoir of dramatic possibilities, his method of dealing with his literary source provides an interesting early example of the way an Elizabethan author with a good sense of form went about changing a piece of prose narrative into drama.

The story which Whetstone found in the fifth novella of the eighth decade of Giraldi Cinthio's *Hecatommithi*[14] resembled, in many of its elements, Thomas Garter's source in the *Book of Susanna*. Both novella and apocryphal story concern corrupt rulers who misuse their power in an attempt to coerce virtuous women into sexual relations. Such a story has obvious attractions for the serious playwright. A question of sexual morality guarantees the initial interest of the audience, while the high position of the offenders provides the writer with an opportunity to consider the problems of justice and morality that arise quite naturally from the dramatic situation.

Cinthio's novella can be quickly summarized. The Emperor of Rome sends his favorite, Juriste, to govern the city of Innsbruck. For a time, Juriste is a model ruler, but eventually the possession of power results in a temptation which he cannot resist. A young man is tried and found guilty of raping a virgin. The law condemns him to death despite his willingness to marry the girl he has ravished. Juriste approves the sentence, but the young man's sister comes to plead for mercy. The judge is so struck by her beauty that he offers to free her brother if she will repay the favor by becoming Juriste's mistress. This, after a tearful plea from her brother, the girl agrees to do. She spends the night with Juriste and leaves in the morning, having heard her lover order the jailer to remove her brother from prison and deliver him to his sister's house. The jailer does as he has been told, but, as the girl learns to her dismay, he has also been told to remove the young man's head from his shoulders before sending him home. Feeling strongly that Juriste has not fulfilled the spirit of his bargain, the girl goes to complain to the emperor, who is shocked by her story and summons Juriste to defend himself. Juriste attempts vainly to maintain his innocence, but finally breaks down and confesses. The emperor orders that Juriste first marry the girl he has wronged and then die for her brother's death, but the girl begs for the life of the man who becomes her husband and the emperor yields to her pleas.

In adapting Cinthio's novella to the demands of the stage, Whetstone makes two major changes in the plot: he alters the nature of the brother's crime,[15] and he preserves the young man's life. In the novella, the brother is a rapist; his crime, "la violenza fatta alla vergine." [16] In Whetstone's play, Andrugio (the brother) and his mistress, Polina, have sinned by mutual consent. Cassandra (the sister) reproaches the God of Love for his treacherous favor to Andrugio in having made "Polina graunt him (earst) even what he would request." Geoffrey Bullough explains Whetstone's change by maintaining that "for the English moralist rape could not be the trivial offense it was in Terence and apparently in Renaissance Italy; Whetstone lightens the brother's crime." [17] He certainly does, but in doing so it is probable that he is doing more than simply compensating for that deplorable lack of moral sense so frequently observed in the non-English. Cinthio, Renaissance Italian or not, did not regard rape as a trivial crime and was not presenting it as such. He wants us, rather, to see it as a very serious offense for whose punishment there were some grounds for mitigation in the offender's extreme youth and in his willingness to make reparation to his victim through marriage.

The Elizabethans would have seen nothing unusually harsh in the condemnation of a rapist to death. Rape was one of the sexual offenses for which capital punishment was prescribed in sixteenth-century England and the law specifically includes the provision that the crime remains capital when the woman is ravished by force "though she do consent after." [18] It seems unlikely that, on the one hand, an Elizabethan audience would automatically consider the judge who enforced the letter of such a law as behaving with undue severity, although on the other hand there is no reason to suspect that they would have regarded him as dangerously merciful if he had pardoned the young man after taking into consideration the arguments in favor of mitigating the law's full rigor. The reaction of such an audience to the law against lovers which Whetstone invents is a different matter. Andrugio's fornication is certainly presented as an offense against morality; nonetheless, no society, Elizabethan or any other, has treated premarital sexual intercourse as deserving of the death penalty, and the law that would seek to punish it so harshly is here looked upon with a kind of awe at its severity—no doubt a very fine thing in theory, but demanding too much of weak humanity. Promos' attempt to apply it to Andrugio and Polina is definitely treated as an example of excessive zeal, not only dangerous to comparatively innocent lovers, but actually encouraging the criminally vicious. "A Good law yll executed" [19] seems to sum up the response expected by the author at this point.

By substituting fornication for the rape in Cinthio's novella, Whetstone prevents the intrusion into his comedy of really serious crime. More than that, he provides a motivating force for the action of his subplot. In that plot, a careful parallel to his main action, Whetstone shows his audience the effects of the reign of Promos, the corrupt judge, upon the underworld of professional vice. This picture owes nothing to Cinthio, who, both in his novella and in the play which he later made of it,[20] concentrates upon the effects of Promos on what is normally a superficially decorous upper-class society. But in Whetstone, Promos' revival of capital punishment for fornication suddenly reveals the kinship between the punks, bawds, and hacksters who inhabit the stews, and the well-bred Andrugio, Polina, and Cassandra. A law against the raping of virgins does not, after all, ordinarily create much of an inconvenience for the professional prostitute, but a law that would make every customer a potential candidate for the executioner's block obviously poses a real threat to such a woman's livelihood.

Such a woman is the harlot Lamia, who, with her pimp, Rosko, meets Promos' threat by becoming the mistress of the ruler's right-hand man, Phallax. Thus protected, she prospers as never before. Whetstone's point is neatly made. Excessively severe attempts to root out ineradicable human weaknesses end by encouraging the criminal indulgence of what they try to destroy. The real vice of Lamia and Rosko goes unchecked while the comparatively harmless frailty of Andrugio and Polina is punished with excessive rigor. Whetstone's play is basically, then, a working out in two plots and on two moral levels of Promos' decision to punish fornication with death. On one level that decision results in the corruption of the instruments of the law and the prosperity of the vicious. On another level it brings about the moral debasement of the ruler himself, forces an innocent girl to sacrifice her virginity, and almost succeeds in destroying an overly eager but otherwise decent pair of lovers.

Whetstone's change in the nature of the young man's crime makes possible this ironic comment on the relationship between law and morality. His other important change from Cinthio's narrative comes when he arranges to save Andrugio from the beheading which was his fate in the novella.[21] We have already considered how necessary it is for the author of a comedy of forgiveness to prevent the intrusion into his plot of really serious crime. The character to be forgiven at the climax of the play must be sincere and determined in his intention to do evil, but that intention must be thwarted if the comedy is not to fall into the aesthetic error of sporting with crime.[22] In *Calisto and Melebea* the heroine is saved from her sinful desires by the intervention of God, who sends her father a warning dream. In *The Vertuous and Godlye Susanna,* the wicked judge's plot to seduce the heroine is thwarted by her virtue and godliness. Their scheme to have her executed is frustrated when God prompts Daniel to trick them into revealing their wickedness. In Cinthio's wicked judge, Whetstone found a sinner whose crimes must have struck him as too heinous to forgive in a comedy. Faced with the problem of eliminating the crime without destroying the plot, which depended on the crime, Whetstone hit upon a solution that enabled him to keep his comedy comic without sacrificing the full effect of the forgiveness of the sinner. He created a humane jailer who, shocked by the story of Promos' treachery, agrees to substitute another body for Andrugio's and to allow the young man to go free. The jailer protects himself by making Andrugio promise not to reveal his escape even to his sister or his lover, Polina. Andrugio's apparent death makes it possible for Whetstone to set up a final scene of a kind which was to become a commonplace in the comedy of forgiveness.

Again and again in Elizabethan romantic comedy, a happy ending is made possible by the revelation that a character who has been presumed dead is, in fact, alive. In Shakespeare alone we have Hero in *Much Ado,* Helena in *All's Well,* Claudio in *Measure for Measure,* Imogen in *Cymbeline,* Hermione in *The Winter's Tale* and Miranda, Prospero, and Ferdinand in *The Tempest.* It is worth noting that the explanation for the popularity of this device has nothing to do with any desire on the author's part to astound his audience. The audience is ignorant of the continued existence of only one—Hermione—of the characters listed above. Such scenes were popular with Shakespeare and his contemporaries because they expressed what their authors were trying to say and created the effect which they were trying to achieve by enabling the author to make a point about the opposition

of mercy and justice. We have already seen that it is abundantly possible for the two to be reconciled in the presence of God, and the
medieval drama presented us frequently with the spectacle of that
reconciliation. The Renaissance drama, however, literally removed
God from the scene. In the Elizabethan comedy of forgiveness we are
concerned with the pardon of men by men, and when a crime has
been committed, pardon becomes a matter of more than individual
charity. John may forgive George the evil that George has done to
John and that forgiveness will cancel George's debt to John. If
George has offended John by calling him a booby, John's forgiveness
can legitimately close the incident. If, on the other hand, George has
offended by murdering John's sister Alice, the case is altered. By his
action, George has offended society, a law has been broken, and justice must take its course in opposition to mercy. The writer of comedy
can resolve this opposition only by devising some method of having
his cake and eating it too. The resurrection of sister Alice is one such
method. In the medieval miracle plays such a resurrection may be,
indeed, a miracle, as it is in *Jehan le Paulu,* but the writer of secular
comedy will usually provide a naturalistic explanation, as Whetstone
does here. In *Promos and Cassandra* the resurrection of Andrugio
makes it possible for Whetstone to end his play in effective forgiveness without denying the claims of justice. Society, speaking through
the emperor, can add its forgiveness of Promos to Cassandra's and can
do so without offense to morality.

The rational claims of justice are, then, met by Whetstone's preservation of Andrugio, but even more important, the emotional demands of the spectator of comedy are also satisfied. The fulfillment
of wishes is clearly one of the major functions of comedy, particularly
romantic comedy. The comic dramatist creates a world in which the
good things the spectator thinks he wants are possible of achievement.
Love, beauty, and happiness exist in the worlds of comedy and they
are gained by the people who inhabit those worlds. Now of all the
wishes common to man, none is more poignant or more impossible
of achievement than the desire to alter the past. There can be few

humans who would not be pleased at the prospect of being able to undo something they ought not to have done but did anyway. There can be few more intense feelings of relief than those of the dreamer who, upon awakening from a nightmare, realizes that the horrors which were so vivid but a moment before do not in fact exist. It is this "sense of awakening from nightmare," as Northrop Frye calls it,[23] that is communicated by the offender in the final scenes of the comedy of forgiveness when it is successful—when, for example, Hero unveils or the "statue" of Hermione stirs into life; and are not Angelo, in *Measure for Measure,* and Alonso, in *The Tempest,* deliberately afflicted with and then awakened from living nightmares by Duke Vincentio and Prospero?

Promos and Cassandra is not a successful comedy of forgiveness. That it was written in English verse in 1578 is in itself almost enough to guarantee its artistic failure. Whetstone was in the unlucky position of having to participate in the creation rather than in the use and development of a dramatic tradition. The ability that he demonstrates for making drama convey its meanings through action, as well as through didactic speech, and his talent for devising action that will reinforce the theme of his play without violating its mood seem to me to forecast the genius of later playwrights, notably of Shakespeare. I do not mean to imply that the Elizabethan dramatists were close students of Whetstone, though Shakespeare may well have profited from reading his play. The workings of literary tradition are so complex that it is seldom possible to point to any one work or any one writer as *the* innovating factor in the development of a form. We can say that Whetstone's effects seem to be different from those of the writers that preceded him and similar to those of the writers that followed him, but for explanation of the fact it is best to content ourselves with the observation that the drama was changing.

A part of the nature of that change becomes clear in the final scenes of *Promos and Cassandra.* The miracle/morality pattern of weak humanity tempted and sinning underlies the structure of the main plot up to this point. Promos, the *humanum genus,* urged on by the vice figure of Phallax, cannot resist the temptation to abuse his power by using it to force Cassandra to have intercourse with him. He compounds his crime by ordering the judicial murder of Andrugio. His crime is revealed, not as in the early morality, before the throne of God, but before the throne of his earthly ruler, the emperor. Cassandra assumes the role of an avenging justice and demands the punishment of her seducer. The emperor orders that Promos marry his victim and then lose his life. The demands of justice are satisfied. The play must now satisfy the demands of mercy. At this point Cassandra is called upon to change her role. She forgives Promos his sins and transforms herself from the advocate of justice to the advocate of mercy. This shift is carefully, if abstractly, motivated by Whetstone. Her actions up to this point have grown out of her love for her brother, but now she must meet a new claim on her loyalties:

> Nature wyld mee, my Brother love, now dutie commaunds mee
> To preferre before kyn or friend my Husbands safetie
> But O, aye mee, by Fortune, I, am made his chiefest foe:
>
> .   .   .   .   .
>
> And shall I seeke to save his blood, that lately sought his lyfe?
> O yea, I then was sworne his foe: but nowe as faithfull Wife
> I must and wyll preferre his health, God sende me good successe:
> For nowe unto the King I wyll, my chaunged minde to expresse.
>
> (p. 506)

Cassandra's last phrase is significant. One of the more complicated problems that the Renaissance dramatist had to learn to deal with was the dramatization of a change of mind. To make convincing the shift in a character from vengefulness to forgiveness or from sinfulness to remorse was something which the secular drama of this period had to learn how to do. The methods of the medieval dramatist in dealing with the problem were really not of much help. The moralities allegorized the event. All the stage was a mind and the characters on the stage represented the forces working within that mind to change it. In the nonallegorical drama a mind changed because God intervened to change it. God sent Melebea's father a dream. God raised the spirit of Daniel. But as the drama grew more secular, such explanations become less satisfactory. This was not because the Elizabethans lost faith in the possibility of God's control over the human mind. Rather, the use of God as an explanation for actions in a play which otherwise concerned itself with a secular society would be an aesthetic violation of the play's mood—of what Madeleine Doran has called its "qualitative unity." [24] It would, if done too flagrantly, be a failure to play the game according to the rules. The elimination of God from the scene forced the playwright to look elsewhere for explanations of what was happening on-stage. The word "forced" is used advisedly for there seems to be no question that the writers of drama turned to the contemplation of psychological problems eagerly or even willingly. For these writers, it seems to have been action that counted above all. Whatever deeper significance their plays hold emerges from the action, and it is the action that provides the outlines into which the characters must fit. Successful characterization for the Elizabethan dramatist was that characterization which made the action plausible, and he seems usually to have felt that the psychological movement implied in the term "change of mind" was sufficiently explained so long as it worked—so long, that is, as it was accepted by his audience momentarily within the framework of his dramatic action.

Whetstone relates Cassandra's "chaunged minde" to the change in her legal relationship to Promos. The logic of that change is clear. A good woman's first duty is to her husband. Cassandra is a good woman and Promos is her husband, so she will do her duty, forgive the man who wronged her, and seek to save his life. The explanation is too simple for the complexities of reality, but it is strong enough to support the action of the drama.

Another important change of mind provides the author with even fewer difficulties. This is the remorse of Promos. Promos' pangs of conscience and his confession are easily explicable. There is no surer inspiration for remorse than getting caught, and Promos gets caught.

The moment in which the sinner must acknowledge his crime is potentially one of tremendous dramatic force, and it is a moment which Shakespeare can endow with its full theatrical impact. In Shakespeare that revelation of guilt is often a revelation to the sinner as well as to the society that discovers him to be guilty—as when, in *The Winter's Tale,* the death of Mamillius suddenly and irrationally convinces Leontes that he has wronged his wife. Whetstone is far from capable of this sort of effect. Cassandra reveals Promos' sin to the emperor and his court and Promos confesses that she has told the truth. Later, when he is about to be executed, he is sorry that he has done wrong and hopes that others will profit by his example. His speeches communicate nothing beyond the platitudes expressed in them.

More interesting than either of these mental struggles is the psychomachia of Cassandra's brother, Andrugio. He is presented with a clear but intricate moral decision and the stages through which he passes in making it are straightforwardly defined and dramatized. He is living a hermit's life in the woods when a passing rustic tells him the news of Promos' fall and impending execution. Andrugio is delighted and gives thanks to God for the destruction of his enemy. It then occurs to him that Promos' fall may give him a chance to better his situation. He goes to the court in disguise and learns that Promos has married Cassandra and is about to be executed for causing Andrugio's death. Andrugio is more than content that this should be the case:

> he must lose his subtyll head
> For murdring me, whome no man thinkes but dead.
> His wyll was good; and therfore beshrewe mee,
> If (mov'd with ruthe) I seeke to set him free.   (p. 507)

"His wyll was good." Promos was quite sincere in his attempt to kill Andrugio, who sees no reason to forgive him for it. Though legally innocent, Promos is to all appearances guilty of murder and in his own mind he is as guilty as if Andrugio were dead. So long as this is true, Andrugio will avoid endangering his own safety—he is, after all, still subject to a legally valid death sentence—in order to save Promos. The motives for Andrugio's change of mind contribute decisively to the significant design of the play as a whole. He overhears his sister pleading for Promos' life and, in a third soliloquy, decides that he must come forward in order to spare her the pain of losing a husband. He faces the fact that his gesture may mean his own death and decides to take the chance:

> Nay fyrst I wilbe spoyld with blooddy knife,
> Before I fayle her, plunged in distres.
> Death is but death, and all in fyne shall dye.   (p. 508)

Andrugio's decision and the process by which he arrives at it balance, with real artistry, Cassandra's dilemma and sacrifice in the opening scenes of the play. Andrugio repays his sister's willingness to give her virginity for his life by being willing to give his life for her happiness. Another reason for Whetstone's second change in Cinthio's novella now becomes clear. By providing for the resurrection of Andrugio, he makes possible the pardon, with justice, of Promos, and he also completes the design of the first half of his play by repeating it in a different key. Both of the important changes which Whetstone makes in his source are evidence, I think, of a first-rate artistic sensibility which was unfortunately confined to a sense of design. A sense of verbal style is lamentably absent, and in that Whetstone was the victim of his period. The sense of style was soon to be supplied to the English drama by two very different artists, Lyly and Marlowe, but in writing a well-designed play whose significance emerges from its action, Whetstone made a contribution to the English drama that deserves recognition.

In *Promos and Cassandra* the complex elements of the denouement of a fully developed comedy of forgiveness are present for the first time. A central figure sins grievously in intention and believes that he has sinned effectively in reality as well. A potentially tragic situation is resolved, however, through the forgiveness of the sinner by those he has wronged, and the demands of justice are satisfied by the revelation that his intended crime has not actually been committed.

Whetstone's choice and use of his source in Cinthio is typical and informative of the methods of the Elizabethan dramatist. The contribution of the novella to English Renaissance drama goes beyond the mere providing of narrative raw material. The example of the *novellieri* gave the Elizabethan dramatists a lesson in narrative discipline which they badly needed. The novella generally is a controlled, tightly organized form, making its effects with economy. As such it served as a useful corrective to the tendency in the sixteenth-century dramatists to be diffuse and windily didactic. (Not that Cinthio, in particular, could be called terse, by modern standards. These things are relative.) The stories are more, however, than simply entertaining anecdotes. They are usually told by the frame-story character who is narrating them in order to illustrate a point or develop a theme, and their significance is insisted on. Such a story provides an excellent ancedotal center around which to build a play. By intelligent expansion and addition, the playwright can comment on and enrich the meaning of his central narrative as Whetstone did by adding a lowlife subplot to his original story and by creating, for Andrugio, a moral problem to set against the central moral problem faced by the heroine. Shakespeare is the master of these methods of commentary and enrichment, but he is not the originator of them. When he came to adapt novella material for the stage, he was able to make use of an already developed method for turning narrative into drama.

The other great source of story which the Elizabethan and Jacobean playwrights drew upon was, of course, the romance. As a narrative form it is at the opposite pole from the novella. Relaxed and diffuse, it presents the would-be playwright with the necessity for the selection, excision, and contraction of an embarrassing richness of incident. The contribution of the romance to the romantic comedy is immense, but the nature of that contribution is difficult to charac-

terize. Its structural effect was to encourage a lack of structure, to lead
the playwright to turn his play into a series of "moving accidents by
flood and field." Such are the plots of the earliest surviving dramatic
romances, *Sir Clyomon and Sir Clamydes* and *Common Conditions*.
The great positive contribution of the form is that of a special atmosphere, hard to define, but easy to recognize, which constitutes one
of the dramatic romance's greatest strengths. That atmosphere might
best be characterized as one in which the marvelous is not only possible, but constantly imminent and finally occurring. It is an atmosphere in which love can flourish and develop the ability to persevere
through trials of time, space, and adversity.

The romance is a journey which ends in lovers meeting, but necessary preludes to the triumph of love are the separations and temptations which test its strength. Because of the opposition which it suggests, the title *The Rare Triumphs of Love and Fortune*[25] (like *All's
Well That Ends Well*) could serve as well for a kind of drama as
for a single play. The play presents, with an almost schematized
clarity, the basic pattern of the dramatic romance. It begins with a
war in heaven between two goddesses, Venus and Fortune, each of
whom is determined to maintain her superiority over the other. Jupiter, called upon to judge between them, asks them to demonstrate
their respective powers upon a pair of lovers, Fidelia, the daughter of
King Phizantius, and Hermione, a foundling, but really the son of
the banished nobelman Bomelio, an adept at magic and currently
a hermit. Hermione, of course, is already a victim of the ill fortune
which has banished his father and left his noble birth obscured, but
his sufferings, as well as those of his lover, have only begun. Fidelia's
brother, the prince Armenio, discovers his sister's love and, filled
with pride of birth, persuades his father to banish Hermione, whom
he considers unworthy of alliance with the royal family. Fidelia tries
to accompany Hermione but the parasite Penulo betrays her plans to
Armenio. Before she is recaptured, she meets Bomelio, who puts a
curse on Armenio which causes him to lose the power of speech.
Bomelio then finds his long-lost son, Hermione, and decides to assist

him in his love by going disguised to the court and spiriting Fidelia away. Pretending to be an Italian physician, Bomelio gains entrance to the court when he claims to be able to cure the stricken Armenio. He diagnoses his malady as the result of a spell which he says can be broken only if Armenio's tongue is washed in blood taken from the tenderest part of his worst enemy. Armenio's worst enemy is his sister, Fidelia, and her tenderest part is her breast, so that the course of treatment is obvious. Fidelia, however, balks at losing so much as a drop of her blood for the comfort of her loathesome brother. Bomelio tells the courtiers he will give her a sedative and take the blood from her while she is asleep, but instead of doing so, he reveals his identity to her and helps her to escape from the court.

Hermione, meanwhile, has been awaiting his father's return at Bomelio's cell. To pass the time he glances through his father's library, which, he is appalled to discover, contains books of a distinctly atheistical cast. He decides to burn them all. When Bomelio returns and discovers his loss, he goes raving mad and pursues poor Fidelia with shouts of "give me my bookes, my bookes give me, give." Mercury descends and puts Bomelio to sleep with music. King Phizantius and the still dumb Armenio enter and Phizantius orders Hermione to leave the kingdom or die. At this point, Venus and Fortune appear together to reconcile the opposing factions. They repeat the prescription for Armenio's cure and add that the sprinkling of Fidelia's blood on the sleeping Bomelio will also end his madness. Fidelia is now eager to be of help. The cures are effected, all the parties are reconciled, and the play ends happily.

For all its comparative naïveté, *Love and Fortune* is very much in the spirit of Shakespeare's late romances. There seems little reason to doubt that Shakespeare knew the play and he may even have seen it staged, for the Earl of Derby's Men, to whose repertory it belonged, played in Stratford-on-Avon less than two years before the court performance of the play recorded on December 30, 1582.[26] J. M. Nosworthy, the editor of the New Arden *Cymbeline*, makes a strong case for Shakespeare's indebtedness to this older dramatic romance.

According to him, "a comparison of *Cymbeline* or *The Tempest* with *Love and Fortune* will show quite clearly that the only distinction that can be drawn is one of quality and effect." [27] Yet there is, I think, a basic and revealing distinction in each case. In *Love and Fortune,* the love between hero and heroine, the motivating force of the play, is a given constant. That love, though it can suffer, cannot change or be changed. It is less a human emotion than, at worst, a literary convenience or, at best, a beautiful ideal. As an ideal, Shakespeare half accepted it, but only half. In four of the six Shakespearean plays we shall examine, love is the motivating force, and in all of these four, as in all romance, love is, in E. C. Pettet's phrase, "subjected to some grievous and abnormal strain." [28] But in these four plays, including *Cymbeline,* the love of the romantic hero is not strong enough to meet that strain. The heroine's love, however, has the necessary strength, and contains the ability to forgive the hero's offense against it. It is the strength of woman's love that makes it possible for these plays to be comedies. Posthumus doubly violates (doubly because the alteration which he finds does not exist) the romantic ideal which Shakespeare states in Sonnet 116:

> love is not love
> Which alters when it alteration finds
> Or bends with the remover to remove.

Imogen fulfills that ideal and her ability to do so makes possible the ending of the play in forgiveness and reconciliation. *The Tempest,* like *Measure for Measure,* is a play not primarily concerned with romantic love, though the love of Ferdinand and Miranda is essential to it. It is, like all romance, a story of trial by fortune, but in *The Tempest* the trying forces are fully controlled by the play's protagonist. As a result, Shakespeare's play is basically different from *Love and Fortune.* Prospero, unlike Bomelio, does not fall victim to the power of fortune. Rather, he directs that power to his own ends. In doing so, he takes the place of fortune, momentarily, in the lives of his enemies. He becomes fortune, but a fortune no longer blind or fickle. He uses the powers of fortune for an intelligent purpose.

In this older romance, the constituents of the basic pattern have not been sophisticated. Love is unalterable. Fortune is its foe. The lovers suffer from the trials inflicted on them, but their love remains constant. The comic ending becomes possible when Love and Fortune (like Justice and Mercy) cooperate to bless the hero and heroine.

Like *Promos and Cassandra,* its near contemporary, *Love and Fortune* is a play from whose scene the Christian God has departed. In *Promos and Cassandra,* however, we have a play which attempts to work out its problems without the help of the supernatural. Whetstone's comedy is in the Christian tradition, but God is not among the *dramatis personae,* and he does not intervene directly in the action of the play. No more does the Christian God interfere with what goes on in our dramatic romance, but in the cast of *Love and Fortune* he has been not so much eliminated as replaced. The problem of dramatizing a change of mind, which we saw exercising Whetstone's talents in *Promos and Cassandra,* is obviously made a good deal simpler if it can be effected by a god from the machine, and that is how it is done in *Love and Fortune.* It is, of course, classical tragedy which invented the useful convention that a course of events which has been determined by the motives and emotions of its human protagonists can be changed by the appearance on stage of a higher power —as Hercules changes the course of events at the end of the *Philoctetes* of Sophocles. Euripidean as well as Senecan tragedy was becoming well known to the educated by the time *Love and Fortune* was performed and the appearance of the gods and goddesses in the play is analogous to the *deus ex machina* of the drama of classical antiquity. It was probably also the result of a need to fill part of the space left by the departure from the stage of the Christian god. It is impossible for a student of the drama to read medieval miracle plays, particularly the French *Miracles de Notre Dame,* without being struck by the resemblance of the intervention of divine power in them to the *deus ex machina* of classical tragedy. It was only natural, therefore, that when it became inadvisable for the playwright to portray his own god on-stage, he should, in a period in which the classics were being eagerly revived, substitute for him the gods of the Greeks and Romans.

As conventional figures, Venus and Fortune ease the playwright's difficulties. They provide an amusing explanation for the twists of the play's action—an explanation that is far easier to dramatize than any purely in terms of human motives would be.[29] So long as Venus and Fortune are on the outs, the course of true love never will run smooth, but when, at the beginning of Act V, Mercury convinces the warring goddesses that they should make peace, we know that the human characters of our play must reflect the heavenly reconciliation. Our expectation is not disappointed. At the moment when the fortunes of all concerned are at their lowest ebb, when Bomelio is raving mad, Armenio struck dumb and the faithful lovers about to be separated by the enraged king:

> Venus and Fortune shew themselves and speak to Phizantius, while
> Hermione standeth in a maze. (1739-740)

Venus and Fortune reveal the hidden truth: Bomelio has been unjustly banished and his son, Hermione, is worthy of the king's daughter. This revelation, like the revelation that Andrugio is alive in *Promos and Cassandra,* makes the happy ending possible by motivating Fidelia's forgiveness of her brother and the sacrifice of her blood for his sake. But while the revelation in *Promos and Cassandra* is the result of forces at work within the mind of Andrugio, the moment of forgiveness and reconciliation here grows directly out of the reconciliation of the heavenly powers. *Love and Fortune* is a romantic comedy which ends with a scene of forgiveness. It is not, however, a fully developed example of the kind of play I shall call the romantic comedy of forgiveness. The essential feature of that form is the combining in one character of the roles of the romantic hero and the *humanum genus* figure. Armenio, the sinner in *Love and Fortune,* is definitely the latter. He is misled by a vice, the parasite Penulo, and the denouement includes his forgiveness and regeneration, but he is not the hero of the play. The manner of his forgiveness and cure is interesting, however, in view of the sinning heroes we will soon be looking at.

Fidelia pierces her own breast for her brother's benefit. This "sweet and fearfull sight the signe of love" is a curious bit of stage business with strong symbolic overtones. One is reminded of that Christ symbol, the Pelican, who feeds her young on the blood from a self-inflicted wound in her breast. The miraculous cure which results from Fidelia's self-sacrifice enables Armenio to end the play by begging forgiveness of those he was wronged:

> Forgive Hermione, forgive me I beseech.
> And you my sister pardon my freends too.　(1800–801)

That forgiveness, like God's pardon of sinning humanity, has obviously been granted in advance by the "sweet and fearfull" action of Fidelia.

It is appropriate to romance and particularly to what Shakespeare was to make of romance, that a denouement in forgiveness and reconciliation should depend upon the shedding, with her consent, of a maiden's blood. It is upon the ability of women to suffer and forgive that Shakespeare builds his vision of an ideal romantic world. The romantic heroines, in a sense, replace Christ and his intermediary, the Virgin, as the forgivers of man's sins when the religious drama of the Middle Ages becomes the secular comedy of the Renaissance.

What woman has ordinarily to forgive in these later comedies is not a cruel brother, but an offending lover or husband. As we have seen, it is the man's love which cannot survive the trials of fortune in Shakespearean romantic comedy. The man may fail the woman who loves him by believing calumnies against her honor, as Claudio fails Hero and Posthumus fails Imogen. Or his crimes may be entirely self-generated like those of Leontes. Or he may (most curious and difficult case of all) simply reject the heroine's love from the beginning, as Bertram does in *All's Well That Ends Well*. Obviously, the easiest of these figures to understand and to forgive is the believer of calumny. His offense may be blamed, in part at least, upon the wiles of a villain, and since we are usually shown him suffering dreadfully from the supicion that the woman he loves has betrayed him, we find it comparatively easy to forgive him for his lapse.

No hero suffers more dreadfully from the false suspicion of a lover's infidelity than does the title figure of Greene's *Orlando Furioso*.[30] This comedy, probably written about 1592, brings us to the beginning of Shakespeare's own career as a dramatist and it is the work of a man who seems to have felt that the young Shakespeare's indebtedness to him passed the bounds of legitimate influence. Be that as it may, there is little doubt that Shakespeare knew Greene's comedies and that they had a significant effect upon his own work in the form. I shall consider two of them, *Orlando Furioso* and *James IV*, which, I think, provided Shakespeare with his most immediate models for the comedies of forgiveness.

Ariosto's epic gave Greene's play a title and a mad hero. Beyond that, the stories the two authors tell are very different. It is, in fact, rather futile to point out, as Greene's latest editor does, such changes in detail as the fact that Greene "makes Angelica the daughter, not of Galaphron, king of Cathay, but of Marsilius, emperor of Africa." [31] The truth is that Ariosto's Angelica does not exist in Greene's comedy. She is replaced by another heroine of the same name. Ariosto's (and Boiardo's) heroine is beautiful, clever, and deceitful. She is not so much fickle as impervious to love—save for a period in the *Orlando Innamorato* when she becomes enamoured of Rinaldo as a result of drinking from an enchanted stream. When she can, she makes use of the men who love her. When she can't, she flees from them. The greatest men in the world desire her and it is hardly surprising that she entertains a dangerously high opinion of herself:

So great her folly grew, so vaine her pride,
As she esteemed all the world at nought,
The which when once the blind boy had espi'd,
(Not blind when any mischiefe may be wrought)
He will no longer this presumption bide,
And for a fit occasion long he sought,
And finding this, he thought himselfe now sped,
And up he drawes his arrow to the head.[32]

Cupid's arrow afflicts Angelica with the love of Medoro, a young squire much her social inferior, whom she finds wounded, cures, and marries, and with whom she lives happily ever after. Ironically enough, it is not Angelica who is plagued by her love for Medoro, but the faithful lover, Orlando. It is the knowledge of her marriage that drives Orlando out of his mind.

All this is completely at variance with Greene's version. There the Angelica loves only Orlando and is steadfastly faithful to him. His madness is the result, not of his beloved's faithlessness, but of his own overly credulous belief in the calumnies which his treacherous rival, Sacrepant, has spread about Angelica. The damning evidence of Angelica's name carved on the trees in conjunction with Medoro's is borrowed from the epic, but in the play it is false evidence, planted by Sacrepant. The play ends, not with the final separation of the lovers, but with their reunion and marriage. In Ariosto that (comparatively minor) portion of the narrative which concerns the love of the title figure is, in fact, antiromantic. The central romantic theme of love persevering through trials and temptations is carried by the story of Bradamante and Ruggiero. Greene, in the course of dramatizing the antiromantic theme of Ariosto's epic, has turned it into a typically romantic narrative.

I should like to speculate for a moment on the genesis and development of Greene's play. It seems likely that it must have struck someone—perhaps Greene himself—that the madness of Orlando provided a really stunning opportunity for Edward Alleyn to display his talents as an actor. Here was a chance for an actor of superb physical presence, with the ability to meet the demands of the most highly inflated poetic bombast, to tear the theater almost literally to pieces. The problem of getting those thrilling moments onto the stage as a part of some sort of coherent narrative was obviously a fairly taxing one for the dramatist, however. Clearly it was almost impossible to devise an exposition that would present the audience with any comprehensible condensation of the events (in Boiardo as well as in Ariosto) that lead up to the insanity of Orlando. Even if some method had been found to preserve Ariosto's story, it would not have been advisable to do so. The rejection of love as an irrational and unworthy emotion might be all very well for the courtly entertainments devised by Lyly to be played by children, but it was no denouement for the dramas of a company which had the distinctly red-blooded Alleyn for a drawing card. Clearly more suitable was a comedy in which the hero got the girl, and that was what Greene decided upon.

In order to do so, he had to alter drastically the character of the girl to be got. The Angelica of Greene's play had to be all that Ariosto's was not—innocent, long-suffering, and true. At the devising of such females Greene was—or turned out to be—something of a specialist. Margaret of Fressingfield, the sorely tried heroine of *Friar Bacon and Friar Bungay*, is his best-known figure of this type, and Dorothea, the Griselda of his *James IV*, is a character whom we soon must consider at some length. Greene's talent for the creation of heroines of this sort was the object of the admiration of a previous generation of scholars and critics. "Wholesome," "bright," "clean-minded," "calm," "serious," "faithful," "virtuous," "lovely," "admirable," "vivacious," "witty," "beautiful," "pure," "unspoiled," and "fresh" are adjectives applied to various of Greene's ladies in the course of little more than a page of one monograph on the playwright.[33] Tastes have changed and it seems likely that most contemporary analyses of Greene's paragons would somewhere find room for "vapid." Be that as it may, Greene's heroines are an important fact in the history of the English drama. I do not mean to suggest, of course, that Greene invented the type. The figure of Griselda had been on the stage since Philippe de

Mézières first dramatized her patient sufferings in the 1390s.[34] In any case, the figure is a literary commonplace, perhaps a literary necessity. Nevertheless, Greene's heroines of romance are the most skillfully realized examples of the type in the English drama before Shakespeare and it seems very likely indeed that Shakespeare learned from Greene in this respect as he did in others, and Greene's heroines are, therefore, important for the understanding and misunderstanding of the greater dramatist.

Angelica, Margaret of Fressingfield, and Dorothea represent the norm for the romantic heroine which the Elizabethan audience expected to find in their dramas when such a figure seemed called for. But here, as elsewhere, Shakespeare was free to create effective theater by supplying expectation with the unexpected. His heroines are not ordinarily stock figures, though they often superficially resemble them. Helena and Isabella are most emphatically not sweet girlish things, nor, really, are Imogen, Hermione, Perdita, and Miranda. In the case of *All's Well* and *Measure for Measure* the substitution of characters of complexity and subtlety for the expected simplicities of the average ingenue has led to a great deal of critical confusion. This confusion is most likely to take one of two forms. The critic may notice that the character is not the comfortable Kewpie doll that his experience of the drama has led him to expect and desire, and he will assume that Shakepeare tried to create a perfectly ordinary heroine and failed, thus demonstrating his talent for playwriting to be rather inferior to that of any competent hack. Or a critic of another variety may deny that there is, in fact, anything at all unusual about the character in question, thus rewriting the play in his mind in order to show us that Shakespeare was merely offering the mixture as before, and to insist that those readers are deficient of palate who fail to recognize the presence of saccharine in the dish.

But, for the moment, we are considering the romantic heroine as she appears in *Orlando Furioso*.[35] The function of Greene's Angelica is to love, to suffer, and to forgive, and she does her job admirably enough. Her love is the ideal romantic emotion, granted to one man only, and for life:

> The Knot of Gordion at the shrine of Ioue
> Was neuer halfe so hard or intricate
> As be the bands which louely Venus ties.
> Sweete is my loue; and, for I loue, my Lord,
> Seek not vnlesse, as Alesander did,
> To cut the plough-swaines traces with thy sword.
> Or slice the slender fillets of my life:
> Or else, my Lord, Orlando must be mine. (458–65)

This is Angelica's reply to Sacrepant's invitation: "Tush, leave the Palatine and go with me." Sacrepant's vengeance for her refusal is the source of the trials that love must undergo in the course of romance, just as Armenio's opposition was the source in *Love and Fortune*. The difference between the two arises from the fact that, while Armenio can only make life unpleasant for the lovers, Sacrepant manages to endanger love itself. The false evidence that he plants for Orlando's benefit soon takes effect:

> *Orlando:* Boy, view these trees carued with true loue knots,
>   The inscription Medor and Angelica:
>   And read these verses hung vp of their loues:
>   Now tell me, boy, what dost thou thinke?
> *Orgalio:* By my troth, my Lord, I thinke Angelica is a woman.
> *Orlando:* And what of that?
> *Orgalio:* Therefore vnconstant, mutable, hauing their loues hanging in
>   their ey-lids; that as they are got with a looke, so they are lost againe
>   with a wink. (623–31)

Angelica, on the one hand, and Orgalio, on the other, express the extremes of possible Renaissance opinion on the strength of woman's love. The opalescent mind of Duke Orsino is able to hold both points of view within one scene of *Twelfth Night*:

> For boy, howeuer we do praise ourselves,
> Our fancies are more giddie and vnfirme,
> More longing, wauering, sooner lost and worne,
> Then womens are.   (II.iv.31–34)

And, later:

> Alas, their loue may be call'd appetite,
> No motion of the Liuer, but the Pallat,
> That suffer surfet, cloyment, and reuolt . . .
>   (II.iv.98–100)

Shakespearean romantic comedy is founded on the truth of the first opinion, but it is the heroes' error of believing that the second applies to the women they love that causes the sufferings which are essential to such comedies as *Orlando Furioso, Much Ado About Nothing, Cymbeline,* and *The Winter's Tale.* The sufferings are, of course, the common property of both lovers though they are the fault of only one of them. Orlando's misapprehension causes him to suffer the pangs of madness. It causes Angelica to suffer from the spectacle of that madness and from the knowledge that it is the result of her lover's believing her guilty of a crime that she could never commit.

Wrongly to suspect one's lover of infidelity is, by romantic standards, a serious crime against love. That crime may become less serious if it is the result of having been taken in by the wiles of a calumniator, and the existence within the play of a Sacrepant, a Don John, or a Iachimo undoubtedly serves to channel the resentment of an audience away from the erring hero. And yet, the sin is not a venial one. The man has failed in his love and the woman has not, and the man must seek in the woman's love the forgiveness that he was not prepared to grant.

Orlando recovers his wits. They are not, alas, brought to him by Astolfo in a bottle from the other side of the moon. When the audience has had enough of Orlando's mad antics—and they constitute about one half of the play—Greene borrows from the Bradamante-Ruggiero plot in Ariosto an enchantress named Melissa who, with her supernatural powers, charms Orlando asleep and cures him with music and pleasing visions, afterward informing him that Sacrepant is the cause of his false suspicions. Orlando kills the villain and saves the day for Angelica's father. The lovers are reunited and the play is brought to a happy climax by the obligatory act of forgiveness:

> *Orlando:* . . . but giue mee leave a while,
>   Humbly as Mars did to his Paramour,
>   So to submit to faire Angelica—
>   Pardon thy Lord, faire Saint Angelica,
>   Whose loue, stealing by steps into extreames,
>   Grew by suspition to a causeles lunacie.   (1396–401)

Angelica, in a paroxysm of irrational charity, takes the sin upon herself:

> *Angelica:* O no, my Lord, but pardon my amis;
>   For had not Orlando loude Angelica,
>   Nere had my Lord falne into these extreames,
>   Which we will parle priuate to our selues.   (1402–405)

Whatever logic there is in this speech is, appropriately, the logic of love. Angelica sees the cause of the weakness of Orlando's love as lying essentially in its strength. It is a good excuse and one that only love could find.

No such excuse is available to Dorothea, the unhappy heroine of *James IV*.[36] It is true that her trials grow out of her husband's love, but not, unfortunately, out of his love for her. Dorothea is an innocent, persecuted wife, a member of the great sorority that might be called the Daughters of Griselda. These ladies are so much alike in serving as whipping girls for fortune that it is most efficient to classify them according to the identity and motives of their persecutors rather than by attempting to isolate personal details that might differentiate one victim from another. Boccaccio's Griselda, in this respect, is something of an anomaly, for, though her persecutor is her husband, which is customary enough, his motives are finally un-fathomable. One day a strange idea pops into his head ("entratogli un nuovo pensier nell'animo")[37] and he begins to mistreat, or to pretend to mistreat, his thoroughly admirable wife. His decision, like God's decision to plague Job, is beyond the comprehension of human reason. Persecuted wives other than Griselda are often the victims of their husbands' mothers or brothers. We have already briefly considered the wickedness of the mother of *Le Roi Thierry*.[38] Her conduct is typical, as a glance at the analogues to Chaucer's *Man of Law's Tale*[39] will show, and she needs little motivation beyond the fact that she is a mother-in-law. Brothers-in-law are likely to misbehave out of fear, or a desire for revenge, when their sexual advances have been repulsed. Sometimes they manage to convince their brothers (in a variation of the Potiphar's wife story) that the woman has been the guilty party.[40] The husbands thus become the believers of a calumny and such stories are basically analogues to *Much Ado* and *Cymbeline*. The sufferings of the heroine of *James IV* have their origin in still another motive—her husband's desire to replace her with someone else.

From Cinthio,[41] Greene borrowed his story of a king (Irish in the original) who marries a king's daughter but falls in love with one of his own subjects. Unable to get the girl to agree to an adulterous relationship, he plots the murder of his wife, who discovers his plan and flees, disguised as a man. The king's hired assassin pursues, over-takes, and (he thinks) kills her, but in fact she is only badly wounded and recovers, still disguised, in the household of a noble knight and his lady. The king believes his wife is dead, but when he tries to marry the girl he loves, he finds she has forestalled him by marrying somebody else. To add to his troubles, the queen's father invades the kingdom vowing revenge for his daughter's murder. Before her hus-band can receive the punishment which he clearly has coming to him, the queen reveals that she is still alive, forgives her husband his trespasses, and reconciles him to her father.

The play into which Greene has turned this story is notably reminiscent of the miracle/morality pattern of sin, contrition, and forgiveness. The king of Scots (he bears no relationship whatever to the historical James IV) is a *humanum genus* figure, tempted, sinning, remorseful, forgiven. This pattern is emphasized by the addition to the play of Ateukin, the king's evil councilor and a good example of what happened to the figure of the old Vice when the religious drama underwent the process of secularization.[42] The function of the Vice is to persuade mankind to do evil, and one of his useful aspects for the writer of narrative drama is that the Vice serves to draw away from the central figure some of the hostility an audience feels toward a hero whose bad actions prevent the happy ending which the audience desires. The Vice serves to absorb some of the blame which attaches to the hero of the romantic comedy of forgiveness, and since such a hero must be reconciled to the world of the play before a happy ending is possible, it is clearly handy to have a scapegoat figure who can carry from the scene the sins of which the hero is guilty. It is important to remember, however, that the ultimate responsibility for the offenses that have taken place remains with the *humanum genus* figure. The Vice is no more, and no less, guilty of the crimes of the man he influences than the pander is guilty of the fornications committed by his customers.

The Vice's first job is to provide an atmosphere of complaisance to crime. In his presence it must be possible for the *humanum genus* figure to feel that sin is not, after all, a terribly serious matter, and even more important, that it can be committed without unfortunate consequences. Like the pander's, the Vice's function is to offer the means for the satisfaction of illicit desires, and so Ateukin functions in Greene's play. The king's desire to commit adultery with the beautiful Ida is revealed in the first scene of the play proper (the play itself is set within a framework in which Bohan, a misanthrope, presents the action as an entertainment for Oberon, King of Fairies). Ateukin introduces himself only after the king has been frustrated by

Ida's stubborn virtue. He tells the king that he knows of his desire and that he also knows

> . . . the meanes
> To worke your graces freedome and your loue   (334–35)

When the king reveals his disquiet over his recent marriage and the improbability of his new wife's being willing to "brooke th'abuse" of his liaison with Ida, Ateukin replies with the comment:

> These lets are but as moaths against the sun,
> Yet not so great. . . .   (360–61)

And he climaxes his speech with the statement that is practically the trademark of the evil councilor: "Your will is law." (365) Before the scene is over, the king has silently acquiesced in the murder, should it be necessary, of his wife.

But the forces of evil do not have things all their own way. There are Virtues to oppose Vices and the forces of good fight their battle for the king's mind. Ateukin is opposed by good councilors, and though they are called the Bishop of St. Andrews, Earl Douglas, Morton, and so on, there is little reason why they should not be named Goodhope, Redresse, and Sad Circumspection. Their *sententiae* are of no avail against the sensually appealing promises of Ateukin. They are quickly defeated and the battle for good must finally be fought by the king's intended victims, Ida and Dorothea. For Ida, that battle is a defense of her virtue against the king's temptations. Her reaction to Ateukin's proposition is unequivocal:

> Oh, how hee talkes, as if he should not die!
> As if that God in iustice once could winke
> Vpon that fault I am asham'd to thinke.   (813–15)

For Dorothea, the problem is more complicated. Although her husband has ceased to love her and has attempted to have her murdered, she must continue to love him. Her success in doing so is extravagant. When, after the discovery of the king's plot, one of her supporters suggests calling in her father to revenge her and defend her right, she replies with the following revelation of romantic love:

> As if they kill not me, who with him fight!
> As if his brest be toucht, I am not wounded!
> As if he waild, my ioyes were not confounded!
> We are one heart tho rent by hate in twaine;
> One soule, one essence, doth our weale containe:
> What, then, can conquer him that kils not me? (1399–404)

She does, however, agree to run away, like Imogen, disguised as a man. Jaques, the French malcontent who is hired to do the murder, overtakes her, wounds her, and leaves her for dead. She is rescued, her wounds do not prove fatal, and while she is still convalescing she faints with grief upon hearing that her husband is likely to be defeated by the forces of her father. Still disguised, she hastens to the scene of battle where James has already taken the first step on the path to regeneration. This happens when he discovers that he has been cheated of the fruits of his evil deeds by Ida's marriage. He first regrets his wife's murder, therefore, because he has not succeeded in gaining by it. However, when the king of England confronts him in battle array James cannot, at first, admit his guilt: "Faith, not by my consent thy daughter died." When it becomes perfectly clear that his father-in-law knows the facts, James rather feebly offers to "repay the ransom for her blood." But England will have none of this, and the armies are about to join battle when Dorothea arrives and reveals that she is still among the living. Her appearance completes the king's contrition:

> Durst I presume to looke vpon those eies
> Which I haue tired with a world of woes,
> Or did I thinke submission were ynough,
> Or sighes might make an entrance to thy soule,

> You heauens, you know how willing I would weep;
> You heauens can tell how glad I would submit;
> You heauens can say how firmly I would sigh.   (2363–369)

James's doubts about the efficacy of his remorse are, of course, entirely unfounded. Dorothea's love is too perfect to allow for the presence of rancour, and her forgiveness is as available as the grace of God. Judged by her love, as by the love of God in the miracle plays, adultery and murder, once repented of, become peccadilloes, bagatelles. To the king's speech she replies:

> Shame me not, Prince, companion in thy bed:
> Youth hath misled,—tut, but a little fault:
> Tis kingly to amend what is amisse.
> Might I with twise as many paines as these
> Vnite our hearts, then should my wedded Lord
> See how incessaunt labours I would take.   (2370–375)

But there is, of course, a rational and emotional difference between the religious spectacle of an almighty and merciful God forgiving the sins of his repentant creatures and a wife forgiving her husband in a purely secular comedy. Once more, the function of comedy is to sport with follies not with crimes (or with *seeming* crimes rather than real ones), and the king's crimes can be forgiven only because they have not, in fact, been committed, Dorothea being living proof of her husband's technical innocence. The resurrection of Dorothea achieves more, however, than the salvation of her husband and the reestablishment of their love. The would-be criminality of the king of Scots has caused a kind of gap in nature. As a result of his actions, the times have fallen out of joint, the good nobles have lost their rightful positions, villains have crept into power, and a bloody war has broken out between Scotland and England. Dorothea's reappearance reestablishes concord. The king of England, when his daughter appeals to him to join her in reconciliation with her erring husband, replies with the following invocation:

Thou prouident kinde mother of increase,
Thou must preuaile; ah, nature thou must rule!   (2384-385)

The primary meaning here is that natural love for his daughter is too strong to allow him to refuse her request, but the speech also carries with it the sense that Dorothea's reappearance has restored the rule of Nature. Out of the forgiveness of her husband have emerged love, peace, and order.

In plays like *Promos and Cassandra, Love and Fortune, Orlando Furioso,* and *James IV,* the essential ingredients of the comedy of forgiveness had been assembled by the beginning of Shakespeare's dramatic career. The *humanum genus* figure, the offender whose forgiveness climaxes the play, is, I believe, a descendant of the protagonist of the medieval miracle and morality plays. His forgiver, the romantic heroine, has a literary history as long as that of romance, and here, I suggest, takes over the functions of those forgiving figures of the old plays, the Virgin Mary and Christ. The "jealous God" of the medieval drama, who judges mankind severely according to his deserts and whose justice must be reconciled with mercy if mankind is to escape eternal torment, is often present later as the ruler whose duty it is to enforce the laws, but whose duty it also is to mitigate the law's rigor whenever possible, and whose stern justice is satisfied by the revelation that the sins of the *humanum genus* figure have taken place only in intent and not in fact. These elements of the comedy of forgiveness had been developed as separate constituent parts of the drama before Shakespeare's time. They had also been arranged in the basic medieval pattern of sin, remorse, and forgiveness, and this pattern Shakespeare was to leave undisturbed.

While insisting on his indebtedness to the traditional drama, I do not wish to give the impression that my view of Shakespeare coincides in any way with that which would see him as "simply" a popular playwright who was "simply" working with traditional materials in order to turn out plays "simply" to please his audience. In the first place, none of these activities is ever simple, and in the second place, I know of no artist to whose work the adjective "simple" can be less aptly applied. The dramatic tradition Shakespeare worked within was richly complex, much more so, I think, than our own. Its ultimate origin was in the medieval drama, and the religious preoccupations of the earlier forms linger on, submerged but recognizable, in the secular theater of the Elizabethans. In addition, the drama in the sixteenth century had served both as the instrument and the object of a bitter religious controversy and, as a result, writer and audience were more sharply aware of the moral and intellectual implications of what occurred on stage. But Elizabethan dramatic tradition drew its strength from secular sources as well. Its indebtedness to the ritualistic, quasi-dramatic customs and celebrations of the various classes of English society has been well explored elsewhere,[43] as have the lessons which it learned as a result of the increased interest in the drama of classical antiquity.

The Elizabethan theater was the product of the mixture of all these ingredients and more. The richness of the resulting gallimaufry, which overwhelmed a good many weaker talents and inspired artists of neoclassic sensibility (like Ben Jonson) to attempt a purification of the brew, seems to have been exactly suited to the genius of Shakespeare. His creative intelligence possessed an almost incredible ability to see and to communicate the possible significances of every moment which the action of his plays led him to dramatize. As a result, it is ridiculous to assume that because he was frequently working with the commonplaces of his dramatic tradition, it is therefore possible to understand his work solely in terms of those commonplaces. Shakespeare supremely had the ability to "make it new." He was not, however, making something out of nothing. Among the materials of his art was the work of his predecessors, and to understand him fully, we must try to understand what he owed to traditions that are no longer our own.

Much Ado About Nothing

Though the appearance of *Orlando Furioso* and *James IV* coincided approximately with that of Shakespeare on the London theatrical scene, and though Robert Greene was notoriously convinced that Shakespeare's borrowing from him was closer to theft than to legitimate influence, in comedy, at least, the *young* Shakespeare was quite guiltless of furthering the tradition which Greene had developed. The author of *The Comedy of Errors, Love's Labour's Lost, The Taming of the Shrew,* and *A Midsummer Night's Dream* could claim literary ancestors of the highest Renaissance respectability: Plautus and Terence, the *commedia erudita,* and John Lyly. In *The Two Gentlemen of Verona,* however, there is a strong pull in the direction of the medieval comic tradition which I have attempted to describe in the preceding chapters.

Geoffrey Bullough has described *The Two Gentlemen of Verona* as "a dramatic laboratory in which Shakespeare experimented with many of the ideas and devices which were to be his stock-in-trade and delight for years to come." [1] This is certainly true of the play's denouement in forgiveness. That climax in pardon comes at the end of the comedy when Valentine's unexpected appearance on the scene prevents his best friend, Proteus, from raping Silvia, Valentine's sweetheart. Nothing is more conducive to contrition than getting caught, and Proteus immediately repents of his evil ways:

> *Prot.:* My shame and guilt confounds me:
> Forgiue me *Valentine:* if hearty sorrow
> Be a sufficient Ransome for offence,
> I tender't heere: I doe as truly suffer,
> As ere I did commit.   (V.iv.73–77)

Valentine's reply is a summation of the Christian attitude toward repentance which, in all the plays we shall discuss, underlies the denouement in forgiveness and gives it its emotional force:

> *Val.*: Then I am paid:
> And once againe, I doe receiue thee honest;
> Who by Repentance is not satisfied,
> Is nor of heauen, nor earth; for these are pleas'd:
> By Penitence th'Eternalls wrath's appeas'd:
> And that my loue may appeare plaine and free,
> All that was mine, in *Siluia*, I giue thee.   (V.iv.77–83)

H. B. Charlton's reaction to "this preposterous episode," is a fair sample of how the scene strikes a modern sensibility:

> Valentine's utmost reach of ineptitude comes with what, again romantically speaking, is meant to be the heroic climax of the play. When he has just learnt the full tale of the villainy of Proteus, the code permits him neither resentment nor passion. Like a cashier addressing a charwoman who has pilfered a penny stamp, he sums up his rebuke— "I am sorry I must never trust thee more." And worse follows immediately. With but five lines of formal apology from the villain, Valentine professes himself so completely satisfied that he enthusiastically resigns his darling Silvia to the traitor. Even Valentine must have seen that the gesture was a little odd, because he quotes the legal sanction. It is the code, a primary article in the romantic faith—"that my love may appear plain and free." But it makes a man a nincompoop.[2]

Perhaps. But Mr. Charlton seems not to realize that Valentine's gesture makes him a *Christian* nincompoop, for it is surely not a "romantic faith" (whatever that may be) or a chivalric code that Shakespeare is invoking here. It is a central tenet of Christianity— the religion which Shakespeare shared with his audience. Proteus informs Valentine that he has experienced "hearty sorrow"—contrition —for his sin. Valentine replies, with complete orthodoxy, that contrition alone makes satisfaction for sin, and that the wrath of the God of Judgment is appeased by repentance. Sinful man must prove

worthy of his own ultimate forgiveness by pardoning those who trespass against him. Such considerations would not, I imagine, make
this episode any more palatable to Mr. Charlton. They do, however,
make its acceptance by Shakespeare's audience more comprehensible
and more interesting, and it is a clear testimony to the power of
the concept of forgiveness that Shakespeare could depend upon the
invocation of it for the success of so arbitrary a dramatic moment as
Valentine's forgiveness of Proteus.

Furthermore, Shakespeare has gone out of his way to include
this moment of forgiveness in the comedy, for Pope, in assuming
that, at this point, "our author probably follow'd the stories just as
he found them in his novels as well as histories," [3] appears to have
assumed wrong. Ernst Sehrt points out that the Valentine/Proteus
plot is an addition to the play's one clear source, Montemayor's *Diana
Enamorada,* and he also rightly emphasizes that Shakespeare's in-
clusion of the story indicates his interest in the forgiveness theme.[4]
There is a model for the forgiveness of Proteus in the play's source,
however. Felix, the Proteus figure, is forgiven in the *Diana Enamorada,* but his forgiveness is granted, not by a friend, but by the woman
he was wronged. One, at least, of Shakespeare's experiments in *The
Two Gentlemen of Verona* was misguided, and he did not repeat it.
By setting up the theme of friendship alongside that of romantic love
and by making his *humanum genus* figure an offender against both
ideals, Shakespeare has dissipated the emotional force of his climax.
In the four comedies which I shall label the romantic comedies of
forgiveness (*Much Ado, All's Well, Cymbeline,* and *The Winter's
Tale*) the *humanum genus* figure offends the woman who loves
him and is forgiven by her.

The Two Gentlemen of Verona demonstrates that, from the beginning, Shakespeare associated romantic comedy with the denouement of forgiveness. That association continues in *The Merchant
of Venice.* Again, however, the structure of the play is not that of
the comedy of forgiveness. Shylock is the serio-comic scapegoat of
the drama rather than a *humanum genus* figure. He is the personified
barrier in a play whose structure is basically that of New Comedy,

where boy and girl are kept apart by a force external to themselves.[5]

It is only with *Much Ado About Nothing*, midway in his career as a dramatist, that Shakespeare writes a play whose form is that of the comedy of forgiveness. If our chronology is correct, he did not go on immediately to develop that form, for the festive comedies *As You Like It*, *Twelfth Night*, and *The Merry Wives of Windsor* were written between *Much Ado* and his next comedy of forgiveness, *All's Well That Ends Well*. From *All's Well* onward, however, Shakespeare's work in comedy was entirely within the tradition I am trying to define. I would assign, then, six Shakespearean comedies to that tradition. Of these six, four are closely related structurally: *Much Ado*, *All's Well*, *Cymbeline*, and *The Winter's Tale*. In these, the romantic comedies of forgiveness, the sin of *humanum genus* has its source in a failure to trust love absolutely. As a result, the hero rejects the heroine's love, and she appears to die. The denouement in forgiveness comes when the heroine is discovered to be alive and the *humanum genus* figure awakens from his nightmare to be pardoned by the woman whose worth he has doubted and whose love he has consequently rejected. In the two remaining comedies of forgiveness—*Measure for Measure* and *The Tempest*—the offense is of a different order. Angelo and Alonso have violated basic tenets of political and social morality and the forgiveness of each comes ultimately from the ruler of his play's world.

All of the four romantic comedies of forgiveness share a common structure, though each differs widely from the others in its tone and in the dramatic strategies that the author uses to gain his final effect of pardon and reconciliation. Dramatic structure is more closely analogous to the structure of music than to that of architecture. It is a structure which exists, not in space, but in time, and which is revealed in the unfolding of a series of artistically related moments. That unfolding does take place, however, within another kind of structure —a conceptual framework, a vision or version of the world, which is sometimes assumed, sometimes implied, and sometimes demonstrated.

As each work of art is unique in its temporal structure, so every play unfolds within its unique world, but the artistic worlds of one time and one artist will frequently have a great deal in common with one another. Shakespeare's romantic comedies of forgiveness take place in versions of the universe that resemble one another in certain basic ways.

As a work of art—or part of one—a dramatic world is related only indirectly and partially to the world of reality. The artist, in consciously or unconsciously creating a setting for his action, selects those aspects of reality which are appropriate to that action. The daffodils, doxies, and dales of Autolycus are examples of one such process of selection; the thickening light, the crow, the rooky wood of *Macbeth* represent another. But the dramatic world I am attempting to describe is something more (or other) than such a verbally created, emotionally appropriate setting for dramatic action. It is rather an idea of the universe which can logically account for the action and which helps to reveal its significance. Such a universe is also an artistic creation, but it is likely to be related to philosophic, religious, and scientific notions of what the cosmos "really" is. The worlds of the four Shakespearean romantic comedies of forgiveness are commonly related to one such notion—a theory or vision of the universe which is sometimes called Empedoclean, after the pre-Socratic philosopher who may have originated the ideas on which it is based. Shakespeare is likely, however, to have absorbed it chiefly from Spenser and particularly from *The Faerie Queene* and *The Fowre Hymnes.*

The world that our four plays seem to share exists in three different but closely related aspects: that of the physical universe, that of human society, and that of the individual mind. The physical universe is constructed from the four elements and the elements are, in their turn, subject to the influence of two forces: Love and Strife. In the beginning, the strife which is inherent between the elements produced chaos:

> The earth, the ayre, the water, and the fyre,
> Then gan to raunge them selues in huge array,
> And with contrary forces to conspyre
> Each against other, by all meanes they may,
> Threatening their owne confusion and decay:
> Ayre hated earth, and water hated fyre,
> Till Loue relented their rebellious yre.[6]

But this triumph of Love at the moment of creation does not imply the disappearance of Strife. The natural enmity between the elements remains and is, indeed, a necessity in maintaining the forms of created things—which is why Ben Jonson describes the beauty of Charis as representing "all the Gaine, all the Good of the Elements strife." [7]

Though this theory of the nature of the physical universe is ultimately classical in origin it was not necessary for Spenser to go to the Greeks, or even to Lucretius, for it. It was, as Rosemond Tuve has shown us, "a medieval commonplace" [8] and Spenser probably absorbed it from a variety of sources. What Spenser did with the concept was to extend its implications to the social and psychological fabric of man's world. "Spenser conceives of friendship as the operation in the world of man of a principle of cosmic love. . . . When Nature reigns in the Universe, order results; when Venus reigns in the realm of man, concord results. . . . In Lucretius there is an exposition of the principle of concord and the principle of discord in the nature of things; in Spenser there is an exposition of these same principles in conflict in the world of man." [9]

What is, perhaps, Spenser's clearest iconographical presentation of the relationship between love and hate comes in stanzas 32 through 35 in Canto X of Book IV of *The Faerie Queene*. There Scudamour is describing the Temple of Venus and the "amiable Dame"— Concord—who is seated at the entrance to it:

> On either side of her, two young men stood,
>   Both strongly arm'd, as fearing one another;

Yet were they brethren both of halfe the blood,
   Begotten by two fathers of one mother,
   Though of contrarie natures each to other:
   The one of them hight *Loue*, the other *Hate*,
   Hate was the elder, *Loue* the younger brother;
   Yet was the younger stronger in his state
Then th'elder, and him maysterd still in all debate.

Nathelesse that Dame so well them tempred both,
   That she them forced hand to ioyne in hand,
   Albe that *Hatred* was thereto full loth,
   And turn'd his face away, as he did stand,
   Vnwilling to behold that louely band.
   Yet she was of such grace and vertuous might,
   That her commaundment he could not withstand,
   But bit his lip for felonous despight,
And gnasht his yron tuskes at that displeasing sight.

Concord she cleeped was in common reed,
   Mother of blessed Peace, and Friendship trew;
   They both her twins, both borne of heauenly seed,
   And she her selfe likewise diuinely grew;
   The which right well her workes diuine did shew:
   For strength, and wealth, and happinesse she lends,
   And strife, and warre, and anger does subdew:
   Of little much, of foes she maketh frends,
And to afflicted minds sweet rest and quiet sends.

By her the heauen is in his course contained,
   And all the world in state vnmoued stands,
   As their Almightie maker first ordained,
   And bound them with inuiolable bands;
   Else would the waters ouerflow the lands,
   And fire deuoure the ayre, and hell them quight,
   But that she holds them with her blessed hands.
   She is the nourse of pleasure and delight,
And vnto *Venus* grace the gate doth open right.[10]

Hatred, then, is coexistent with love. They are blood brothers, but (like Don Pedro and Don John, or Edgar and Edmund) they are half-brothers and natural enemies. An orderly cosmos, a peaceful society, a quiet mind depend upon their reconciliation by concord, but concord is constantly threatened by hate. The source of chaos is present within order itself.[11]

Nature composed us of four elements and though they may war within us for mastery, they are kept in order so long as concord retains the ascendancy within our minds. So long, that is, as love continues to master his recalcitrant brother in all debate. If strife or hatred is allowed to gain the victory, a psychological chaos taking the form of jealousy, wrath, or even madness will result. From such ascendancy within one mind, hatred can spread its power throughout a society, with a resulting violence and disorder that, at least in Shakespearean tragedy and late romance, may be reflected in physical nature. Othello compresses the whole complex interrelationship into his great ironic lines:

> Excellent wretch: Perdition catch my Soule
> But I do loue thee: and when I loue thee not,
> Chaos is come againe.   (III.iii.90–92)[12]

But the clearest Shakespearean example of this Empedoclean/Spenserian cosmos in operation comes in *King Lear,* where the king's error in allowing hatred to overcome the natural ascendancy in his mind of his love for Cordelia provides an entrance for evil into the play and results in the social chaos of war, the physical chaos of the storm, and the psychological chaos of Lear's madness.[13]

This Spenserian cosmos can easily be adapted into a natural environment for romantic comedy. Comedy, one of whose functions is to exalt love, will clearly find itself at home in a world which depends upon love as a primary cosmic principle. As comedies, the plays we are considering inevitably concern themselves primarily with the social and psychological levels of the Spenserian world— though in the late romances, where the pull toward tragedy is especially strong, a relationship of the psychological and social worlds of man to the supernatural powers who watch and rule them is frequently suggested. These social and psychological worlds depend for their happy existence upon love, and upon two varieties of love.

The comedies of forgiveness, like all romantic comedies, celebrate the love of man for woman, but by their very nature they are also celebrations of that variety of love which the Bible calls charity. Romantic love is celebrated as a source of happiness for the man and woman who love each other, and as the socially acceptable form of the force upon which the continued existence of society depends— sexual desire. Charity is celebrated also as a virtue in itself and as a social necessity, for the comedy of forgiveness proclaims that human nature is such that any social structure must finally depend on mutual forbearance—on forgiving and being forgiven. More than that, romantic love itself turns out in these plays to be dependent upon the virtue of charity. The love of man for woman (but not of woman for man) is seen as too frail an emotion to sustain the pressures that are frequently put upon it. Man's love fails, and woman must charitably forgive the failure.

The error of the *humanum genus* figure in four of our comedies consists in this failure of love. As a result of deception or lack of self-knowledge (or both), the romantic heroes fail the women who love them, and by this failure hatred gains the ascendancy within their minds. As a result, the fabric of the play's society is threatened by strife, and love and order are finally restored only after a revelation of truth and a consequent repentance and forgiveness. This is the pattern of *Much Ado*, *All's Well* (though Bertram is something of a special problem), *Cymbeline*, and *The Winter's Tale*.

The world of *Much Ado About Nothing* is one in which, at the beginning of the play, love has lately reasserted its ascendancy over hate. Don Pedro, the good and rightful ruler of the play's society, has just defeated in battle his villainous and illegitimate half-brother, Don John. Don John's power to hurt has, as a result, been severely circumscribed. He has, in his own words, been "trusted with a mussel, and enfraunchised with a clogge." But his nature as a "plain-dealing villaine" has not altered:

> if I had my mouth I would bite: if I had my
> liberty, I would do my liking: in the mean time,
> let me be that I am, and seeke not to alter me.   (I.iii.35–38)

In Spenserian terms, Love is in control for the moment, but his half-brother, Hate, though frustrated, is by no means destroyed, and continues to gnash his iron tusks at the spectacle of human happiness. But though the principle of strife is personified by Don John, it is by no means concentrated solely in him. What Don John stands for is present and potentially ascendant in all the characters of the play. There is, for example, elemental strife as well as elemental attraction between men and women, and Beatrice opens the play by demonstrating as much. In Leonato's words:

> there is a kind of mery warre betwixt Signior
> Benedick, and her; they neuer meet, but there's
> a skirmish of wit betweene them.   (I.i.62–64)

This merry war progresses from skirmish to skirmish until it occurs to Don Pedro that there is a means by which this strife can be resolved into concord through love. That means is illusion. By tricking Benedick into believing that Beatrice loves him and Beatrice into believing that Benedick loves her, Don Pedro removes what is, for this pair, the barrier to love—the fear of not being loved in return. Love is born from a shared illusion.

Don Pedro's function is to create love. Don John's is to destroy it, and the means for destruction is the same as the means for creation. Don John arranges a charade which is opposite in purpose, but not very different in technique, from those devised by Don Pedro. Claudio, in falling in love with Hero, "has fallen in love with a pretty face and a modest manner." [14] By making it appear that the face and manner conceal a Hero who has been having an affair with another man, Don John convinces Claudio that he has fallen in love with an illusion and that the reality he has truly perceived in Hero does not exist. Here is the error of *humanum genus* and it

is certainly no more than an error, a "mistaking" as Claudio calls it
later. As such, it cannot deserve, in itself, our very strong censure.
Unfortunately, the world of the play (and perhaps of reality) is so
constituted that the most excusable of mistakes can have the most
horrible consequences. As a result of his deception by Don John,
Claudio gives the principle of hatred its chance to gain the superiority
within the play. The always tenuous ascendancy of concord is destroyed, and the fabric of the society of Messina begins to be threatened by the force of strife.

This process starts in Claudio's mind. His love for Hero cannot
survive the false appearance of her treachery. But love is not replaced by indifference. Love, in the Spenserian cosmos, presupposes
the containment of hate, and the defeat of love entails the victory
of hate. Claudio's love is replaced, therefore, by a rage to hurt, to
destroy, to gain revenge. Under the influence of his hatred, Claudio
devises as cruel a revenge as possible. By repudiating Hero at the
altar where they should be married, he forces her to suffer about as
painful an emotional shock as it is possible for a man to inflict upon
a woman. But the public nature of the occasion means that Claudio's
hatred will result in more than the suffering of the woman who loves
him. The social fabric of the play's world will be endangered by it.
The near hysterics of Claudio are followed by the less emotional
but still brutal lines of Don Pedro:

> What should I speake?
> I stand dishonourd that haue gone about,
> To lincke my deare friend to a common stale. (IV.i.64–66)

The ruler's condemnation is followed by the father's:

> Grieued I, I had but one?
> Chid I, for that at frugall Natures frame?
> O one too much by thee: why had I one?
> Why euer wast thou louely in my eies? (IV.i.129–32)

Removed from their context, these lines and the lines that follow them would be entirely appropriate to the intensest tragedy. The love of father for child, and especially for daughter, was to become for Shakespeare, in *Lear* and in the late romances, the most common type of the natural affection on which human society depends. With the cracking of that bond, there is a danger that chaos will come again.

Much Ado is a comedy, however, and the danger is forestalled. At the very moment of Leonato's renunciation of his daughter, the force of love begins to reassert itself. Beatrice's instinctive "O on my soule my cosin is belied," (IV.i.148) is followed by the calm charity of the friar. His certainty that "there is some strange misprision in the princes," (IV.i.187) is based on more than a charitable desire to think well of Hero, however. The friar represents, to be sure, the love of God, which for the Renaissance and medieval Christian was what love as a cosmic principle meant. But he also stands for a more human aspect of love—the ability of charity to arrive, at least occasionally, at the truth about reality through the dispassionate observation of appearance. It is precisely "by noting of the lady"[15] that the friar, relying on his reading, observation, and experience, is impelled to the conviction that Hero is innocent.

Love has been dethroned, so the friar must set about restoring it to power. His means, of course, is illusion. Through the pretense that Hero is dead, the friar hopes to "change slaunder to remorse," and the religious aspect of the heroine, which will come to be insisted on in the later comedies of forgiveness, is here lightly hinted at in the friar's line, "Come lady, die to liue. . . ." (IV.i.55)

Love continues to assert itself even after the friar has left the stage. The scene of Don John's triumph—the victory of hatred which is dramatized in Claudio's repudiation of Hero—turns out to be a prelude to the triumph of the love that the deceptions of Don Pedro have managed to create between Beatrice and Benedick. It is a major triumph that reduces the volatile and voluble Beatrice to the embarrassed, the almost monosyllabic declaration, "I loue you with so much of my heart, that none is left to protest." (IV.i.288–89) And Benedick's exuberant "Come bid me doe any thing for thee," comes from the man who not long before had offered to do his prince "any service to the worldes end . . . rather than holde three words conference, with this harpy. . . ." (II.i.271-79) And yet even into this moment of what would seem total victory for love, the hatred unleashed by Claudio's error intrudes itself, for Benedick is answered with Beatrice's "Kill Claudio." His decision to do as she asks represents, to be sure, Benedick's highest possible affirmation of his love for Beatrice, but his action should not be viewed merely as that of a chivalric knight following unquestioningly the orders, however fantastic, of his lady. There is a large element of chivalry in Benedick's decision to defend Hero's honor, but his decision to do so is not automatic. He agrees to challenge Claudio only after he has convinced himself of the justice of Hero's cause by receiving, in answer to his "Thinke you in your soule the Count Claudio hath wronged Hero?" Beatrice's reply, "Yea, as sure as I haue a thought, or a soule." (IV.i.331–33) Here Benedick is giving evidence of his willingness to follow the Emersonian injunction and to "give all to love," trusting his instinctive, love-inspired belief in the decency of Beatrice and trusting her instinctive belief (also love-inspired) in the purity of Hero.

It would be comforting and tidy if we could let it go at that, but Shakespeare is seldom comfortable or tidy. The idea of giving all to love certainly receives support in this scene and in the play, but that support is no assurance that if we give everything to love, all will be well, for in agreeing to carry out Beatrice's command Benedick is agreeing to give a great deal to hate. Beatrice hates Claudio, and well she might:

> Is a not approued in the height a villaine, that
> hath slaundered, scorned, dishonored my kinswoman?
> (IV.i.303–4)

Beatrice is right. She has seen and heard Claudio do all that she accuses him of, and her desire for revenge certainly is justified by what she thinks she knows. And yet we know that in her accusation of Claudio, she is committing Claudio's error. Claudio believes that he has seen and heard Hero convict herself of unchastity. Beatrice knows that she has listened in horror while Claudio slandered, as cruelly as possible, her innocent cousin. But neither of them has witnessed what he thinks he has witnessed. Beatrice has not seen a deliberate and cold-blooded act of villainy and Benedick knows that she has not, in much the same way that Beatrice knows Hero is innocent:

> Two of them have the very bent of honour,
> And if their wisedomes be misled in this,
> The practise of it liues in *Iohn* the Bastard,
> Whose spirites toyle in frame of villanies. (IV.i.188–91)

All of the good characters have, at this point in the action, become the victims of the consequences of Claudio's original error. Hatred has taken good advantage of the opportunity provided it by Claudio's thoughts and actions. It has so permeated the world of the play that even love itself has become the servant of the principle of strife.

But we must now ask ourselves precisely what Claudio, as *humanum genus,* is guilty of. Clearly Shakespeare did not intend that we should blame him for believing in the tableau presented for his benefit by Don John. Don Pedro, whom we are meant to like and admire, is equally taken in and the very similar charades got up for the benefit of Beatrice and Benedick demonstrate that even the wittiest and wariest can be fooled by appearance. To fall victim to illusion in this play is to rank oneself with the good, for in *Much Ado* as in *Othello,* only the villain is never fooled. But if, in Claudio's own words, he "sinned . . . not,/ But in mistaking," (V.i.283–4) then clearly he is more to be pitied than censured and Don John was the cause of it all.

The critical reaction to Claudio has fallen generally into one of two categories. Traditionally, he has been seen, in Andrew Lang's excellent phrase, as "the real villain as well as the *jeune premier* of the piece," [16] and the critics have assumed that Shakespeare simply botched the job of creating a standard *jeune premier*. In recent years, however, a number of writers on the play have taken a quite different approach to the character. Recognizing correctly that Claudio cannot be blamed for being deceived by Don John, they move to the further conclusion that he cannot be blamed for anything. According to T. W. Craik, "Most critics blame Claudio's credulity and/or his public repudiation of Hero. . . . In reality, Claudio is exonerated, chiefly by the facts that Don John (as villain) draws all censure on himself and that Don Pedro (hitherto the norm, the reasonable man) is also deceived." [17] Let us look at that repudiation and see to what extent Claudio can be so exonerated.

In the repudiation scene we see a girl whom we know to be entirely innocent and loving met at the marriage altar by the man who is supposed to become her husband and forced to listen to—among others—the following sentiments from the man she loves:

> There Leonato, take her backe againe,
> Giue not this rotten orenge to your friend.
>
> . . . . .
>
>   would you not sweare
> All you that see her, that she were a maide,
> By these exterior shewes? But she is none:
> She knowes the heate of a luxurious bed:
> Her blush is guiltinesse, not modestie.
>
> . . . . .
>
> But you are more intemperate in your blood,
> Than Venus, or those pampred animalls,
> That rage in sauage sensualitie.   (IV.i.32–62)

It may ultimately be Don John's fault that Claudio thinks and says these things, but Claudio thinks and says them. His passionate outrage causes him to behave cruelly, and we, especially since we know that Hero is innocent, are repelled by his cruelty. To be sure there are good reasons for his behavior—more and better excuses than Shakespeare gives to any of his other *humanum genus* figures. Claudio is taken in by a villain, and Don Pedro is also deceived. As a result of Don John's trick, Claudio is convinced that his honor has been endangered, and he determines not simply to avoid what he thinks is a trap set for him, but to revenge himself for almost being duped. To some extent, Claudio's cruelty to Hero is inspired by social considerations. He and Pedro think Hero has misbehaved and are resolved that she shall be punished for her conduct. Some critics would have us believe, therefore, that Claudio's outburst against Hero in the church scene represents nothing more than the emotion proper to a proper Elizabethan whose proprieties have been outraged, and that the denunciation of Hero would have been automatically approved by an Elizabethan audience: "Had [Claudio], as in the sources, quietly told Hero and her father that the nuptial rites could not be celebrated, the Elizabethan audience would have felt that justice had not been done." [18] But surely this statement contradicts itself, for if the young man's behavior is proper in the sources, why should it not have remained proper in Shakespeare's play? An interesting point has been raised, however. Shakespeare could have done the whole thing differently if he had wanted to.

If Shakespeare had wanted to create a Claudio who was in all respects an exemplary *jeune premier,* he might have done so easily. Any hack dramatist could dash off a scene in which a manly but deeply wounded Claudio asks his friend and prince to explain to Leonato why the marriage cannot take place. Shakespeare does not do so because he does not want to do so. Shakespeare wants to show us in Claudio a man in love whose love has not been able to survive the severe strain to which it has been subjected. In the terms of Sonnet 116, Claudio has admitted impediments to the fulfillment of his love. He has bent with the remover to remove without realizing that the remover is not Hero but Don John. The real source of

Claudio's outburst against Hero is not outraged propriety. Nor is it, as C. T. Prouty has suggested,[19] the chagrin of a man who believes that the value of the goods offered him in a *mariage de convenance* has been misrepresented. Claudio's brutal denunciation of Hero is the result of his former love for her—a love that has been transformed into a hatred all the more intense because it was formerly love. Though his hatred has been released by a villain, it is an ugly emotion and Claudio expresses it in as ugly a way as possible so as to ensure that we will dislike him for it. Shakespeare wants us, for the moment, to dislike Claudio intensely, and later, when Beatrice ends one of her magnificent tirades against this "goodly Count Comfect" with the finely Sicilian "O God that I were a man! I woulde eate his heart in the market place," (IV.i.308–9) she is expressing and consequently relieving some of the emotion that we have stored up against her enemy.

Yet it is this speech that begins to rebuild the character of Claudio a bit. The very vehemence of the attack reminds us that it is made on false grounds, that Claudio is not precisely the villain Beatrice takes him for. We have already seen that Beatrice's attack on Claudio resembles Claudio's on Hero. There are, however, differences that are certain to affect decisively the audience's reactions to each outburst. Beatrice's attack is basically a defense, a counterattack in which she tries to save her cousin's honor, and she is inspired more by love for Hero than by hatred for Claudio. Most importantly, the object of the attack is not a person for whom Beatrice has ever felt any unusual affection. Claudio's tirades against Hero are very different. They spring entirely from a love-destroying hatred and they are a direct attack upon the very heart of the comic mystery— romantic love. They are an expression of the hatred that love contains, and the terms which Claudio uses betray a revulsion against sexuality itself. One of the defenders of Claudio's treatment of Hero has approved of this aspect of it on the grounds that it "shows an abhorrence of such carnality," the effect of which is to "idealize Claudio even as he denounces the innocent Hero."[20] But is an abhorrence of carnality really likely to idealize a romantic hero? Even in tragedy the disgust of Hippolytus with the idea of sexuality makes us uncomfortable, and Hamlet's tirade against Ophelia provides his least heroic moment. In romantic comedy, whose purpose is to idealize and celebrate sexual love, such "abhorrence" is distinctly out of place.

In fact, some of Claudio's worst offenses are those against the form and spirit of comedy. Had his hatred and denunciation of Hero taken place in reality (as his defenders tacitly assume they have) most men would probably find them in some degree offensive. Occurring as they do in a comedy, they become very difficult to pardon. We have—we members of the audience—gathered together, after all, in the expectation of enjoying a spectacle designed to convince us, however momentarily, that beauty exists and that happiness and love are goals possible to attain. The wedding to which *Much Ado* brings us in Act Four is precisely one of those festivities with which comedy should properly end. By preventing us from vicariously enjoying the pleasures symbolized by that ceremony, by rudely refusing us the spectacle of love and happiness attained, Claudio aligns himself with those interrupters of festivity which comedy has always contained and whose defeat has always provided a large part of the comic pleasure. Claudio, in terms of comic character functions, is transformed from a romantic hero into a barrier figure—a personified impediment to the happiness toward which comedy moves.[21]

The writers of comedy discovered early that the pleasures of arriving at a happy ending were all the more intense if the journey had been difficult, and Plautus and Terence (presumably having learned from Menander) became adept at the devising of barriers to felicity. These (usually personified) barriers, though they exercised the agility of the characters on stage, did not demand anything more of the audience than an amused attention. The Shakespearean comedies we are discussing are different. The fact that here the barriers have been placed within the minds and feelings of the characters who are destined for happiness means that we must participate emotionally in the achievement of the happy ending. An on-stage happy ending in these plays is dangerously easy to attain. The forgiveness of the offenders by the offended is all that is needed. But if we in the audience are to participate in that felicity, we must also participate vicariously in the means to it. *We* must pardon the offenders. If we cannot, the play does not, for us, end happily, and we are denied the comic experience.

Having allowed his *humanum genus* figure to offend both the moral and aesthetic sensibilities of the audience, Shakespeare must now set about cajoling us into forgiving Claudio his trespasses. The two methods he uses to do so are excuse and penance. By personifying the origin of evil in Don John, Shakespeare has provided a scapegoat upon whom to heap Claudio's misdeeds at the end of the play. By allowing Don Pedro to share Claudio's errors, Shakespeare lightens them. He has taken unusual care in *Much Ado* to provide his *humanum genus* with a strong defense against the enmity of the audience. In the rest of his comedies of forgiveness, he is by no means so tender toward his erring heroes. But despite the excuses with which he is provided, a residue of guilt remains with Claudio, and he must expiate it. Through his hatred and cruelty, he has enabled evil to enter the world of comedy. To deserve our forgiveness, he must be put through a process of penance.

That process resembles, in its elements, the sacrament of penance as it is described by Aquinas. Claudio experiences contrition, confesses his sin, and agrees to make satisfaction. His contrition is the result not, as the friar had hoped, of the news of Hero's death, but of the confession of Don John's accomplice, Borachio, who makes it clear that Claudio's hatred and cruelty have been the product of a terrible illusion. When Borachio's speech has run like iron through his blood, Claudio turns to Leonato for the imposition of punishment:

> Impose me to what penance your inuention
> Can lay vpon my sinne, yet sinnd I not,
> But in mistaking.   (V.i.282–84)

Don Pedro joins him:

> By my soule nor I,
> And yet to satisfie this good old man,
> I would bend vnder anie heauy waight,
> That heele enioyne me to.   (V.i.284–87)

The weight is not extraordinarily heavy. Leonato asks them to make
their confession public:

> Possesse the people in Messina here,
> How innocent she died, and if your loue
> Can labour aught in sad inuention,
> Hang her an epitaph vpon her toomb,
> And sing it to her bones. . . .   (V.i.290–94)

Further "satisfaction" will be Claudio's alone. In order to redress
the wrong he has done to the honor of Leonato's family, he must
marry Leonato's niece. In the comedy of forgiveness, however, contrition and confession are usually enough. The sins of the *humanum
genus* figure are revealed to have failed of their full effect. Claudio's
outburst of venomous hatred has injured Hero, but has not destroyed
her. The death of Hero is the last of the play's illusions and, like the
double deception of Beatrice and Benedick, its effects are beneficent.
When Hero unveils, Claudio awakens from the nightmare that has
been imposed upon him by the wisdom of the friar. With that
awakening, the happiness within the play is complete. The force of
love is once again ascendant over hate. The comic world has been
restored to its natural condition. Within the play, Claudio is un-
reservedly forgiven. When the friar says of Hero, "Did I not tell
you shee was innocent?" Leonato replies:

> So are the Prince and Claudio who accusd her,
> Vpon the errour that you heard debated.   (V.iv.2–3)

Whether or not the audience joins wholeheartedly in this charity
is definitely less certain. It is clear, I think, that Shakespeare meant

us to, that he wished us to pass on to the concluding dance with minds untroubled by doubts as to Claudio's worthiness, and it seems likely that, in his own time, he achieved his desired effect. M. C. Bradbrook betrays the usual modern uneasiness about Claudio's contrition when she says, "Claudio cannot now be . . . allowed more than a pretty lyric by way of remorse." [22] It is possible that an Elizabethan audience would have found more, and what they found might have inspired them to a stronger sympathy with the offender. Shakespeare presented them with the spectacle of a man falling victim to false appearance and, as a result, becoming possessed by the force of hatred, in other words, with the spectacle of a man behaving like a man. In fact, Claudio's crime is being human. There is no worse offense, but surely an audience of human beings should not indulge itself in a complacent sense of superiority to such an offender. The Elizabethan dramatic tradition would have disposed *Much Ado*'s first audience to see in Claudio, and figures like him, images of its own frailty, and the religious connotations which Shakespeare gives to the penance of Claudio would have emphasized that resemblance.

Miss Bradbrook is unqualifiedly right, however, when she goes on to say, "The full story was not to be told till Shakespeare wrote *Cymbeline*, and depicted remorse in Posthumus, with constancy in Imogen." [23] The way to *Cymbeline* runs through *All's Well*, and before we can give our attention to Posthumus, we must look at Bertram, the most thoroughly unlovable of all Shakespeare's romantic heroes.

5

All's Well That Ends Well

In *All's Well That Ends Well*, the world of comedy is threatened not so much by strife as by mutability. Change, the second great enemy of love, beauty, and happiness, has brought the once charmed worlds of Rossillion and Paris to the point of final dissolution. Within the first fifteen lines of the play we learn that the fathers of this world are dead and that its king is near death, the victim of an incurable disease, against which he refuses to struggle. Constantly throughout the first part of the play, the old—the countess, Lafew, the king—remember and lament the past. They remember the nobility and honor of the dead Count Rossillion, the wisdom and skill of Helena's father, Gerard de Narbon, and their memories communicate the sense that irreplaceable virtues are in danger of passing from the world. The elegiac, autumnal tone of these opening scenes is close to that of the quatrains of Sonnet 73 with their images of bare boughs, twilight, and dying fire, and the effect of this beauty in *All's Well* is that described in the couplet of the sonnet: we love that best which we must leave ere long. Like all autumnal beauty, it has a double force. It reminds us simultaneously that it will soon disappear, and that its decay will one day be our own.

All's Well presents us with a dying world and if, as has been suggested, it is a problem play, its problem is a basic one—how do you rejuvenate a constantly dying race? The answer is one that we all know, and one that is suggested at the play's very opening when we discover, on-stage, not only an old man and an old lady, but a young man and a girl. Here, then, is our solution, and being members of the audience at a comedy, we recognize it. In romantic

comedy, boy and girl mean love, love means marriage, marriage
means sexual intercourse, means procreation, means the re-creation
of an always dying world. And, of course, we are right. No sooner
is the beautiful girl left alone than she confesses to us her passionate
love for the handsome young man:

> My imagination
> Carries no fauour in't but *Bertrams*.
> I am vndone, there is no liuing, none,
> If *Bertram* be away.   (I.i.93–96)

If we are not surprised by this news, however, we are no more
startled to learn that there are obstacles in the way of this love's
fulfillment. In Act One, Scene One of a comedy, how could it be
otherwise? Bertram and Helena are separated by more than Bertram's
imminent departure:

> 'Twere all one,
> That I should loue a bright particuler starre,
> And think to wed it, he is so aboue me.
> In his bright radience and colaterall light,
> Must I be comforted, not in his sphere;
> Th'ambition in my loue thus plagues it selfe:
> The hind that would be mated by the Lion
> Must die for loue.   (I.i.96–103)

With remarkable economy, in little more than a hundred lines,
Shakespeare has established his basic comic situation: a noble but
dying world stands in need of the rejuvenating force of sexual love.
That love is potentially present in Bertram and Helena, but, as
always in romantic comedy, a barrier exists between boy and girl—
in this case, the barrier of a great disparity in social position. As
members of the audience, we appear to know where we are and we
can settle ourselves to enjoy the destruction of the barrier and the
vicarious pleasures that attend the fulfillment of love and the artistic

creation of happiness. Though the heroine despairs of the possibility of achieving her desires, though she seems content, with Viola's mythical sister, to sit like patience on a monument, smiling at grief, we know better. Love in romantic comedy, will find out the way.

It is at this moment in the play that Shakespeare, for the first time, does something slightly odd. It will not be the last time, for of all Shakespeare's comedies, this is certainly the oddest, the most uncomfortable, perhaps the least popular, and it is probable that in those elements that cause its oddity and discomfort, the clues to its special significance are to be found.

As amateurs of the various forms of literary romance, any audience, whether Elizabethan readers of chivalric or pastoral narrative, or moderns with an experience of Victorian fiction or Hollywood movies, would have, I should imagine, a not wholly formed but nonetheless definite expectation at this point in the play's action. We are expecting, surely, some sort of sign from the hero, some indication of the state of his emotions—the declaration of a passion that he, too, realizes to be hopeless, perhaps. Or even better, an expression of his determination to defy the prejudices of society, followed, of course, by the heroine's refusal to let him make the sacrifice. But instead of "Enter Bertram," the stage direction at this point reads, "Enter Parolles." Instead of the *jeune premier* we are presented with the parasite, with one who is immediately identified for us as a liar, a fool, and a coward, and instead of a tender passage between hero and heroine, we are treated to some fifty lines of bawdy on the absurdity of remaining a virgin. It is not surprising that Shakespeare has been strongly reprehended for creating the scene. Quiller-Couch would like to cut it (and "the whole Parolles business") right out of the play, "like a wen." He finds it offensive and worse: ". . . such chat is more than offensive; it is pointless lacking a listener; and as we wish Helena to be, and as Boccaccio conceives Helena, she would have dismissed Parolles by a turn of the back. Shakespeare degrades her for us by allowing her to remain in the room with this impertinent." [1]

A shift in taste since Quiller-Couch's time has made it easier for the modern reader to enjoy Shakespeare's jokes about sex and tempts us to regard Edwardian attitudes toward them as quaint if not neurotic. We should not be too quick to dismiss Quiller-Couch's objections as absurd, however. They are absurd, but the absurdity they demonstrate is common to a great deal of the adverse criticism of *All's Well*. Again and again in the critical remarks on this comedy (and in one's own reactions to it) one notices the unconscious assumption that *All's Well* should really be another play altogether, and that Shakespeare wrote the one we have either by mistake or through a combination of perversity and incompetence. *We*, the argument appears to run, know perfectly well what should happen in the play, but Shakespeare seems to be unable to get it through his head what it is that we want him to do. *We* know what Helena is like but the author fails to provide us with a Helena who is "as we wish Helena to be." *All's Well* obstinately refuses to be as we like it.

Our expectations are consistently disappointed, our hopes are frustrated, and the romantic comedy that, after the first hundred lines, we had settled down comfortably to enjoy is again and again pulled out from under us in the most annoying and awkward way. So consistently does this occur that one must end, finally, by entertaining the suspicion that in writing *All's Well* Shakespeare had something other than our undisturbed comfort in mind, and by acknowledging the fact that an understanding of the play can be arrived at only through an attempt to deal with it on its own terms, as Shakespeare wrote it.

Parolles' bawdy is a case in point. His interchange with Helena is an odd and unexpected incident, but its reasons for being in the play are clear enough. Parolles tells some home truths, none of which Helena gives the slightest sign of ever having doubted. "Virginity," he tells her and us, is "too cold a companion." It is unnatural, self-consuming, suicidal, and, finally, unattractive:

Losse of Virginitie is rationall encrease, and there
was neuer Virgin got, till virginitie was first lost . . .

    .   .   .   .   .

your virginity, your old virginity, is like one
of our French wither'd peares, it looks
ill, it eates drily, marry 'tis a wither'd peare:
it was formerly better, marry yet 'tis a
wither'd peare.   (I.i.138–74)

Helena does more than tolerate this "offensive chat." She listens to it and she clearly allows it to influence her state of mind. As G. K. Hunter points out, this dialogue

> is a free and frothy play upon the ideas which are fermenting . . . in Helena's (or rather Shakespeare's) mind, and the topic it turns upon— the use of virginity and the manner in which it can be laid out to best advantage—is obviously germane to the situation of a virgin yearning for honest marriage to a young nobleman.[2]

Its obvious effect upon Helena is to make her stop merely yearning and begin planning how she may lose her virginity, as she puts it, "to her own liking"—to Bertram and in marriage. She casts off the hopeless melancholy of her first soliloquy and substitutes for it the self-confidence of her second:

> Our remedies oft in our selues do lye,
> Which we ascribe to heauen: the fated skye
> Giues vs free scope, onely doth backward pull
> Our slow designes, when we our selues are dull. (I.i.232–35)

This change from despair to determination is entirely in keeping with the comic spirit. Comedy, traditionally, is anything but dedicated to the preservation and exaltation of virginity, and Helena's desire to lose hers lawfully entirely befits a comic heroine. And yet her determination to marry Bertram unquestionably makes Helena something of an oddity among the usual heroines of romance. It is the function of the lady, ordinarily, to appear, at least, to be the pursued rather than the pursuer in a romantic narrative. According to Andrew Lang, "Every one would prefer the worm in the bud to feed on the damask cheek rather than to see 'Vénus toute entière à sa proie attachée,' as Helena attaches herself to Bertram." [3] Again, Shakespeare appears to have failed or refused to write this comedy as we would like it. An instructive example of how Lang's "every one" expects a heroine like Helena to behave can be found in Trollope's *Framley Parsonage*. There, too, the heroine, Lucy Robarts, is the daughter of a poor and recently deceased physician. There, too, the hero, Lord Lufton, is a great aristocrat of proud family. Lucy loves Lufton, but Lufton also loves Lucy, and far from pursuing him, Lucy refuses Lufton when he proposes and continues to refuse him until, in Volume III, his heretofore recalcitrant mother proposes for him.

In fact, *All's Well* is not a romantic comedy in the usual sense of the term. If we look to this play to gratify the expectations commonly raised by romantic comedy, we will be disappointed and our frustration will make an understanding of the play impossible. It has been suggested that these frustrated expectations are a largely modern phenomenon and that the Elizabethan audience for whom the play was intended would have accepted it, with little discomfort, as a perhaps slightly odd but still quite satisfactory romantic drama. This is the argument of W. W. Lawrence in his excellent essay on the play, and by an intelligent examination of Shakespeare's source in Boccaccio and of analogous medieval stories, Professor Lawrence certainly manages to demonstrate the absurdity of objecting to Helena's "indelicacy" in pursuing Bertram, or to her use of the bed trick in catching him.[4] It is, however, in the play's departure from the traditional story that the argument from narrative and dramatic convention breaks down. Boccaccio's novella tells the story of a "clever wench" (to use Lawrence's term) who by curing the king gets herself married to a tough, unwilling aristocrat, who is nonetheless, "rather a good fellow." [5] The new husband refuses to sleep with his lowborn wife and tells her that he will not do so until she has a child by him. His wife accepts the challenge and proves herself worthy of her husband by fulfilling the condition he has imposed upon her. When the clever wench reveals how clever she has been, the aristocrat accepts her as his wife. It is, as a matter of fact, a good story, and, straightforwardly dramatized, it could have made an amusing play. Shakespeare, however, did not choose to dramatize it straightforwardly. "The blackening of the character of Bertram is one of the most sweeping changes made by Shakespeare in the story as a whole." [6] Indeed, by turning Bertram "into a thoroughly disagreeable, peevish and vicious person," [7] Shakespeare has altered his story in a very basic way. Instead of a clever wench who must prove herself worthy of an aristocratic husband, we have an unworthy husband who must be made worthy of his wife. Shakespeare has chosen to transform his hero into an erring mortal in need of regeneration and forgiveness. Like the anonymous author of *Calisto and Melebea*, Shakespeare has changed his narrative source into a play of forgiveness, and it is as a comedy of forgiveness rather than as a purely romantic comedy that *All's Well* should be examined and judged. *All's Well* was never meant to please in the way that *As You Like It* or *Twelfth Night* please. Though the comedy of forgiveness is a subspecies of the genre romantic comedy, it is different enough in its conventions and in the expectations which it is designed to arouse and fulfill, to require that it be examined critically on the basis of criteria slightly but distinctly different from those by which we ordinarily judge purely romantic comedy. As a purely romantic comedy, *All's Well* is unquestionably a failure; as a comedy of forgiveness it may be only partially successful, but the successes it does achieve are frequently of a high order.

That we should mistake *All's Well* for a purely romantic comedy is not entirely our fault, for Shakespeare only gradually reveals to us that it is not. Indeed, one could say that for the first act and a half, the characters themselves are under the impression that they are appearing in an almost typical boy/girl romance. Helena and the countess, who learns of her love, believe that the barrier to love and happiness is the disparity in rank between Helena and Bertram. With her future mother-in-law's blessing, Helena sets about to destroy that barrier. In Elizabethan terms, Helena is the victim of Fortune, who has assigned her a worldly position which is inappropriate to her deserts. Helena's project in the first half of the play is to raise herself in Fortune to a position of equality with Bertram. Mark Van Doren has pointed out that one of Helena's favorite words is "nature," [8] and well it might be, for if the goddess Fortuna has been niggardly in her gifts to Helena, the goddess Natura has been abundantly generous, and it is through the gifts of Nature that Helena means to overcome the opposition of Fortune. The king says of her:

> Shee is young, wise, faire,
> In these, to Nature shee's immediate heire:
> And these breed honour. . . .   (II.iii.140–42)

Though she does not name them, Helena is clearly thinking of the power of her youth, intelligence, and beauty when she contemplates her chances of winning Bertram:

> The mightiest space in fortune, Nature brings
> To ioyne like, likes; and kisse like natiue things. (I.i.238–39)

But, as Helena realizes, she must have a means by which to show her merit. That means is a symbolically powerful one—the king's disease.

Miss Jessie L. Weston[9] has made modern readers sufficiently conscious of the antiquity and symbolic force that is contained in the Arthurian motif of the dying king. Something of the same aura surrounds the king of France in *All's Well*. His figure is at the center of the play's sterile, dying world, and Helena's cure of him is an impressive and significant demonstration of her restorative power. That power is of two interrelated kinds. By restoring the king to his natural state of health, she is demonstrating again that she is the darling, the "immediate heir" of Nature. But the play strongly insists that she is more. Her cure of the king is "supernatural and causeless" (to quote Lafew). It is a direct result of the grace of God, whose instrument Helena is. "The greatest grace lending grace," (II.i.164) she will cure the king, and she challenges him to try her ability with the words, "Of heaven, not me, make an experiment." (II.i.157) This duality in Helena's nature is insisted on throughout the play. For Lavatch, the clown, she is at one moment "the sweete Margerom of the sallet, or rather the hearbe of grace," (IV.v.16–17) but she has previously been Helen of Troy:

> Was this faire face the cause, quoth she,
> Why the Grecians sacked *Troy* . . .   (I.iii.58–59)

Helena is a beautiful and sexually attractive girl who is also a recipient of God's grace and a means by which it is transmitted to others. It is possible that her name has been chosen with both aspects of her nature in mind. She is, on the one hand, Helen, for whose beauty men launched ships and burned towers. On the other hand, she is Helena, who was the daughter of the notoriously merry old Coelus, Earl of Colchester, and one of the first and most famous of British saints. Her major accomplishments were to give birth to Constantine the Great and to discover the True Cross, by means of which she healed the sick and raised the dead. Though Protestant historians tended to take a jaundiced view of her story, she was by no means forgotten by Shakespeare's contemporaries.[10] One of the London churches and the parish Shakespeare lived in during the 1590s[11] were called after her and her name would presumably have had sacred connotations for the average Londoner.

It is impossible to say which of the two aspects of Helena—the sacred or the profane—is more important. Shakespeare keeps them constantly in balance and to emphasize one at the expense of the other is to throw both character and play out of kilter. The scene in which Helena is introduced to the king is a good example of

Shakespeare's strategy in preserving this balance. The scene ends with Helena at her most hieratic and sibylline, declaiming in highly formal rhymed verse her intention of serving as God's instrument in the cure of the king. But the episode begins with suggestions of a quite different kind. The job of convincing the king that he should give Helena an audience is assigned to old Lafew, and he goes about it bawdily—imitating the encomium of a pander, in order to amuse the king and arouse his interest:

> I haue seen a medicine
> That's able to breath life into a stone,
> Quicken a rocke, and make you dance Canari
> With sprightly fire and motion, whose simple touch
> Is powerfull to arayse King *Pippen,* nay
> To give great *Charlemaine* a pen in's hand
> And write to her a loue-line. (II.i.68–74)

Helena, Lafew is pretending to suggest, will put the debilitated king into a tumescent state,[12] and he makes his exit with the line:

> I am *Cresseds* Vncle,
> That dare leaue two together, far you well. (II.i.97–98)

As with the earlier bawdy of Parolles, these speeches have functions beyond that of getting a laugh. They ensure that in our admiration for Helena's spirituality, we shall not forget her sexual attractiveness. And yet it seems possible that Shakespeare deliberately set Lafew's *double-entendres* within an action that would itself suggest spirituality for this scene is strongly reminiscent of another, previously dramatized by Shakespeare (or a collaborator), and familiar to his audience, in which the ruler of France is in grave danger and a simple country maiden is brought to him with assurances that she is the instrument of heaven sent to save the day. The resemblance to St. Joan may be fortuitous or unconscious, but even so, it can contribute to our idea of Helena.[13]

That idea is complex, to say the least. Compounded of St. Helena and Helen of Troy, with hints of St. Joan and Cressida, Helena can fairly be called Shakespeare's most complicated comic heroine. Her complexity is the result of her function in *All's Well*, for the play demands a heroine who combines, in their highest degrees, the attributes of sacred and profane love. On the human, secular level it is necessary that Helena regenerate a dying world in the ordinary human, secular way—sexually and procreatively. But on another level that regeneration must take place in ways other than the physical. The virtue as well as the bodily existence of a dying world must be re-created, and to achieve that, Helena's spiritual forces will be necessary.

The full extent of Helena's task is not apparent until she has cured the king. Before that, we had accepted her assumption that the barrier to the comic ending was, indeed, the disparity in rank between hero and heroine. Now we find out that we have been wrong. The barrier that stands between Helena and Bertram is Bertram. The scene in which we make this discovery is an equivalent to the church scene in *Much Ado*. But though Claudio's outburst there is more violent in language and emotion than Bertram's in the later play, the effect of both as violations of the comic spirit is the same, and, if anything, Bertram's interruption of festivity leaves us more frustrated and uncomfortable than Claudio's.

The festive quality of the scene within which Shakespeare has placed Bertram's rejection of Helena is interesting. There is a ceremoniousness about the business of Helena's choice of a partner that has caused it to be staged as a ballet[14] and compared to a Levantine slave market.[15] It is also reminiscent of another and very common ritual—a children's game, a choosing or kissing game, like "Post Office." Indeed, the whole incident resembles a children's party with the old folks, the king and Lafew, looking benignly on while the birthday girl selects her partner. And as frequently happens on such occasions there is one guest who spoils the fun by refusing to play if he has to be "it." The petulance of Bertram at this moment reveals suddenly that the object of Helena's pursuit is not a fairy-tale prince, a romantic hero, but a spoiled, immature, self-centered snob. Like Claudio, Bertram denies us our comic pleasures, but while Claudio acts as badly as Bertram, he at least acts upon the discreditable motives of a grown man—outraged honor, however misguided, and sexual revulsion, however irrational—and he is suffering while he acts. Bertram does not have even these excuses for his offense.

To be sure, Bertram's refusal to accept Helena as his wife is in part a matter of principle. He is a ward of the king, so that the king has the legal right, as his guardian as well as his lord, to marry him where he chooses. Bertram, however, has the legal right to refuse his guardian's choice of a partner if the proposed marriage entails what was called "disparagement" [16]—marriage to a person of a lower social class. He attempts to exercise that right:

> A poore Physitians daughter my wife? Disdaine
> Rather corrupt me euer.   (II.iii.124–26)

The king then tries to persuade Bertram with the familiar Renaissance argument that true nobility is not the exclusive possession of the aristocracy.[17] An aristocrat may be essentially ignoble while commoners frequently display noble qualities. These are commonplaces hallowed by repetition through the centuries, but the king does not stop with them. He proceeds to point out that he can endow the already naturally endowed Helena with the additional gifts of Fortune, thus making her the equal in every way of Count Rossillion:

> If thou canst like this creature, as a maide,
> I can create the rest: Vertue, and shee
> Is her owne dower: Honour and wealth, from mee.
>   (II.iii.153–55)

The king is not proposing to force Bertram to marry his inferior. Rather, he will raise Helena to Bertram's material and social level. In the reigns of Elizabeth and James I, it would have been unwise to deny the monarch's ability to do this, and Bertram does not attempt it. Instead, he rejects Helena as a woman: "I cannot loue her, nor will strive to doo't (II.iii.156)

Bertram, at this point, stops trying to justify himself, and the king, in turn, abandons all attempt to reason with him and produces the royal power. The result is impressive and gives one an inkling of why contemporary courtiers were shaken even by the distant memory of one of Elizabeth's losses of temper.[18] Bertram capitulates completely and admits what he had never denied—that the king has it in his power to ennoble Helena. He does not, however, recant his refusal to love her and we must ask ourselves what, finally, inspires or accounts for that refusal.

The "children's party" quality of the scene of rejection underlines one of Bertram's most important characteristics—his extreme immaturity. Bertram is very young, chronologically nineteen, perhaps, and psychologically even younger. He is young, however, in an odd way. His reaction to the situation he finds himself in is not that of an ordinary late adolescent. It is understandable enough that he should oppose the king's insistence that he marry a woman of the king's choosing, but his behavior after he has been forced to capitulate is less comprehensible. One would expect him, after the marriage ceremony, to take stock of the situation. He would find himself married to a young, intelligent, and charming girl whose influence with the king was likely to procure him great worldly advantage. He would also discover that he had acquired a wife of great beauty and sexual attractiveness. Under the circumstances it seems likely that for the average nineteen-year-old—for the average man of any age, perhaps—having to "bed" Helena would be, not the final indignity, but the first consolation.

Bertram's refusal to consummate his marriage cannot, surely, be attributed simply to his refusal to recognize Helena's true nobility. It must also be the result of his failure to feel sexual desire for his young and attractive wife. As we have seen, Shakespeare has been at great pains to make it clear that Helena is, in fact, more than ordinarily desirable and that the reason for Bertram's refusal to "bed" her is clearly not to be discovered in Helena. Whatever its source, nothing could be more inimical to the spirit of romantic comedy than this refusal of sexual love. That the ostensible hero of a comedy should reject, for any reason, the pleasure, beauty and happiness of the act of love is shocking enough to the comic sensibilities. Claudio, Posthumus, and Leontes, however, are at least provided with a comprehensible reason: they have wrongly suspected the women they love of unchastity, and, as a result, their love has turned to hatred. Bertram's rejection of love, by comparison, is simply perverse, and in refusing to make love to Helena, he refuses not only his own pleasure, but the means which nature has provided for the defeat of mutability. By doing so, he sets himself against the emotional movement of the play he is appearing in, and leaves his audience baffled, frustrated, and annoyed.

But, of course, our frustration and annoyance are only beginning. Shakespeare will proceed to have Bertram behave more and more unpleasantly until the final moments of the play. It is only natural, perhaps, that, confronted by this series of unpleasant actions on the part of a "hero," we should search for an explanation of them, a tidy, logical "reason" for Bertram's bad behavior. Since, for example, it is clear that the reason for Bertram's refusal to "bed" Helena is not to be discovered in Helena, where, we ask ourselves, is it to be discovered? A common solution, and one that is to some extent justified by the play, is to find it in Parolles. It is tempting to try to ameliorate, somewhat, the play's central difficulty by shifting the blame for Bertram's ignobility onto a figure who can be seen as his bad angel, as a version of the old Vice, who tempts Bertram and leads him astray. If Parolles could be so seen, could be found to function in the play as a surrogate for the audience's dislike of his master, if we could legitimately allow Parolles to serve as a scapegoat for Bertram, as Don John serves for Claudio, and Iachimo serves for Posthumus, the difficulty of forgiving Bertram at the play's end would be considerably eased.

Evidence for so regarding Parolles can be found within the play. He is described precisely as the ignoble misleader of noble youth by several of the more clear-seeing figures in the comedy. The Old Countess characterizes him as:

> A verie tainted fellow, and full of wickednesse,
> My sonne corrupts a well deriued nature
> With his inducement. (III.ii.90–92)

And when, toward the end of the play, Lafew has decided to marry his daughter to Bertram, he similarly excuses his future son-in-law:

> No, no, no your sonne was misled with a
> snipt taffata fellow there, whose villanous
> saffron wold haue made all the vnbak'd and
> dowy youth of a nation in his colour. (IV.v.1–4)

These statements, of course, influence our view of the relationship between Parolles and Bertram. They do not, however, completely define that relationship for they do not accurately describe what has been presented to us by the action of the play. There are undoubtedly elements of the old Vice and the evil councilor in Parolles, but they are not of a kind or of an intensity to serve as full excuses for Bertram's actions. Parolles is unquestionably a low fellow and far from suitable company for the young, but we never see him actively misleading, tempting, or corrupting Bertram. It is Bertram who has the evil impulses and suggests the ignoble actions. Parolles need do no more than second the motion. He is a parasite, a yes-man, rather than a corrupter of youth. The scene in which Bertram decides to desert his wife and run away to Italy is an excellent example of the relationship:

> *Ros.*: Vndone, and forfeited to cares for euer.
> *Par.*: What's the matter sweet-heart?
> *Rosill.*: Although before the solemne Priest I haue

sworne, I will not bed her.
Par.: What? what sweet-heart?
Ros.: O my *Parrolles*, they have married me:
Ile to the *Tuscan* warres, and neuer bed her.
Par.: *France* is a dog-hole, and it no more merits,
The tread of a mans foot: too'th warres.   (II.iii.276–82)

Far from leading Bertram into temptation, Parolles is lamentably slow to discover exactly what he is expected to agree to. The most we can blame Parolles for is his failure to disapprove of Bertram's plans. He does perform a portion of the Vice's function in that he provides an atmosphere of complaisance to sin, but as an active tempter, he is highly ineffective. Even when he serves as a go-between for Bertram in the attempted seduction of Diana, we discover that, far from encouraging Diana to commit adultery, Parolles is double-crossing his master and trying to get the girl for himself.

That "the relationship of the two is not that of misleader and misled" [19] is clearest in the last act of the play. By the time of Bertram's return to France, the true character of Parolles has been made clear to him as a result of the plot concocted for that purpose by the two French lords. Bertram has dismissed Parolles from his favor, and if Parolles had been previously responsible for Bertram's ignoble actions, we would be justified in expecting Bertram to begin acting decently once he had been removed from the influence of his bad angel. Nothing of the sort happens. In the final scene of the play, Bertram's behavior surpasses, in loutishness, everything he has achieved up to that point. His treatment of Diana makes it quite clear that nothing outside his own character is needed to inspire Bertram to dishonorable actions.

Parolles is a symptom rather than a cause of Bertram's disease— for Bertram's very nature is diseased. Just as the king's natural state of health is corrupted by his illness, so Bertram "corrupts a well-derived nature." To cure him Helena must, in a sense, repeat, on a spiritual and psychological plane, the miracle of the king's restoration to health, and Parolles serves as the fistula, the symptom by which

Bertram's malady can be recognized. Bertram's admiration for this fool and coward is a logical complement to his detestation of Helena. A part of Bertram's corruption is the result of his inability to perceive the true nature of others. He can see neither Parolles nor Helena for what they truly are. This failure of perception is, itself, only an indication of another and, to the Elizabethan, far more dangerous failure—for Bertram is also unable to perceive and to differentiate between the nobility and ignobility within his own character. His admiration for Parolles provides an example of the first of these failures. Parolles' unmasking and subsequent forced assumption of his true role in the world of the play will, as we shall see, provide an action analogous to that in which Bertram is similarly dealt with. It is as symptom and as analogue, rather than as tempter, that Parolles functions most importantly in *All's Well*.

Bertram's refusal to go to bed with Helena cannot, then, be explained either as the result of Helena's lack of sexual desirability or of the malign influence of Parolles. Neither can we justifiably suspect that Bertram is unable to feel ordinary sexual desire. His determined pursuit of Diana is sufficient proof that he is capable of heterosexual lust. But it is perhaps time to call a halt to our search for motivations and to think, for a moment, of the significance of Bertram's recalcitrance in terms of the action of the play as a whole. That recalcitrance appears to be at the center of the play's meaning, but there is little reason to believe that Shakespeare therefore felt called upon to account for it either with strict psychological realism or by providing any of the tidy "motives" which some academic critics still naïvely regard as explanations for human action. Bertram's intransigence is Shakespeare's *donné*. He dramatizes it, considers it, comments on it, but he does not explain it. Some of its implications for the play as a whole are clear enough. Man sometimes inexplicably rebels against his own good—against both what is good for him and what is good within him. This is what Bertram does, not only in his treatment of Helena, but consistently throughout the play. To look for motives in the ordinary sense of the word will be to look in vain, for Bertram acts, not out of a rational desire for his own good, but from an inexplicable but by no means uncommon desire for self-damage. Or, to put it in Elizabethan terms:

> Of ourselves and by ourselves, we are not able either to think a good thought, or work a good deed: so that we can find in ourselves no hope of salvation, but rather whatsoever maketh unto our destruction.[20]

The two French lords, Shakespeare's chorus to the third and fourth acts of *All's Well,* comment specifically upon Bertram as his own enemy, and extend their remarks to include us all:

> *Cap. E.:* Hee hath peruerted a young Gentlewoman heere in *Florence,* of a most chaste renown, & this night he fleshes his will in the spoyle of her honour: hee hath giuen her his monumentall Ring, and thinkes himselfe made in the unchaste composition.
>
> *Cap. G.:* Now God delay our rebellion as we are our selues, what things are we.
>
> *Cap. E.:* Meerely our owne traitours. And as in the common course of all treasons, we still see them reueale themselues, till they attaine to their abhorr'd ends: so he that in this action contriues against his owne Nobility in his proper streame, ore-flowes himselfe.   (IV.iii.13–24)

Shakespeare has been at some pains to show us, in the incident of Bertram's attempted seduction of Diana, a man not only contriving against his own nobility, but inspired to do so by an absurdly and ironically misguided sensuality. In order to "flesh his will," Bertram is ready to betray anything. He breaks, first, his marriage vows, then violates his personal honor with a string of lying promises to Diana, and finally, in agreeing to give Diana his "monumental ring," he symbolically betrays the honor of his family. Family honor, the motive upon which he has insisted in refusing to consummate his marriage with Helena, he is willing to pawn for a few moments of adulterous lust in the pitch dark with Diana. The dark contains, not Diana, but the detested Helena, and Bertram is unaware of the difference.

Helena's substitution of herself for Diana is immediately inspired by Bertram's taunting assertion that he will not sleep with his wife until he has had a child by her. By deceiving him, Helena saves her husband from the violation of his marriage vows and of his honor. In addition, Helena is able to trick Bertram into performing his necessary role in the physical regeneration of the dying world of Rossillion, for lust will serve as well as love for that, and Helena need only direct lust toward its morally and legally sanctioned object. The fact that she is able to do so without lust's being aware of what is happening inspires her to make a profound and disquieting comment upon the nature of male sexuality:

> But O strange men,
> That can such sweet vse make of what they hate,
> When sawcie trusting of the cosin'd thoughts
> Defiles the pitchy night, so lust doth play
> With what it loathes, for that which is away. (IV.iv.24–28)

Although Helena's knowledge is the result of her deception of Bertram, it is clear that her comments are not meant to be limited to those (surely rare) unfortunates who are victims of the bed trick. The truth that lust is more a mental than a physical phenomenon has been fully revealed by Bertram's passionate response to the mistaken thought that the woman he detests is the woman he desires. But the application of the truth goes beyond Bertram, beyond the deceived to the self-deceived, for the cozened thoughts of the lustful are ordinarily self-cozened and we deceive ourselves into accepting the loathsome as a substitute for the desirable. Helena's statement suggests an even deeper insight into the duality of sexual desire, however, for men, she ambiguously tells us, make sweet use of *what* they hate. Sexual desire makes it possible for men to enjoy not only a partner they detest, but an act they detest. Lust, as opposed to love, contains a hatred for the sexual act itself.

Bertram's attempted seduction of Diana and his deception by the bed trick reveal the corruption of his nature and, by implication, the corruption of all male sexuality when it is dominated by lust. Bertram selects the corrupt and ignoble alternative when forced by his sexual desires to find an object for them. He rejects the sexuality which is sanctioned and, indeed, enjoined upon him by his marriage vows, because he prefers an adulterous liaison which he can obtain only by ignoble lying and bribery. He believes that he seduces Diana because of his overwhelming sensual desire for her, and yet he is able to satisfy that desire by a brief moment in the dark with another woman, with the very woman whom he professes to loathe so intensely that he will not have sexual relations with her. By this irrational rejection of his own good, Bertram is doing more than demonstrate the truth of the proposition that "Passion and reason self-division cause." Bertram is not self-divided; he is self-deceived and self-ignorant. He seems totally unaware of the ignobility of his own nature and, as a result, he is in a perilous state, indeed. Again the comments of the French lords are to the point:

> *Cap. G.:* The webbe of our life, is of a mingled yarne, good and ill together: our vertues would bee proud, if our faults whipt them not, and our crimes would dispaire if they were not cherish'd by our vertues.
> (IV.iii.77–80)

Bertram is ignorant of his faults and consequently ignorant of his virtues. Until she has brought her husband to a state of self-knowledge, Helena will not have completed her task of restoring the dying world of Rossillion. The honor of Bertram's father has not reappeared in the son, and so long as that is the case, the world of Rossillion is only superficially alive, for honor is the soul of that world, and

> this is honours scorne,
> Which challenges it selfe as honours borne,
> And is not like the sire. . . . (II.iii.144–46)

Helena has cured the king and, by obtaining Bertram's ring and becoming pregnant by him, she has fulfilled the tasks which her husband imposed upon her. The dying world of the play's opening scene has been restored to health and fertility. It now remains for Helena to restore Bertram to that state of honor which, we are told, is naturally his. This she can do only by forcing self-knowledge upon him.

The method by which this end is achieved is both predicted and explained by the analogous action of Parolles' unmasking. The two French lords undertake this project specifically in the hope that it will force Bertram to confront the true nature, not so much of Parolles, as of himself:

> I would gladly haue him see his company
> anathomiz'd, that hee might take a measure
> of his owne iudgements, wherein so curiously
> he had set this counterfeit (IV.iii.37–40)

Their hopes, for the time being, prove fruitless, for Bertram's self-esteem needs harsher methods for its correction than the revelation of someone else's weakness. The plot of the drum does, however, provide Shakespeare with a method of demonstrating how a man may be forced to act in accordance with his own nature.

The basic difference between the unmasking of Parolles here and the unmasking of Bertram in the last act is that Parolles learns nothing about himself because he has never been the victim of any illusions about what he is. He, like everyone else in the play, except Bertram, is perfectly well aware that Parolles is a coward and a knave. In order to profit by Bertram's credulity, Parolles is willing to pretend to be what he is not, but he knows that he is playing a role and he curses himself when he begins playing it too realistically:

What the diuell should moue mee to vndertake
the recouerie of this drumme, being not ignorant of the
impossibility, and knowing I had no such purpose?

(IV.i.34–36)

Again the comments of the French captains underline the point: "Is it possible that he should know what hee is, and be that he is?" It is, indeed, possible, though unlike Parolles, most of us manage to prevent ourselves from knowing what we are. There is, however, nothing immoral about ignobility so long as one cannot be and does not pretend to be noble. Pretensions to nobility can be dangerous to society for they may lead to misplaced trust. In deflating Parolles' pretensions, the French lords are performing a public service, and the way in which they go about it has a strong resemblance to the way in which Helena goes about the cure of Bertram. Like Bertram in his desire for Diana, Parolles, in his desire for life, is ready to promise anything, compromise anything, betray anyone. Like Bertram, the blindfolded Parolles is caught in the dark, and just as Bertram commits adultery with his wife, Parolles betrays his comrades to his comrades. When the blindfold is removed from his eyes, Parolles realizes that he has revealed his true nature beyond hope of concealment or excuse. His reaction is to accept that nature and decide to live by it:

Rust sword, coole blushes, and *Parrolles* liue
Safest in shame: being fool'd, by fool'rie thriue;
There's place and meanes for euery man aliue.
Ile after them.   (IV.iii.370–73)

By becoming a tame toady to Lord Lafew, he discovers the place in the world that is proper to him.

It is necessary to keep the unmasking of Parolles in mind when one approaches the last scene of the play—a highly uncomfortable piece of theater which has been generally held to result in the failure

of the comedy as a whole. Parolles thinks he is safe in defaming his
fellow soldiers—Captain Dumain, for example:

> I know him, a was a Botchers Prentize in *Paris*,
> from whence he was whipt for getting the Shrieues fool
> with childe, a dumbe innocent that could not
> say him nay.　　　　　　　　　　　　　　　(IV.iii.207–10)

By doing so, he hopes to save his life. Bertram thinks he is safe
in defaming Diana:

> She's impudent my Lord,
> And was a common gamester to the Campe.
> 　　　　　　　　　　　　　　　　(V.iii.187–88)

By doing so, he hopes to save his reputation. When the truth dawns
upon Parolles, he has no choice but to become himself and to turn to
the charity of his fellow men in the hope that they will accept him as
he is. The truth which dawns upon Bertram is more complex. He realizes, first that the girl whom he thinks he has seduced and whom he
has had no compunction about slandering, is, in fact, innocent, and
has revealed to the king, the countess, and the court of France that
Bertram is a lying, promise-breaking seducer. Like Parolles when
the blindfold is removed, Bertram must face the fact that the truth
about him is irretrievably known, but we have also the sense that
for the first time the truth about Bertram has been revealed to Bertram himself.

In Bertram's case, then, the blindfold is removed from the inner
eye of conscience, and *humanum genus* is able, as a result, finally
to see the evidence of his own corruption. That revelation is no more
fortuitous than the unmasking of Parolles. The French lords have
played a socially valuable practical joke which results in the return
of Parolles to his appropriate station in the world. Like them, Helena
has arranged a salutary discomfiture—that of her erring husband. In
doing so, she has once again served as the instrument of God's grace.

As Clifford Leech puts it, "Helena, in her curing of the King, is a dispenser of divine grace, and in her definitive subjection of Bertram she is setting his foot on the path of Christian virtue." [21] For Bertram, the descent of grace equals the access of self-knowledge, and because "the turning of the heart unto God is of God," [22] the means by which that "turning" is achieved must be of God, too. Helena is the instrument which heaven has employed in working out its designs:

> Whatsoever God doeth, he bringeth it about by his instruments ordained thereto. He hath good angels, he hath evil angels; he hath good men, and he hath evil men; he hath hail and rain, he hath wind and thunder, he hath heat and cold; innumerable instruments hath he, and messengers . . .[23]

Helena is such an instrument and messenger.

The Old Countess, reflecting on her son's flight to Italy, asks:

> What Angell shall
> Blesse this vnworthy husband . . . ?   (III.iv.26–27)

The answer, of course, is Helena, as the countess goes on to explain in the lines that follow:

> he cannot thriue,
> Vnlesse her prayers, whom heauen delights to heare
> And loues to grant, repreeue him from the wrath
> Of greatest Iustice.   (III.iv.27–30)

These lines describe Helena, but they do so in terms that inevitably suggest the Virgin Mary. The Arden editor believes that "a straightforward reference to the Virgin as intercessor is too Popish to be probable," [24] but a more "Popish" activity than a barefoot pilgrimage to Santiago da Compostella is difficult to imagine, and yet Helena has just left on such an errand when these lines are spoken of her. Shakespeare evokes the Virgin here because Helena's function in the play is similar to that of the Mother of God in the "Popish" scheme of things. Both serve as means through which the grace of God can be communicated to man. Nor is this similarity surprising, for, considered historically, the charitable heroines of the comedy of forgiveness are literary descendants of the Virgin in the medieval narrative and dramatic "Miracles of Our Lady." Ordinarily their function is simply to be sinned against and to forgive, but unlike Hero, Imogen, and Hermione, Helena is called upon to serve as the active agent in the regeneration of the erring hero.

Two main objections, largely inspired by that regeneration, have been raised to the happy ending of *All's Well*. The first of these sees the forgiveness of Bertram as a violation of poetic justice. For Dr. Johnson, Bertram's felicity is not deserved. Bertram is merely "dismissed to happiness," [25] after a series of sneaking profligacies, and Dr. Johnson cannot, therefore, reconcile his heart to him. Against this objection no defense is possible except a very basic one. Poetic justice is *not* served by the comedies of forgiveness. It is not meant to be served, because these comedies celebrate another virtue—charity. The second objection is more complicated in its implications. Critics of this play have felt (as far as I know, without exception) that the final scene of the play fails because Bertram's regeneration is unconvincing. There can be no doubt that, indeed, the scene does so fail for a modern audience. We do not believe in the regeneration. It is not communicated to us.

The reasons for that failure of communication need careful consideration, however. The general feeling seems to be that Shakespeare fell back on a rather shallow theatrical convention for the denouement of this play. According to Quiller-Couch, "*All's Well* has no atmosphere save that of the stage. . . . It is a thing 'of the boards'" [26] and such a "thing," we assume, does not deserve the name of great drama and is unworthy of a great dramatist. Robert Y. Turner, in a recent essay, has shown how common a theatrical event such arbitrary regenerations were in the drama of Shakespeare's time, but, as Turner points out, this use of a literary commonplace "will not justify Shakespeare's workmanship. It merely tells us that *All's Well* is a failure of one kind and not another." [27] And yet, theatrical conventions of this sort are not simply arbitrary or purely formal. They succeed because they refer to and draw upon the shared beliefs of an audience.

The final scene of *All's Well* draws upon and refers to a belief in the reality of the descent of grace upon a sinning human. The Elizabethan audience believed in such an occurrence not as a theological abstraction, but as an everyday psychological possibility. What happens to Bertram would, I think, have been clear to Shakespeare's contemporaries. The scales fall from Bertram's eyes, he sees what he has done, and he is filled with shame and a sense of the necessity for pardon:

> We have a common experience of the same in them which, when they have committed any heinous offence or some filthy and abominable sin, if it once come to light, or if they chance to have a through feeling of it, they be so ashamed, their own conscience putting before their eyes the filthiness of their act, that they dare look no man on the face, much less that they should be able to stand in the sight of God.[28]

Out of such an experience, a new man is born:

> After his repentance he was no more the man that he was before, but was clean changed and altered.[29]

A Renaissance audience would not, I think, have considered even Bertram incapable of that alteration.

By referring the characters and events of *All's Well* to the Christian concepts which help to explain them, I am not, I hope, maintaining that this comedy is a Christian allegory, a Christian parable, or a Christian homily. It is a secular comedy concerned with this world and with the relationships between men and women in this life. It was, however, written for a Christian audience and it draws naturally upon a Christian view of the world. It is, furthermore, cast in a traditionally Christian dramatic form—that of the play of forgiveness.

The Romance and the
Comedy of Forgiveness

Students of Shakespeare inevitably feel called upon to account for the late romances. Oddly enough, we seldom seem to find it puzzling that one man should have written both *As You Like It* and *King Lear*; but that the same man should have gone on to produce *Cymbeline* strikes us as peculiar, and to account for the peculiarity we imagine that something peculiar had happened to Shakespeare. He had become serene, or bored, or old; he had undergone nervous breakdown and/or religious conversion. Indeed, Shakespeare's possible state (or states) of mind in his later years is a subject limited only by the possibilities of the human psyche, for in fact we do not have the vaguest notion of his spiritual or emotional condition then or at any other period in his career. The late romances themselves are the only evidence we have for Shakespeare's mental state at the time he wrote them, and the state of mind we attribute to Shakespeare will probably be that which his art induces in us. If the late romances leave us bored, or serene, or nervous, we will explain the fact as resulting from the boredom, or serenity, or nervousness of the man who wrote them.

Clearly, such lines of thought are circular, and though amusing—like merry-go-rounds—they end by transporting us nowhere. If we must explain the existence of the romances—and it seems we must —it is better to regard them, not as sources for Shakespeare's biography, but as documents in the history of Shakespeare's art. As such they can be viewed in two ways: as evidence of what happened to Shakespearean tragedy and as evidence of what happened to Shakespearean comedy. E. M. W. Tillyard, in *Shakespeare's Last Plays*, sees them as the former, as workings out of the full tragic pattern, with the re-creation of a new order, as well as the destruction of an old. For him, "the transitional plays between the full tragic period and the romances are *Antony and Cleopatra* and *Coriolanus*," [1] and the earlier comedies do not underlie the romances because, although "in some of Shakespeare's comedies—in *Much Ado*, for instance—there is the risk of destruction . . . in the end . . . the audience finds itself in the same old world, only aired, exercised, and regaled with marriage bells." [2] Given Tillyard's view of these late plays—and it is an admirably cogent one—his presentation of their development is perfectly logical. However, one can also legitimately see these plays as primarily comic and primarily the outgrowth of a comic tradition—or, rather, as the union of two comic traditions, that of the romance and the comedy of forgiveness.

Between *All's Well* and *Cymbeline*, Shakespeare worked with three plays which clearly influenced his development of the romance form. The first of these, *Promos and Cassandra*, we have already considered and we will consider what Shakespeare made of it in a later chapter. The second, the tragi-comedy of *King Leir*, Shakespeare transformed into his greatest tragedy. In doing so, he discarded the triumphant conclusion of the old play, but the final happiness of father and daughter in *King Leir* clearly remained in Shakespeare's mind as an effective dramatic possibility. He realized that possibility in the third of the plays that lead to the romances—*Pericles*. We have no idea what sort of raw material Shakespeare was working with when he came to write the last three acts of that play, but it has been suggested that he had an entire five-act romance of which he decided to touch up the first two acts and rewrite the third, fourth, and fifth.[3] In any case, he undertook the completion or rewriting of a play in a very old narrative and dramatic tradition. *Pericles* is the romance of a wandering knight who, in the course of his life upon the stage, passes through a series of moving accidents by flood and field, is tested by the vicissitudes of Fortune, and emerges from his trials to collect the well-deserved reward of a happy ending. Such stories and the plays made from them move in space over the known world and frequently cover close to a generation in time. They almost invariably involve the separation of lovers and they achieve their denouements in scenes of reunion. Similar stories have survived in dramatic form from the fourteenth century in the secular Dutch *abel spelen* of *Gloriant, the Duke of Brunswick,* and *Esmoreit, the King's Son of Sicily,* a play in which, as in *The Winter's Tale,* the king of Sicily wrongly suspects his wife of adultery and casts out their only child, a boy who grows up in the rival kingdom of Damask, where he and the king's daughter fall in love with one another. Such narratives were adapted to the purposes of religious didacticism in the French *Miracles de Notre Dame.* Except, as we shall see, for a portion of the fifteenth-century miracle play of *Mary Magdalene,* no real examples of the tradition in English drama survived until the 1560s, the period when the dramas of *Sir Clyomon and Sir Clamydes* and *Common Conditions* first held the stage. From that time on, the type is more or less constantly in evidence. It is clearly plays of this sort that Sidney is primarily annoyed at in his famous attack on the contemporary drama in the *Defense of Poesie* in 1583; and throughout Shakespeare's lifetime such plays were frequently performed. The most famous of them is probably *Mucedorus,* which the King's Men chose to revive in 1610/11,[4] but there are others more strikingly in the tradition which Shakespeare was to transform. Most of these plays are anonymous, of little or no literary merit and, one would imagine, seldom seriously considered by critics of Shakespeare, and yet they serve to indicate the sort of theatrical raw material which Shakespeare worked with in his last plays. In the anonymous *John of Bordeaux,* for example, we have, as in *Pericles,* the story of a noble soldier who is separated from his loving wife and children by the vicissitudes of Fortune—which goddess is seconded in her machinations by the evil magician, Vandermast, and the good magician, Friar Bacon. It is the latter who, Prospero-like, at one point has "frendlie faunes and Satters" and a "nimph" entertain the wandering hero with music and a banquet.[5] Thomas Heywood, in *Four Prentises of London,* creates four romantic protagonists without changing the basic pattern for any one of them, and adds for good measure a princess of France who, like Imogen, falls in love with an honorable social inferior and follows him into battle disguised as a page. Imogen reappears in the anonymous *Weakest Goeth to the Wall,* where she is named Odillia and, though daughter of the Duke of Brabant, has the audacity to fall in love with a foundling. This noble young fellow turns out to be the son of Lodowick, Duke of Bullen, the Fortune-persecuted knight of the play, who, like Pericles, is separated from his sorely tried wife and daughter. In the *Trial of Chivalry,* the action is more concentrated in time and space, but the trappings of chivalric romance are all present and, to the student of *The Winter's Tale,* the play is particularly interesting for one of its major *coups-de-théâtre,* a scene in which the heroine, Katharina of France, kneels at what she believes to be the tomb of Ferdinand of Navar, the lover she has scorned, and confesses her love to what she takes to be "his whole proportion cut in white alabaster." The statue proceeds to embrace her and she is informed that:

> 'tis no sencelesse Image,
> But the true essence of your wished Loue.[6]

All of these plays are difficult to date with much precision, but they seem to belong to the decade between 1590 and 1600. The important thing about them, so far as Shakespeare's artistic development is concerned, is not their individual existence, but the tradition that they represent. There is no reason to suppose that Shakespeare read or saw *The Weakest Goeth to the Wall* or the *Trial of Chivalry*—though he may well have done so. The point is that, as an Elizabethan man of the theater (and of the popular theater) Shakespeare must necessarily have been saturated in the tradition which such plays exemplify. These romantic, wandering knight, Fortune-my-foe melodramas were one of the staples of the Elizabethan theatrical diet. And they were theatrical rather than literary. There is small joy to be obtained from reading them, but the reader with a share of theatrical imagination will recognize at once the force and vitality which they must have had on stage. Of all the products of the Elizabethan theater, they go least successfully into print, and it seems clear that only a small proportion were printed, and even these few have failed to win a sympathetic reading from later students of the period. This may explain the existence of what appears (to me at least) to be an odd myth about the Jacobean drama. "Towards the end of the first decade of the seventeenth century, it was obvious that Beaumont and Fletcher had created a new type of drama, the heroic romance, which was immensely popular. Sensitive and obedient to the public demand, Shakespeare wrote his own tragi-comic romances." [7] Surely this is not what happened at all. Beaumont and Fletcher could no more have "created" the heroic romance than they could have "created" tragedy or comedy. Rather, Shakespeare and Beaumont and Fletcher (who had previously parodied the form with great artistic and small popular success) turned their attention to the romance at approximately the same time. Because they were the first English dramatists of great literary merit to do so, the kinship of their romances with the artistically cruder productions that preceded them is not, perhaps, as clear as it might be.

The transformation of the old romance that Shakespeare was to effect in *Cymbeline* and *The Winter's Tale* is only half completed in *Pericles*. Perhaps because the play was written with a collaborator, *Pericles* remains, so far as its action is concerned, solidly in the Fortune-my-foe tradition. The Shakespearean portion of the play transcends that tradition through the beauty of its poetry, through the dramatic strength of the brothel scenes, and, above all, through the Shakespearean ability to infuse a sense of the wonderful into such moments as the revival of Thaisa, the recognition of Pericles and Marina, and the reunion at the temple of Diana. This transcendence occurs, however, without really changing the nature and significance of the traditional romance action. The romance ordinarily gives us the sense that man is the creature of chance, that he is limited in his ability to control his destiny, and that his virtue must consist in a courageous and honorable behavior through the trials that are thrust upon him. These trials are never meaningless, however, for there are powers above man who judge and finally reward (or punish) his conduct.

> In *Antiochus* and his daughter you haue heard
> Of monstrous lust, the due and iust reward:
> In *Pericles* his Queene and Daughter seene,
> Although assayl'de with *Fortune* fierce and keene,
> Vertue preservd [8] from fell destructions blast,
> Lead on by heauen, and crown'd with joy at last.
> (Epil. 1–6)

So "antient Gower" sums up the play in the final chorus, and, in fact, the significance of the action of *Pericles* is finally as simple as this statement of it. It is Shakespeare's art that sets *Pericles* above the other plays in its tradition, but that art is exercised in the raising of a simple action to the highest poetic power rather than in the investing of such an action with a more complex significance.

What Shakespeare does, for the first time, in *Pericles* is to create the special atmosphere of romance. That atmosphere I have already described as one in which miracle is constantly possible and finally occurs. Northrop Frye characterizes the romance environment as follows:

> The hero of romance moves in a world in which the ordinary laws of nature are slightly suspended: prodigies of courage and endurance, unnatural to us, are natural to him, and enchanted weapons, talking animals, terrifying ogres and witches, and talismans of miraculous power violate no rule of probability once the postulates of romance have been established.[9]

Shakespeare's romances are moving toward the presentation of such a world though (save for *The Tempest*) they stop short of it. In

Pericles, Cymbeline, and *The Winter's Tale* the miraculous can usually be explained naturalistically—as with the resurrection of Thaisa, or the coming to life of Hermione's statue. In addition to such natural marvels, however, these romances are characterized by a phenomenon that never occurs in the earlier plays of Shakespeare: the direct intervention in the world of the play of divine power.

In this use of the theophany, Shakespeare is returning to a romance tradition older than that of his immediate predecessors in the romantic drama. The romances of the 1590s abandoned the appearance on-stage of the god who rules the play's action. In the 1580s, however, in the plays of Lyly and others, theophanies abound, and we have already examined, in *The Rare Triumphs of Love and Fortune,* a pre-Lyly romance in which the gods spend almost as much time on-stage as the human protagonists. Even earlier, in *Sir Clyomon and Sir Clamydes,* Neronis, daughter of the King of the Strange Marshes, has, like Imogen, disguised herself as a boy and fled to the wilderness to escape an unwanted suitor. There she discovers the tomb of her persecutor, but just as Imogen takes the body of Cloten for that of Posthumus, Neronis wrongly assumes that the grave is that of her lover, Sir Clyomon. Filled with despair, she resolves to kill herself, but, in the nick of time, and prompted by her prayer to the gods, Providence descends and advises her to read the epitaph before she does anything rash. Neronis discovers that in fact Sir Clyomon is alive and the grave is that of her worst enemy. She praises "mightie Ioue on hie" and Providence gives her words of advice and comfort:

> *Provi.:* Well, let desparation die in thee, I may not here remaine,
> But be assured, that thou shalt ere long thy knight attaine.

> *Ascend.*
> *Nero:* And for their prouidence diuine, the Gods aboue ile praise,
> And shew their works so wonderfull, vnto their laud alwaies.[10]

Providence is here filling the role that had not long before been the property of the Virgin Mary in the *Miracles de Notre Dame,* and ultimately the origin of the theophany in romantic drama is to be found in the descent of the Virgin or of Christ in the pre-Reformation miracle plays.

Some of the other wonders of *Pericles* can also be paralleled in the medieval drama. The birth, on shipboard, of Marina, her mother's death and subsequent "miraculous" preservation is very closely analogous to one of the major incidents of Part II of the *Play of Mary Magdalene,* a fifteenth-century dramatic potpourri which, in its first part, consists of a half-morality play, half history of the heroine's conversion, and in the second, of a saint's-life miracle continuing the story of the now-sanctified Magdalene. The Magdalene's main achievement as a saint was, according to the drama, the conversion of the king and queen of Marseilles from their devotion to Islam. One of the results of their conversion is the pregnancy of the previously childless queen, and the king, in gratitude, decides to sail to Jerusalem to be baptized by St. Peter himself. His wife insists on making the journey with him and while on shipboard (the theatrical facilities appear to have included a practical ship)[11] in the midst of a tempest, she goes into labor. In *Mary Magdalene* she delivers the baby and dies on-stage. Precisely as in *Pericles,* the sailors thereupon demand that the corpse be thrown overboard so that the storm will abate. Instead of placing his wife's body in a chest, however, the king of "Marcylle" leaves it and the newborn child on a rock in the middle of the ocean, and proceeds to the Holy Land and his baptism. The ceremony over, he returns by the same route and, upon reaching the rock, discovers that a miracle has occurred:

> O thou myty lord of heven region,
> yendyr is my babe of myn own nature,
> preservyd and keptt from all corrupcyon!
> blyssyd be that lord that the dothe socur,

And my wyff lyeth her fayer and puer!
fayer and cler is hur color to se!
a! good lord, yower grace with vs Indure,
My wyvys lyfe for to illumyn.
A, blyssyd be that puer vergyn,
from grevos slepe she gynnyt revyve!
A! the sonne of grace on us doth shynne!
now blyssyd be god, I se my wyff a-lyve! [12]

However inferior as poetry (and it is surely far from negligible) this comes closer in spirit to the great moments of Shakespeare's romances than any other drama I know.

That *Pericles* is in the medieval tradition is not a point that needs laboring. Shakespeare is conscious of the old-fashioned quality of his play and emphasizes it by making "antient Gower" his chorus. To be sure, the story of Apollonius of Tyre, the ultimate source of the play, dates from the fifth century A.D., but before it came to Shakespeare it had been thoroughly absorbed into the medieval romance tradition.[13] That tradition, in its Elizabethan development, provided Shakespeare with a form capable of containing the vision of the world which he presents in his last plays. The form did not come to him completely ready-made, however. In the romances that follow *Pericles*, Shakespeare makes one basic alteration in the Elizabethan dramatic romance as he found it. In place of the wandering knights so fair who serve as the protagonists of *Sir Clyomon and Sir Clamydes, John of Bordeaux, The Four Prentices of London, The Weakest Goeth to the Wall,* etc., Shakespeare substitutes what I have been calling the *humanum genus* figure—the sinner who repents and is forgiven. In doing so, Shakespeare, as we shall see, is returning to the practice of the earlier writers of the *Miracles de Notre Dame,* who sometimes made precisely the same substitution in adapting romance materials to the purposes of religious narrative and drama. The result of such a substitution is basic in that the whole action of the play has an entirely different source from that which accounts for the vicissitudes of *Pericles* and the plays like it. It is not the opposition of Fortune, but the sin of Posthumus, of Leontes, of Alonso that is the origin of the action in the later plays. Thus, in the romances we are about to consider, Shakespeare imposes on the disordered series of thrilling adventures that constitute the actions of such plays as *Pericles,* a meaningful pattern of sin, repentance, and forgiveness.

Cymbeline

The most familiar critical comment on *Cymbeline* is, as in the case of *All's Well,* one of Dr. Johnson's hammer blows:

> This play has many just sentiments, some natural dialogues, and some pleasing scenes, but they are obtained at the expence of much incongruity.
>
> To remark the folly of the fiction, the absurdity of the conduct, the confusion of the names and manners of different times, and the impossibility of the events in any system of life, were to waste criticism upon unresisting imbecillity, upon faults too evident for detection, and too gross for aggravation.[1]

It would be pleasant if those of us who think the play great could comfort ourselves with the reflection that the eighteenth century was simply too antipathetic to the spirit of romance to appreciate *Cymbeline's* merits. Our own time, we would like to think, has inspired in us the possibility of a sympathy with art of this kind, and we can see the magnificence that was invisible to Dr. Johnson. Unfortunately, however, if we turn to a critic who speaks with something like Johnsonian authority in the twentieth century, we find a judgment on *Cymbeline* which, while it is gentler, is far from a total contradiction of the strictures of Dr. Johnson:

> The play contains a great variety of life and interest, and if we talk of "inequalities" and "incongruities" it should not be to suggest inanity or nullity: out of the interplay of contrasting themes and modes we have an effect as (to fall back on the usefully corrective analogy) of an odd and distinctive music. But the organization is not a matter of a strict and delicate subservience to a commanding significance, which

penetrates the whole, informing and ordering everything—imagery, rhythm, symbolism, character, episode, plot—from a deep centre: *Cymbeline* is not a great work of art of the order of *The Winter's Tale*.²

This is Dr. Leavis issuing a *caveat* on the criticism of Shakespeare's late plays, and though he clearly feels that Dr. Johnson went too far, the value which Dr. Leavis, in turn, places on the play is not a notably high one: *Cymbeline*, though it contains some good things, is finally not a great work of art. In the face of critical artillery of this magnitude, those of us in whom *Cymbeline* provokes the sort of reaction which we usually associate with great art hesitate to defend our position. Quiller-Couch, however, refused to surrender his admiration for *Cymbeline* and counterattacked Dr. Johnson with a weapon that is typical of Quiller-Couch's critical tradition: "I turn on Dr. Johnson," he says, "and demand '. . . why do you not include mention of the marvellous portrayal of Imogen?' . . . For Imogen is the be-all and the and all of the play." ³ I am, by analogy, tempted—not to turn on Dr. Leavis: I would not dare—but to ask him respectfully, "What of Posthumus, and the significant and unifying action of which he is the center? Doesn't this, in fact, inform and order the play?" My question would be futile, however, for Dr. Leavis has anticipated it: "Posthumus's jealousy . . . is real enough in its nastiness, but has no significance in relation to any radical theme, or total effect, of the play." It will, of course, be the contention of this essay that Posthumus is the central, *humanum genus* figure of the play, that his jealousy is at the heart of the play's "radical theme" and that the total effect of *Cymbeline* depends absolutely upon a sympathetic understanding of Posthumus' contrition and an emotional involvement in his forgiveness.

It would, however, be wrong to concentrate exclusively upon Posthumus in analyzing the play, for to do so would be to throw the play out of focus as drastically as the Victorians did by their overemphasis on Imogen. The hero and the heroine share the significant action of the play between them, and in that sharing is a clue to Shakespeare's organization of the play's events. Dr. Leavis has objected that "the organization is not a matter of strict and delicate subservience to a commanding significance." I should like to begin my defense of the play by examining one aspect of that "organization"—the arrangement of the play's narrative parts.

Faced with what could well be an overwhelming abundance of romantic incident, Shakespeare has set about ordering it according to the standard Elizabethan critical precepts for the proper construction of drama—according, that is, to the principles of the five-act structure. *Cymbeline* is a play concerned, like all romantic comedy, primarily with love, but unlike most comedy of its kind, its lovers are married before the curtain rises. The play belongs to that type of romantic comedy in which love is tested, in which, temporarily, one of the lovers fails the test, in which the lovers must undergo an ordeal as the result of that failure, and in which, finally, the ordeal is survived and the lovers—one penitent, one forgiving—are reunited. In telling his story, Shakespeare has devoted his first two acts (the protasis) to the test of love. The action is evenly divided between Posthumus and Imogen and Act Two ends with the soliloquy in which Posthumus demonstrates that he, like Claudio in *Much Ado,* has failed the test. Tricked into the mistaken belief that he has found alteration in Imogen's love, Posthumus allows his love to undergo an answering alteration and bends with the remover (whom he believes to be Imogen, but who is really Iachimo) to remove. The third and fourth acts—the epitasis—concern themselves with the ordeal that follows love's failure. That ordeal is Imogen's, and Posthumus does not appear while it is taking place. The catastrophe (Act Five) opens with the reappearance of Posthumus and concentrates almost exclusively upon him and his penitence until the final scene of reunion, reconciliation, and forgiveness. Such is the organization of the narrative. Whether or not it strictly but delicately subserves a commanding significance one can discover only by examining the play in detail.

Cymbeline opens with an expository scene between two gentlemen, one knowing, the other conveniently if inexplicably ignorant. We learn that the king's daughter (and only child since the kidnapping of her brothers) has angered her father by marrying a poor but honorable gentleman in preference to her stepmother's clod of a son by a previous marriage. The scene also establishes the atmosphere of the court—an atmosphere permeated by sycophancy; a court where the courtiers mimic the king's displeasure outwardly while rejoicing in their hearts at its cause. This image of a society where the ignoble must be flattered and fawned on while merit can only be supported *sotto voce* is brilliantly sustained by the comic scenes between Cloten and his two companions. Cloten, however, is only a sign of what is rotten in Britain. Cymbeline himself is the cause of his country's degeneration.

Like the France of *All's Well*, the Britain of *Cymbeline* is diseased, and the king is at the center of its misfortune. But the king of France, though physically sick, was morally sound. Cymbeline is in a sense his opposite and his moral weakness has its source where Bertram's did—in ignorance of merit. But Bertram's inability to see the true worth of others was a personal shortcoming. Cymbeline's is a national catastrophe. As a result of it, the wickedness of the literally bewitching queen and the coarse stupidity of her son are lavishly rewarded, while the true nobility of Posthumus is not only unrecognized, but actively persecuted. Cymbeline's failure to perceive has already caused the banishment of the virtuous Belarius, and, as a result, the loss of the two male heirs to the British throne. Now the king will banish the husband of his sole remaining child. Until the last scene of the play, Cymbeline knows and sees nothing but what is false. His ignorance and misapprehension are total, and serve as the source for the partial ignorances and misapprehensions of the other characters, and the near tragic misunderstandings that result from them. At the play's beginning, the king's moral blindness has created around him a dangerous atmosphere of sycophancy and deceit.

Posthumus and Imogen stand out boldly from this background.

Their love, beauty, and virtue serve as a contrast to the king's ignorance, the queen's wickedness, and Cloten's complacent and boorish stupidity. Their marriage also represents the one visible hope for the society of the play. The courtiers rejoice at Posthumus' victory and Cloten's defeat, not only because good has triumphed, but because their own chance for a better future depends upon that victory. From the beginning, then, the happiness of the world of the play is seen as bound up with the love of Posthumus and Imogen.

The nature of that love demands analysis. It is characteristically described, throughout the protasis of the play, in two opposed sorts of metaphor—in terms derived either from commerce or from theology. In the opening scene, for example, the First Gentleman says of Imogen's love for Posthumus:

> To his Mistris,
> (For whom he now is banish'd) her owne price
> Proclaimes how she esteem'd him. . . .   (I.i.61–63)

In the next scene Posthumus, too, describes their marriage commercially:

> I (my poore selfe) did exchange for you
> To your so infinite losse. . . .   (I.ii.59–60)

And in defending their marriage to her father, Imogen repeats the metaphor with a different conclusion as to the relative value of the commodities involved:

>   he is
> A man, worth any woman: Ouer-buyes mee
> Almost the summe he payes.   (I.ii.96–98)

Set against this materialistic imagery (and these examples could be multiplied)[4] are the lines in which the love of Posthumus and Imogen is discussed in terms usually reserved for the love between deity and mortal. In the first of the examples given above, the First Gentleman continues his description with the words:

> and his Virtue
> By her electiõ may be truly read, what kind of man he is.
> (I.i.63–64)

Denotatively, election means any act of choice, and its connotations, both Elizabethan and modern, are political as well as theological, and yet the theological overtones of the word are very strongly at work here, and in her choice of the commoner Posthumus, the Princess Imogen is compared to God, who chooses those who merit eternal bliss.[5] The term is used again, in an opposite sense, but with an even stronger religious connotation, by the Second Lord in Act One, Scene Three, where in response to Cloten's incredulous, "And that shee should loue this Fellow, and refuse mee," he says (aside), "If it be a sin to make a true election, she is damn'd." (I.iii.22–24) Here the election is that by the mortal of God. Imogen has been offered a choice between matrimonial salvation and matrimonial damnation and has chosen correctly. Finally, in Act One, Scene Seven, in his flattery of Imogen, Iachimo returns to the first meaning when he speaks of her:

> great Iudgement,
> In the election of a Sir, so rare,
> Which you know, cannot erre.   (I.vii.203–5)

Imogen is sometimes, then, seen as the deity who bestows her grace upon her worshiper, sometimes as the worshiper who adores her god, the point being that Posthumus and Imogen adore one another. "I professe my selfe her Adorer, not her Friend," (I.v.69–70) says Posthumus to Iachimo, while to Imogen the tokens and statements of Posthumus' love are as precious as the mercy of God:

> if he should write,
> And I not haue it, 'twere a Paper lost
> As offer'd mercy is. . . . (I.iv.4–6)

And when Cymbeline, having just banished Posthumus, and furious at Imogen's defiance, asks, "Past Grace? Obedience?" she replies, "Past hope and in dispaire, that way past Grace." (I.ii.84–85) Cut off from Posthumus, she is like the mortal who feels himself cut off from the love of God.

Finally, in Act I, Scene Four, when Imogen is lamenting to Pisanio the brevity of her leavetaking of Posthumus, she wishes that she had

> charg'd him
> At the sixt houre of Morne, at Noone, at Midnight,
> T'encounter me with Orisons, for then
> I am in Heauen for him. (I.iv.38–41)

J. M. Nosworthy, in a footnote, points out that,

> the times mentioned are three of the seven canonical hours of the Divine Office. The obvious interpretation is that Imogen sees herself as a goddess whom Posthumus is to worship at certain hours, but I doubt whether it is the correct one. I take "encounter me" to mean "join me" (cf. O.E.D. encounter, vb. 6 = to go to meet) and would interpret: I would have charged him to join with me in prayer at those times because I shall then be praying for him.[6]

Mr. Nosworthy is quite right. Imogen never sees herself as a goddess. Her manner of expression in these lines is such, however, that we think of her as resembling an interceding saint, or the Virgin Mary. Like Helena, in *All's Well,* Imogen is one whose "prayers . . . heaven delights to heare/ And loves to grant."

Posthumus and Imogen, in the first throes of love, regard one another as deities. In life, the reaction is so common as to be conventional. We must, however, decide just how *we* are meant to assess the love Shakespeare describes in these exalted terms. With regard to Posthumus and Imogen as characters, our reaction seems clear enough. They are experiencing the emotions proper to a newly married couple, and we enjoy the spectacle. But the characterization of their love in theological terms is not entirely the work of the lovers themselves. The term "election" is applied to Imogen's choice of Posthumus by three different observers of their love. Furthermore, the terms used are not usually from the conventional vocabulary of diluted Petrarchan love-worship. They are chosen, rather, to suggest the real concerns of theology. It is almost as if Shakespeare wished to reinvest the love of Posthumus and Imogen with something of the exalted spirit of medieval idealization—to see in it a kind of secular salvation, the beginning of a new life.

There is, however, a danger in the application of a theological vocabulary to a romantic love—the danger of awakening the cynicism of an audience that knows there is more to love than an encountering of orisons. To describe love in the vocabulary of Tartuffe is to run the risk of provoking the reactions which Tartuffe provokes. An instinct for avoiding this sort of danger explains, I think, Shakespeare's probably unconscious strategy in juxtaposing commercial metaphors for love against those drawn from theology. The two kinds of imagery combine to produce a complex but single effect: they join to describe a love that is at once physical and spiritual, both of this world and out of it. This combination is what romantic love should be—of the spirit, a "marriage of true minds," and of the body, a matter of things (in the bawdy Elizabethan sense of that basic word). The love of Posthumus and Imogen is established at the play's opening as romantic love of the highest order, a love that contains and holds in balance both the physical and the spiritual. This is the reciprocated love that, in the course of the protasis, will be tested and (partially and temporarily) subjugated.

Iachimo is the active destroyer of that love, but his opportunity for mischief is provided by the muddle-headed Cymbeline's banishment of Posthumus. The physical separation of lovers as a trial of love was, of course, a favorite theme both of romance and lyric poetry (Donne's *Valediction Forbidding Mourning* is particularly *à propos* here). The standard romantic hero passes that test and, indeed, mere separation does not diminish Posthumus' love for Imogen. It does, however, affect that love by destroying the balance in it between the physical and the spiritual—or, rather, by causing a confusion of the two. Prevented, by separation, from the physical enjoyment of love, Posthumus, very naturally indeed, becomes a bit obsessed with love's physical aspect and begins to consider Imogen's spiritual value solely in terms of her ability to remain physically chaste. Instead of properly assuming that Imogen's spiritual value ensures her physical chastity, he begins to think of her physical chastity as the guarantee of her spiritual value. Iachimo's cynicism completes Posthumus' confusion. For Iachimo, "love" is simply and entirely a thing. Imogen's ring, which is a symbol of her love for Posthumus, is for Iachimo an equivalent physical object. Posthumus knows perfectly well that there is a difference.

> the one may be solde or giuen, or if there were wealth enough for the purchases, or merite for the guift. The other is not a thing for sale, and onely the guift of the Gods.
>
> *Iach.*: Which the Gods haue giuen you?
> *Post.*: Which by their Graces I will keepe. (I.v.83–88)

Posthumus here surrenders his position in the process of defending it. His confusion as to the nature of his and Imogen's love for one another leads him to admit Iachimo's basic proposition: that Imogen's love is a thing in Posthumus' possibly temporary possession. It is not, or not entirely. It is, as Posthumus knows but forgets at the moment of knowing, "the guift of the Gods," comparable to God's grace and hence (outside Calvinism) something whose continued possession is merited either by faith in its existence or by an avoidance of sin. Posthumus fails to merit the grace of Imogen's love both by Lutheran and Catholic standards, for he first loses faith in Imogen and then proceeds to sin against her by attempting to have her murdered. Like the Christian sinner, however, he can only destroy the love within himself. He cannot succeed in destroying the love that is felt for him. Imogen's love, like God's for man, remains constant and is available to her erring husband when, penitent, he once more desires it.

Although Imogen's love is *like* the love of God, it is not the love of God, nor is it a symbol of that love. It is a human love and Iachimo sets about to try to destroy it. He begins by undermining Posthumus' half of that mutual emotion. Posthumus allows himself to be convinced that Imogen's ring and Imogen's love can be equated and the one wagered against the other. *Humanum genus* listens to the voice of the tempter and makes his first mistake by half believing what he hears.

To cover Iachimo's shift of place from Italy to Britain, Shakespeare has contrived a brilliant interlude—that in which the queen enters with her ladies to gather flowers, "Whiles yet the dewe's on ground." (I.vi.3) These opening lines evoke a crowd of poetic invitations to take love at the prime and gather rosebuds while we may ("Mignonne, allons voir si la rose . . ."). This morning scene is as incongruous in association with the queen as is the *aubade* provided for Imogen by Cloten, and its incongruity increases as we realize that the queen's purpose in gathering blossoms is the distillation of poison. As Iachimo has set about to turn love into murderous hate, the queen proposes to transform the sweets of nature into the means of death. But she wishes to work a similar change on human material as well, for we immediately see her attempting to seduce the physician Cornelius from his honest practice of medicine and Posthumus' servant Pisanio from his loyalty to his master. Indeed, the rest of the protasis is taken up with a series of attempts to seduce the good from their devotion to virtue. The queen tries to suborn Cornelius and Pisanio. Iachimo and Cloten try to talk Imogen into betraying her husband. Finally, in the only successful "seduction" of the play, Iachimo manages to transform Posthumus from a decent human being into a murderous and deluded fool.

Iachimo's trial of Imogen's love for her husband has been characterized as "crassly blundering," [7] but that is to do less than justice to the shrewdness of Imogen's virtue as well as to Iachimo's skill as a seducer. Iachimo grounds his attempted seduction on the accusation that Posthumus has denied the spirituality of love, that he has treated it as a thing to be bought and sold, that he has hired prostitutes with the very money which (in Iachimo's view) Imogen has paid him for loving her. This coarsening and literalizing of the commercial metaphor of the play has an effect on Imogen, who is half convinced by Iachimo's calumnies until she realizes the motive for them—her seduction. So Iachimo fails, but he revenges himself for his failure with Imogen by his success with Posthumus.

For Iachimo, as for Iago, love means the sexual act, and beauty (as in the bedchamber scene) is only an excitement to desire. Female virtue is a myth. What he does in the last scene of Act Two is to convert Posthumus to his view of life. His method of converting him is similar to the method he employed unsuccessfully against Imogen—he calumniates the object of love. Posthumus believes him, however. He listens to the voice of the tempter and thus completes the process of conversion that had begun at their first encounter. By agreeing to a test of love, Posthumus has offended against love. True love would feel no necessity for a test, would reject the suggestion of one as degrading, and would simultaneously know that love is too important to risk destroying by admitting the possibility of its destruction. Posthumus, in his naïveté and lack of confidence, agrees to Iachimo's proposal and falls an easy victim to his villainy.

The soliloquy with which the protasis ends is painful and disturbing. It is strongly reminiscent of Claudio's diatribe against Hero in the church scene of *Much Ado,* but there is here a stronger misogyny, and a masochistic dwelling on more specifically brutalized images of the loved one's supposed sexual encounters:

> Perchance he spoke not, but
> Like a full Acorn'd Boare, a Iarman on,
> Cry'de oh, and mounted. . . .   (II.iv.212–14)

Like Claudio, he rejects the woman he has loved and, along with her, all women and all the supposed characteristics of the female:

> Could I finde out
> The Womans part in me, for there's no motion
> That tends to vice in man, but I affirme
> It is the Womans part: be it Lying, note it,
> The womans: Flattering, hers; Deceiuing, hers;
> Lust, and ranke thoughts, hers, hers: Reuenges hers: . . .
>   (II.v.216–21)

Shakespeare is here having Posthumus regale us with the clichés of Pauline antifeminism, but he is doing so in a context that transforms Posthumus' ravings by implication into the purest philogyny. Shakespeare is making use of what Bertrand Evans has called "disparate awareness." [8] The audience knows that the source of Posthumus' hatred for Imogen is a lie, and our knowledge of Imogen's innocence turns Posthumus' attack on women into a hymn of praise. We know that lying, deceiving, flattering, lust, etc., are the characteristics not of the woman Imogen, but of the man Iachimo, and we realize that they—and particularly the rank thoughts and revenges—are becoming characteristic of Posthumus as well. As always in Shakespearean romantic comedy, it is the man's love that fails to meet the test. It is the weakness of the hero that allows strife its entrance into the world of the play. In *Cymbeline,* as in *Much Ado,* love presupposes the overcoming and containment of hate. The destruction of love automatically results in the triumph of hate with its inevitable consequences of suffering, war, and death.

The protasis ends with the triumph of hatred in the mind of *humanum genus.* The epitasis begins with preparations for war and plans for murder. Posthumus' cruel orders to Pisanio seem to Imogen, in her ignorance, to provide her with the opportunity to escape from the treachery, hatred, and persecution of the court back to the haven of Posthumus' love for her. Milford Haven, where she is to meet her husband, becomes the play's symbolic goal, a "port after stormy seas" where reconciliation and love will occur. Posthumus was described as leaving haven when he left Britain and Imogen's love. (I.iv.i) His return, Imogen naturally assumes, will be to the shelter of their love for one another. She does not know that that love has been destroyed and that she must now go on a journey which, though it will bring her to haven at last, will necessitate her passing through a wasteland of nightmare horrors.

But "haven" is not simply safe harbor. It is, in Elizabethan pronunciation, a homonym for "heaven," [9] and the sense of supernatural powers who observe and (perhaps) regulate our destinies grows stronger throughout the rest of *Cymbeline* until it culminates first in the descent of Jupiter, and finally in the procession in honor of the gods which ends the play. So Imogen's journey is undertaken under the observation of the gods and with the fulfillment of heaven's will as her final destination, and her movement from the court is a movement into the power of the ruler of the heavens—the sun itself. "The heat o' th' sun" becomes an important symbol throughout Acts Three and Four. Until this point in the play, we have seen Imogen only in the false-valuing, unnatural context of Cymbeline's court, where she is imprisoned, enclosed, stifled. Her extreme whiteness, both physical and spiritual, is insisted upon. Iachimo, as he slavers over her in the bedroom scene, describes her body, seen by candle-light, as "whiter than the sheets," and Posthumus tortures himself with the remembrance of her sexual timidity:

> Me of my lawfull pleasure she restrain'd,
> And pray'd me oft forbearance: did it with
> A pudencie so Rosie, the sweet view on't
> Might well haue warm'd olde Saturne;
> That I thought her
> As Chaste, as vn-Sunn'd Snow.   (II.iv.205–10)

Her rosiness was the superficial result of her modesty (which is seen as sexually arousing) while essentially she is as cold and white as "unsunn'd snow." It is this coldness and whiteness that, in Pisanio's phrase, must now be exposed

> to the greedy touch
> Of common-kissing *Titan:* . . . (III.iv.184–85)

Like Rosalind and Celia before her, and Perdita after her, Imogen is moved from the evils of the court into a heightened and transforming nature. Much more than Arden or Bohemia, however, the Welsh mountains are shown to be tormenting as well as salutary. They are rough, desert wasteland—the background for Imogen's ordeal. To be sure, she finds love as well as suffering in them. Guiderius and Arviragus provide her with comfort and love when she is sick with weariness and despair, and they save her by killing the monster, Cloten, who pursues her. They are pre-eminently creatures of nature. Their nobility is inherent and their love of the disguised Imogen is the result of the natural promptings of an unrecognized blood relationship. Their nurture has been natural. They, like Posthumus, represent the banished virtue of Britain and their virtues make the point that banishment to the wilderness is safer for one's honor than banishment to civilized Italy. When we first see them, they are worshiping the sun and, in physical opposition to their sister, they are "hot summers Tanlings." (IV.iv.37) But they feel themselves to be incomplete, unfinished, unfulfilled. They are dissatisfied with life in a state of nature and determined to prove their honor in the accepted civilized manner—in war.

Cloten is, in a sense, their opposite: a born savage made worse by civilization. It is appropriate that Guiderius should destroy this pretender to the throne that is rightfully his, but Cloten has more important functions than to serve as a foil for Cymbeline's lost sons. As a persecutor, a would-be seducer of Imogen, he is set against and parodies the airs and graces of "yellow Iachimo," and Iachimo's autoerotic gloating over the sleeping Imogen makes a nice contrast with Cloten's straightforward plan to rape her after murdering Posthumus.

Imogen is pursued through the wilderness by a monster intent on rape and murder. At the moment he overtakes her, however, she has drunk the "poison" prepared for her by the queen and is lying "dead" in the cave of Belarius. Her unreal death coincides with the real killing of her pursuer by Guiderius. The slaying of this absurd dragon is played as farce:

> I haue tane
> His head from him: Ile throw't into the Creeke
> Behinde our Rocke, and let it to the Sea,
> And tell the Fishes, hee's the Queenes Sonne, *Cloten*. . . .
>
> (IV.ii.197–200)

This, in an abrupt change of mood from the grotesque to the pathetic, is followed by the entrance of Arviragus with the "corpse" of Imogen. The "wench-like words" of mourning which follow culminate in the exquisite dirge with its catalogue of the evils that Imogen has now escaped: "the heat o' th' sun," "the furious winter's rages;" "the frown o' th' great" and "the tyrant's stroke" of Cymbeline's persecution; the "lightning flash" and "thunder-stone" of the gods; and, finally, the "slander" of Iachimo and the "censure rash" of Posthumus. This pathos, however, again modulates immediately into one of the most bizarre scenes Shakespeare ever wrote.

That Imogen wakes to find beside her a headless corpse which she takes to be that of Posthumus is clearly no spur of the moment inspiration on Shakespeare's part. He lays the groundwork for it carefully in Act Two, Scene Three, when Imogen tells Cloten that she esteems him less than "the mean'st garment" of Posthumus, a remark that inspires Cloten to put on Posthumus' clothes in an effort to add insult to the injuries he has planned for the woman who has dared to reject him. Staging problems are created by the scene, for the actors playing Posthumus and Cloten must be able to wear one another's clothes—unless two identical costumes were created for them with, perhaps, a third for the headless dummy which the scene requires. The purely practical difficulties raised by the scene are complex enough to make it clear that Shakespeare was determined to stage the incident. It is difficult to imagine why. To be sure, Shakespeare wants Imogen to be convinced of her husband's death, and this is the basic *raison d'être* for the scene, but surely it would not have been difficult to devise a less grotesque means of misleading the heroine. Shakespeare, however, wants this moment of grotesquerie, this "ludicrous situation" which yet contains a grief that is "deep, genuine, movingly presented" and "compels simultaneous tears and laughter." [10] But to what end? Does this scene have any significance, or is it simply a piece of supreme theatrical virtuosity indulged in, as similar moments are in the work of Beaumont and Fletcher, for its own sake?

Part of the answer may, perhaps, be indicated by the role which Cloten plays throughout the epitasis. Posthumus is absent from the scene during acts Three and Four, and yet he is in a sense present insofar as during these acts Cloten is providing us with a parody of him. Like Posthumus', Cloten's "love" for Imogen has been turned to hate by what he conceives to be her ill treatment of him. As a result, he meditates bloody thoughts of revenge against her:

> I loue, and hate her: for she's Faire and Royall,
> And that she hath all courtly parts more exquisite
> Then Lady, Ladies, Woman, from euery one
> The best she hath, and she of all compounded
> Out-selles them all. I loue her therefore, but
> Disdaining me, and throwing Fauours on
> The low *Posthumus*, slanders so her iudgement,
> That what's else rare, is choak'd; and in that point
> I will conclude to hate her, nay indeede,
> To be reueng'd vpon her.   (III.v.90–99)

This is approximately equal in sense, if not in eloquence, to Post-humus' soliloquy at the end of Act Two, where, by accepting

Iachimo's lies as truth, he turned himself into a version of Iachimo. By setting about to have his wife murdered, he turns himself into a version of Cloten as well. Cloten, in attempting to suborn Pisanio, says:

> Sirrah, if thou would'st not be a Villain, but do
> me true service: vndergo those Imployments wherin
> I should have cause to vse thee with a serious
> industry, that is, what villainy soere I bid
> thee do to performe it, directly and truely, I would
> thinke thee an honest man.   (III.v.137–42)

Neither style, morality, nor logic differ drastically here from Post-humus' letter to Pisanio:

> . . . thou (Pisanio) must acte for me, if thy Faith be not tainted with
> the breach of hers; let thine owne hands take away her life . . . if thou
> feare to strike . . . thou art the Pander to her dishonour, and equally
> to me disloyall.   (III.iv.28–34)

Posthumus, then, has adopted the mindless savagery of Cloten, and Cloten, by putting on Posthumus' clothes, underlines the resemblance. When Guiderius lops off Cloten's head, the resemblance becomes perfect. I take Cloten's headless body to be a deeply ironic and excessively macabre joke—a deserved mockery of Posthumus. For he, too, has lost his head. By allowing himself to consider the love between him and Imogen to be a matter simply of things, he has reduced himself to the status of a thing—a mindless corpse. Remove the heads from both Cloten and Posthumus and Cloten will equal Posthumus. "I dare speak it to myself," says Cloten, "for it is not Vainglorie for a man, and his Glasse, to confer in his owne Chamber; I meane, the Lines of my body are as well drawne as his; no lesse young, more strong. . . ." (IV.i.8–12) Cloten is quite right. As a thing, he is the equal of Posthumus, and Posthumus has chosen, for the time, to change himself into a thing.

When we next see Posthumus, however, he is in the process of changing himself back into a man—or rather, of changing himself into a new man, for the experience of Posthumus in the catastrophe of the play is made a pagan equivalent to Christian regeneration. This process begins with the erring human's conviction that he is a miserable sinner who has done what he ought not to have done. The moment of that conviction, which is merely presented in the descent of grace upon Bertram in *All's Well*, is fully explored and dramatized in *Cymbeline*. Nowell's catechism divides the experience of repentance through which Posthumus is living into two main parts: "the mortifying of the old man, or the flesh; and the quickening of the new man or the spirit." [11] Posthumus experiences the pagan equivalent of this "mortifying" through the opening scenes of Act Five, until his reunion with Imogen—the moment of the "quickening of the new man." The catechism's description of this mortification makes a useful comment on the emotions of Posthumus in these scenes:

> The mortifying of the old man is unfeigned and sincere acknowledging and confession of sin, and therewith, a shame and sorrow of mind, with the feeling whereof the person is sore grieved for that he hath swerved from righteousness, and not been obedient to the will of God. For every man ought, in remembering the sins of his life past, wholly to mislike himself, to be angry with himself, and to be a severe judge of his own faults, and to give sentence and pronounce judgment of himself, to the intent he abide not the grievous judgment of God in his wrath. This sorrow some have called contrition, whereunto are joined in nearness and nature an earnest hatred of sin, and a love and desire of righteousness lost.[12]

The acknowledgment of sin is also the source of another basic Christian virtue—charity. It is the knowledge of our own sinfulness that inspires us to forgive the sins of others, and the forgiveness of our fellow humans is the sign of true contrition and the *sine qua non* of divine forgiveness. Luther is forceful on the subject:

When [the Christian] sees the mote in his brother's eye, he should go look at himself in the mirror before passing judgment. He will then find beams in his eye big enough to make hog troughs.[13]

Though Luther insists that God's forgiveness does not depend upon our forgiveness of others, he makes it clear that such forgiveness is, nonetheless, a necessity:

It is also necessary for us to provide proof by which we testify that we have received the forgiveness of sin. Such proof is to consist in everyone's forgiving his brother his trespasses.[14]

Nowell's catechism goes even further:

Unless other do find us ready to forgive them, and unless we in following the mercifulness and lenity of God our Father do shew ourselves to be his children, he plainly warneth us to look for nothing else at his hand but extreme severity of punishment.[15]

Posthumus' first soliloquy in Act Five is an expression both of sorrow for his own trespasses and of forgiveness for the woman who, he thinks, has trespassed against him:

> You married ones,
> If each of you should take this course, how many
> Must murther Wiues much better than themselues
> For wrying but a little?   (V.i.2–5)

According to the Arden editor:

The hero's remorse of conscience is unconvincing. Since he still believes in Imogen's guilt, his attitude towards her should remain unchanged, however much he may repent of the supposed murder. To term her alleged offence "wrying but a little" seems contrary to the moral code of the play, though as Professor Ellis-Fermor points out, it is not necessarily inconsistent with the feelings of a human being illuminated by grief and seeing with new eyes.[16]

Professor Ellis-Fermor's point is admirable, but Mr. Nosworthy's introduction of it seems to me to betray a lack of sympathy with Posthumus' moral and spiritual condition. Posthumus is saying that it is wrong to kill your wife because she has slept with another man. Clearly—and Mr. Nosworthy seems to realize this—the "moral code of the play" is not one which would encourage the *crime passionel.* When Posthumus refers to Imogen's supposed adultery, he is comparing it in his mind with his own sin—murder. By comparison with murder, adultery is "wrying but a little." This is certainly not an amoral view of the matter, nor does it suggest that adultery is not wrong. Adultery is a sin, an offense against God which God will forgive if the sinner's repentance (or faith) justifies forgiveness. Adultery is also an immoral act and an offense against man—which man will forgive if he has the slightest sense of his own moral condition:

> If we will have of God forgiveness, there is none other remedy but to forgive the offences done unto us, which be very small in comparison of our offences done against God.[17]

Posthumus thinks he has seen the mote in his wife's eye and has killed her for it. Now he looks in the mirror and sees a murderer in whose eyes are beams big enough to make hog troughs. By forgiving his wife he demonstrates that *he* deserves forgiveness.

Shakespeare's comedies do not, of course, advocate a relative morality in the modern sense. They do insist, however, that man should judge man by the light of self-knowledge. That light had temporarily gone out in Posthumus' mind. In contriving the murder of Imogen, he has acted like an animal, or like a Cloten. Self-knowledge must necessarily be a knowledge of sinfulness, and it will lead to remorse and the forgiveness of a wife who, he thinks, has wronged him. If Shakespeare had satisfied Mr. Nosworthy's desire to have Posthumus' attitude toward Imogen remain unchanged, he would have repeated his characterization of Claudio in *Much Ado,* giving us a far less sympathetic protagonist and a play with a more simple-minded and less humanely Christian view of human emotions and conduct.

Posthumus is penitent, but he is also human, and he tries, though feebly, to shift some of the intolerable blame which he deserves to the account of others:

> Oh *Pisanio,*
> Euery good Seruant do's not all Commands:
> No Bond, but to do iust ones.   (V.i.7–9)

This expresses a natural desire to share the guilt of Imogen's murder, but at the same time it repudiates precisely that attitude toward Pisanio as the instrument of his master's crimes which we have seen Posthumus sharing with Cloten in the play's epitasis.

Posthumus goes on to consider himself and Imogen as the creatures of omnipotent gods and to accuse those powers of injustice in having permitted him to arrange the murder of his wife:

> Gods, if you
> Should haue 'tane vengeance on my faults, I neuer
> Had liu'd to put on this: so had you saued
> The noble *Imogen,* to repent, and strooke
> Me (wretch) more worth your Vengeance.   (V.i.9–13)

In addition to revealing Posthumus' new sense of his own unworthiness, this attack upon the justice of the gods has the effect of celebrating that justice. Posthumus' misogyny, in his previous soliloquy, is turned into a defense of women by our knowledge of Imogen's innocence. Here our knowledge that Imogen is alive justifies the ways of God to men at precisely the moment they are being questioned, and the purpose of the gods in inflicting this ordeal upon the hero and heroine begins to emerge at this point in the play. The regeneration of Posthumus is now taking place and his reunion with Imogen will set the seal of the gods upon the completion of the new man. Posthumus betrays a sense of what is happening to him:

> But alacke,
> You snatch some hence for little faults; that's loue
> To haue them fall no more: you some permit
> To second illes with illes, each elder worse,
> And make them dread it, to the dooers thrift. (V.i.13–17)

The last two lines of this passage have occasioned pages of explication, but Furness' paraphrase in the *Variorum* edition makes their meaning (which is surely not so obscure as the editors would have us believe) perfectly clear:

> The gods permit some people to go from bad to worse, heaping crime on crime, until at last they make them fairly loathe this evil course, which is a good thing for the culprit.[18]

Posthumus, having doubted the justice of heaven, now begins to see some glimmer of meaning in the workings of his fate. The gods, he recognizes, have two methods of rescuing a man from his self-created evil. They may either save a sinner they love by removing him from the world, or they may further torment the evil-doer until he comes to dread his own actions. Posthumus supposes that the gods have taken the first course with Imogen, and the second with Posthumus, whom they wish to punish:

> But *Imogen* is your owne, do your best willes,
> And make me blest to obey. (V.i.18–19)

Posthumus' acceptance of the will of the gods is bound up, however, with a rejection of life. The only blessing he desires from heaven is the speedy death he has characterized as the reward of those whom the gods love, and he will seek death by all the means he can, short of deliberate self-destruction. Posthumus, though in the process of becoming a new man, is still in a state of wanhope as a result of his ignorance that Imogen is alive. But if this ignorance has the effect of making him reject life, it also preserves him from desperation, for if he is ignorant of Imogen's survival, he is also ignorant of her innocence. The knowledge that he has avenged with murder an adulterous act, which, in fact, never occurred, would upset his precarious balance between an acceptance of his unhappiness and complete despair.

Posthumus' departure to seek for death in battle is followed immediately by the entrance of the Roman and British armies, among them Posthumus in disguise. Granville-Barker has pointed out that the "elaborate pantomime" of the battle scene "really looks not unlike an attempt to turn old-fashioned dumb-show to fresh and quaint account." [19] Like a dumb show, certainly, the battle scene contains a moment of silent significance in which Shakespeare is underlining a point of large importance to the play:

> Enter Lucius, Iachimo, and the Romane Army at one doore: and the Britaine Army at another: Leonatus Posthumus following like a poore Souldier. They march ouer, and goe out. Then enter againe in Skirmish Iachimo and Posthumus: he vanquisheth and disarmeth Iachimo, and then leaues him. (V.ii.s.d.)

Bertrand Evans has remarked on the meaningful complexity of this apparently simple encounter:

> Our awareness must supply all the meaning of this meeting; what is actually staged is only a means of prompting the real drama in our heads. Deceived by Posthumus's masquerade as a common soldier, Iachimo is ignorant that he has in fact been vanquished by a nobleman, a paragon—what is more by the very man he had wronged and whose wrong the "enfeebling air" of the island now truly revenges: this irony goes "beyond beyond." Posthumus, recognizing Iachimo and not himself recognized, thereby holds the advantage. Yet in seeing and striking Iachimo only as an impersonal enemy, a member of the Roman forces,

he does not really see him at all. Iachimo's advantage over Posthumus is thus far greater than Posthumus's over Iachimo: Posthumus's recognition of Iachimo is surrounded by irony while he remains ignorant of how the villain betrayed him.[20]

Clearly our minds must be full and busy if we are to comprehend this scene, yet surely our awarenesses must supply even more than Professor Evans demands, for I must disagree with his assertion (which, in fact, I do not think I understand) that Posthumus strikes at Iachimo "only as an impersonal enemy" and that "he does not really see him at all." Posthumus reveals later (V.v.411–13) that he has seen Iachimo very clearly here. It is true that Posthumus is still ignorant "of how the villain has betrayed him," but he is not ignorant of the fact that Iachimo is a villain. That Posthumus believes him the seducer rather than the calumniator of Imogen is hardly likely to make Iachimo less an object of his hatred. Iachimo is Posthumus' worst enemy and here Posthumus has the villain at his mercy. He spares him, and we must ask ourselves why.

There is, perhaps, more than one reason. Posthumus is a man of honor, and he has given his word, in Act One, Scene Five, that if Iachimo succeeds in seducing Imogen, Posthumus will not attempt to revenge himself upon the seducer. In the battle scene, however, these two meet, not in a private cause, but as soldiers in opposing armies, and the code of honor would not require Posthumus to spare his enemy in such circumstances. Posthumus' chivalry may contribute to his decision to treat his enemy mercifully, but the soliloquy which he has just delivered suggests that his action has been prompted by something morally more important than the rules of the game.

In the previous scene, we have heard Posthumus forgive what he thinks has been a trespass against him. Since he also thinks that he had previously had the trespasser murdered, he cannot really demonstrate his charity effectively in action. The trespass which he has been called upon to forgive is adultery, and the party offended by adultery must necessarily have been offended by more than one other person. Posthumus thinks that both Imogen and Iachimo have despitefully used him. He has said that he forgives Imogen. Now we *see* him forgive Iachimo. By sparing Iachimo's life, Posthumus demonstrates that, since he is capable of pardoning others, he deserves the pardon of the gods.

But the final meaning of this moment of silent action remains to be considered. Posthumus, in pardoning his enemy, makes possible the happy ending of the play, for the happiness of the world of *Cymbeline* depends upon the continued existence of its villain. Iachimo alone can bring the play to a comic conclusion, for only he possesses the knowledge which can explain the events of the play, and it is the gaining of knowledge, the moment of revelation, that will make possible the triumphant ending of *Cymbeline*. By choosing to forgive his enemy, Posthumus merits the pardon of the gods, who, we may suspect, have so arranged events that the charitable action contains its own reward.

The battle continues and the British win it. What we are shown and told of the triumph strongly emphasizes one point: Cymbeline's kingdom is saved only by the clandestine support of the virtue which he has ignorantly and unjustly banished from it. The secret return of Bellarius, the princes, and Posthumus alone saves the day. Posthumus, in helping to achieve the victory, has not been able to find the death he has looked for, so he deliberately allows himself to be taken prisoner as a Roman by the British in the hope that they will execute him. His captors put him in chains and leave him alone. The soliloquy which follows their departure is important enough to our theme to require consideration in its entirety:

> *Post.* Most welcome bondage; for thou art a way
> (I thinke) to liberty: yet am I better
> Then one that's sicke o th'Gowt, since he had rather
> Groane so in perpetuity, then be cur'd
> By'th' sure Physitian, Death; who is the key
> T'vnbarre these Lockes. My Conscience, thou art fetter'd
> More then my shanks, & wrists: you good Gods giue me

The penitent Instrument to picke that Bolt,
Then free for euer. Is't enough I am sorry?
So Children temporall Fathers do appease;
Gods are more full of mercy. Must I repent,
I cannot do it better than in Gyues,
Desir'd, more than constrain'd;²¹ to satisfie
If of my Freedome 'tis the maine part, take
No stricter render of me, then my All.
I know you are more clement than vilde men,
Who of their broken Debtors take a third,
A sixt, a tenth, letting them thriue againe
On their abatement; that's not my desire.
For *Imogens* deere life, take mine, and though
'Tis not so deere, yet 'tis a life; you coyn'd it,
'Tweene man, and man, they waigh not euery stampe:
Though light, take Peeces for the figures sake,
(You rather) mine being yours: and so great Powres,
If you will take this Audit, take this life,
And cancell these cold Bonds. O *Imogen*,
Ile speake to thee in silence.   (V.iv.7–33)

Posthumus continues to long for death. Death will free him from the chains upon his flesh and from the flesh which chains his soul. But Posthumus appears to believe that the gods will not allow him to die until he has freed his conscience from the guilt which fetters it. By his "murder" of Imogen, he has sinned against the gods and the knowledge of that sin fetters his conscience to his body. He will be free only when he has achieved the forgiveness of the gods. Posthumus asks himself how he can gain that forgiveness, and presents himself with the thoroughly Christian answer: through penitence. The process of penance is the instrument that will pick the lock on the chains that bind his conscience, and free him forever. But of what does that process consist?

The answer contained in Posthumus' soliloquy is a traditional one. He proposes that there are two possible means of achieving the forgiveness of the gods: contrition and satisfaction. Contrition he considers under the names of sorrow and repentance, but whether he intends any subtle theological distinction thereby is doubtful. When he asks, "Is't enough I am sorry?" his incredulity is that of the repentant Christian who cannot believe his contrition alone will release him from the deserved sentence of divine justice. And yet, as we have seen previously, contrition, according to Aquinas, is enough, and it always served to guarantee the salvation of the *humanum genus* figure in the medieval plays of forgiveness. Posthumus' answer to his own doubt about the efficacy of simple repentance—that God is a loving father—is also traditional:

> Repentance is never too late, so that it be true and earnest. For, sith that God in the Scriptures will be called *our Father*, doubtless he doth follow the nature and property of gentle and merciful fathers, which seek nothing so much as the returning again and amendment of their children.[22]

It is when Posthumus begins to consider the possibility of "satisfaction" that his soliloquy becomes more than ordinarily complex. It is complicated first by the conscious irony of the speaker. In offering to pay for Imogen's murder with his life, Posthumus is being disingenuous. Far from offering the gods a thing of value, he offers what he would most willingly part withal. But Posthumus is being, if that is possible, openly disingenuous, and his irony in asking the gods to show a superhuman mercy (as he thinks they have done with Imogen) by destroying him completely is an irony directed at himself. He is offering the gods a poor bargain, but he knows it, and he says so.

In his dramatic character as a pagan Briton, however, Posthumus is necessarily unaware that he is touching on an important theological controversy. The possibility of "satisfaction," bound up as it was with the whole concept of the efficacy of works, was a major subject for contention in the quarrel between the Church and the reformers. Aquinas holds that satisfaction for sin is possible, given the infinite love and mercy of God. Luther holds that it is impossible and insists instead that salvation is obtainable through faith alone. Anglicanism, as usual, manages to take a middle position. The "Homily on Repentance" follows Aquinas by defining the first two parts of repentance as "contrition of the heart" and "unfeigned confession." It then adds a sop to Lutheranism by inserting a third part—faith—and alters Aquinas' "satisfaction" to "amendment of life"—presumably in order to tone down the contaminating suggestion of justification by works.[23] Posthumus' remarks would, I should think, be acceptable both to orthodox Catholicism and to Anglicanism because of their irony and the conditional mode of their expression. *If* satisfaction is the main part of penance, Posthumus is willing to pay for his sin with his life. His speech is certainly in the spirit of Aquinas' observation that satisfaction for sin cannot be "measure for measure . . . man cannot make satisfaction to God if *satis* (enough) denotes quantitative equality; but he can, if it denote proportionate equality . . . and as this suffices for justice, so does it suffice for satisfaction." [24] At the same time, the speech's admission that Posthumus' offered "satisfaction" is inadequate keeps it safely Protestant, while his paganism avoids the necessity for a statement of faith in anything more controversial than the power of Jove.

The final complexity of this speech has its source in the irony of which Posthumus is unconscious: the fact that he is not really guilty of the crime he wishes to expiate. The gods (including, one may say, the audience) know that Posthumus, like all *humanum genus* figures in the secularized comedy of forgiveness, has sinned through intention only. As a result, his expiation by contrition alone is aesthetically as well as theologically sufficient.

That contrition, with the charity he has demonstrated in sparing Iachimo, clearly earns Posthumus the forgiveness of the gods, and his prayer to them brings its own odd answer. The theophany which follows this soliloquy has been denied to Shakespeare on stylistic grounds by critics of intelligence and sensibility. Their arguments have been countered by an equally strong line of commentators who are convinced that the scene is authentically Shakespearean, and it is the latter group whose position appears to me the stronger. The arguments of those who would deny the scene to Shakespeare are clearly desperate. Their supposition is that the King's Men, for reasons of theatrical display, decided to foist in a theophany at this point in the play's action and because Shakespeare was "at Stratford with his hands full of local and domestic affairs . . . they asked X to draft the script," and Shakespeare, "being the easy-going dramatist he was . . . would do his best to fit it in." [25] One difficulty with this theory, it seems to me, is the problem of just where, in 1610, the King's Men were able to exhume an "X," a "playhouse hack," who seriously believed that it was *the thing* to write drama in fourteeners. Hacks, of all men, are most conscious of what is fashionable in a literary way and fourteeners had not been fashionable in the theater for well over twenty years. The opening speeches of the scene are in fourteeners, and they are Shakespearean fourteeners, as G. Wilson Knight has abundantly and, I think, irrefutably demonstrated.[26] But if it is impossible to believe that a playhouse hack should have complied with a hypothetical request from the King's Men by providing this piece of highly old-fashioned verse, why should Shakespeare have chosen to cast a portion of the theophany in so outmoded a form? That question is best answered by investigating what the form contains.

Posthumus' dream-vision opens with the apparition of the spirits of his parents and his two brothers. Their function is to ask the gods a very basic question: Why does the good man suffer? Why, specifically, have the gods, after rewarding Posthumus' virtues with the love of Imogen, taken that gift from him and brought him to his present miserable state? And why, most importantly of all, have the gods allowed the evil man to triumph by successfully tempting the good man to sin?

> Sic. Why did you suffer *Iachimo,* slight thing of Italy,
> To taint his Nobler hart & braine, with needlesse ielousy,
> And to become the geeke and scorne o' th'others vilany?
>
> (V.iv.73–75)

Jupiter's reply is in the Christian tradition:[27]

> Whom best I loue, I crosse; to make my guift
> The more delay'd, delighted. Be content,
> Your low-laide Sonne, our Godhead will vplift:
> His Comforts thriue, his Trials well are spent:
> Our Iouiall Starre reign'd at his Birth, and in
> Our Temple was he married: Rise, and fade,
> He shall be Lord of Lady *Imogen*,
> And happier much by his Affliction made.   (V.iv.106–13)

God punishes those whom he loves and they are happier as a result of their afflictions because of the contrast between their sufferings and their eventual felicity. This is Jupiter's message, and given the complexity of the action that has preceded it, its burden, we may justifiably think, is rather a simple-minded one. It is difficult to find this theophany a "central and dominating" [28] statement of the play's meaning. If the vision really sums up and contains the significance of *Cymbeline*, then the play is a good deal less interesting than the rest of it would lead us to suspect. But there is not the slightest reason to take the epiphany as the summation of the play. The version of reality given us in *Cymbeline*, as always in Shakespeare, is highly complex. Like Jaques' melancholy, it is compounded of many simples and one of the simplest of these is the truth contained in the theophany. That truth—even though all's not quite right with the world, God *is* in his heaven, and we suffer for our own good—is, in terms of the play, perfectly valid but only partial. It is the sort of simple truth with which children are reassured after a first encounter with un-justifiable suffering.

This simplicity is, I think, the explanation for the archaism of the verse in the scene's opening lines. By using fourteeners, Shakespeare, I would suggest, is deliberately creating an aura of "the olden times." "The good old days" are always simpler than the present and this scene is summoning up a nostalgia for the simpler solutions of a supposedly less complex time by employing the devices of the drama which had been popular thirty years before *Cymbeline*. Such a strategy has two results. On the one hand, the charm associated with a remembrance of things past would lend an added strength to the message of the scene, while, at the same time, its "old-fashioned" quality underlines the partialness and simplicity of its meaning by contrast with the more "modern" complexity of the action which surrounds it.

It is important, too, that the deity who descends is a mythological one. I must take issue with J. A. Bryant's recent insistence that "there is no question of a pagan Jupiter here. Jupiter is the One God, called Jupiter in this play simply because the setting happens to be pre-Christian Britain." [29] This airborne, sulphurous-breathed old gentleman is not, I think, meant to convey to us the full impact of God's awful majesty. He is the kind of apparition Ben Jonson was making fun of when he pointed out that, in his revised *Everyman In His Humour*, "Nor creaking throne comes downe, the boyes to please." [30] The boys who are meant to be pleased by Shakespeare's fundamentally benevolent but rather testy father figure are not simply the very young, but also the boys contained within all men. This Jupiter is the remembered God of childhood, who loves us but punishes us for our own good. He is not destroyed, but amplified and subtilized in the God of the grown man. *Cymbeline,* like the rest of the romances, contains much that appeals to a highly sophisticated childishness, but its world is, nonetheless, a grown-up world. To take this Jupiter as an entirely satisfactory divinity for that world would be to oversimplify a complex work of art.

The immediate effect of the vision of Jupiter is to present Posthumus, not with a solution, but with a further mystery. He awakens from his dream to discover upon his breast the "tablet" which Jupiter instructs the ghosts to leave there. This prophecy, with its jumble of lion's whelps, tender air, and stately cedars, disappoints Posthumus' desire for revelation:

'Tis still a Dreame: or else such stuffe as Madmen
Tongue, and braine not: either both, or nothing,
Or senselesse speaking, or a speaking such
As sense cannot vntye. Be what it is,
The Action of my life is like it, which Ile keepe
If but for simpathy.   (V.iv.151–56)

Jupiter's descent has provided a refutation of one pessimistic version (expressed here by the ghosts but echoing that of Gloucester in *Lear*) of the human condition: that we are mortal flies spitefully tormented for the sport of the gods. Now Posthumus proposes another view, equally pessimistic, which echoes that of Macbeth in his "Tomorrow, and tomorrow, and tomorrow" speech: our lives are tales "told by an Idiot, full of sound and fury/ Signifying nothing." But Posthumus qualifies that pessimism by admitting the possibility that his life may be not "senseless," but merely "a speaking such/ As sense cannot un-tye." Not meaningless, but incomprehensible. He will finally dis-cover, however, that it is neither. In retrospect, his sufferings, like the prophecy of the gods, will be found to have a meaning, and Jupiter, though we may not accept him as a revelation of complete godhead, will stand as a sign that the universe is controlled by an omnipotent and omniscient intelligence.

The demonstration of this divine omniscience comes in the last scene of the play, where it is set against an example of human nes-cience, the ignorant Cymbeline, who alone possesses no fragment of the truth which the other characters will now proceed to assemble for our admiration. The rush of knowledge into this royal vacuum constitutes the action of the play's denouement. And yet Cymbeline does begin the scene in possession of one almost instinctive truth: the gods have preserved his kingdom through their instruments—his as yet unrecognized sons and the disguised Belarius and Posthumus. What more the gods have done and what instruments they have em-ployed is revealed by Shakespeare in a scene whose technical bril-liance comes close to obscuring the significance of what occurs. But the revelations of the last scene are more than a series of astounding *coups-de-théâtre,* and their meaning may be clearer if we concentrate our attention not upon Cymbeline but upon Posthumus.

The first revelation to Posthumus is the revelation we have previously seen made to Claudio and Bertram—he learns how vilely he has sinned. Unlike Shakespeare's earlier *humanum genus* figures, however, Posthumus has the advantage, in terms of audience sympathy, of having already repented the crime of which he thinks himself guilty. But only at this point does he realize the full horror of what he has done, for he discovers that he has commanded the murder not of a wife who has wryed a little, but of an entirely innocent and loyal woman. The effect of Iachimo's confession is to make Posthumus loathe himself completely:

> Aye me, most credulous Foole,
> Egregious murtherer, Theefe, any thing
> That's due to all the Villaines past, in being
> To come. Oh giue me Cord, or knife, or poyson,
> Some vpright Iusticer. Thou King, send out
> For Torturors ingenious: it is I
> That all th'abhorred things o' th'earth amend
> By being worse then they. I am *Posthumus,*
> That kill'd thy Daughter: Villain-like, I lye,
> That caus'd a lesser villaine then my selfe,
> A sacreligious Theefe to doo't.   (V.v.246–56)

But he is wrong, and his error is immediately revealed. Imogen is alive and Pisanio, far from having been the agent of Posthumus' villainy, has served as the good instrument of the gods. The gods, who have "to instrument this lower world," [31] have "innumerable instruments," [32] both good and evil. Against the wickedness of the queen, Cloten, and Iachimo, they have set the virtue of Imogen, Cornelius, Pisanio, and the banished princes. Their purpose—or one of their purposes—has been the regeneration of Posthumus. As a result of their mysterious workings, Posthumus has been tested, has sinned, repented, and been forgiven. But their efforts have not been confined to the individual alone. The kingdom of Britain has been cured as well, and its virtues, personified by the lost princes, the lost Imogen, Belarius, and Posthumus himself, have been restored to it.

The virtuous, of course, are rewarded and *humanum genus* is regenerated and restored to a greater felicity than he had lost. But the fate of the evil instruments is instructive, too. The *Homilies,* in urging us to accept the chastisement of God without grumbling, point out that we may survive our trials to enjoy the destruction of those who have served to plague us:

> We should rather submit ourself in patience than to have indignation at God's rod: which peradventure, when he hath corrected us to our nurture, he will cast it into the fire, as it deserveth.[33]

To be cast into the fire is the well-deserved fate of two such instruments—the queen and Cloten, but the treatment of Iachimo is instructive to a different end. We have seen that his defeat at the hands of the disguised Posthumus has served to signify the genuineness of Posthumus' repentance. It has also served to inspire the contrition of Iachimo, who sees his defeat by a seeming peasant as the result of "the heauinesse and guilt within my bosome." (V.ii.8) Unlike the queen, who "repented/ The euils she hatch'd, were not effected," (V.v.74–75) Iachimo is capable of the first essential step toward regeneration and, as a result, he can participate in the play's happy ending. Like Posthumus, his knowledge of his sinfulness makes him want to die, and he asks for death in terms that remind us of Posthumus trying to bargain with the gods:

> my heauie Conscience sinkes my knee,
> As then your force did. Take that life, beseech you
> Which I so often owe. (V.v.492–94)

Posthumus has learned, however, that not death but "amendment of life" is the only proper satisfaction for sin:

Post.: Kneele not to me:
The powre that I haue on you, is to spare you:
The malice towards you, to forgiue you. Live
And deale with others better.   (V.v.497–500)

This speech is taken up by Cymbeline and its charity extended to the defeated Romans and to all the actors in the drama:

Cym.: Nobly doom'd:
Wee'l learne our Freenesse of a Sonne-in-Law:
Pardon's the word to all.   (V.v.501–3)

Man will spare those whom the gods have spared and he will do so in the knowledge that his sufferings have been to a meaningful and comprehensible end. The "senseless" prophecy of Jupiter reveals its meaning and, by testifying to the omniscience and omnipotence of the gods, leaves us with the knowledge that:

The fingers of the Powres aboue, do tune
The harmony of this Peace.   (V.v.551–52)

Of the four romantic comedies of forgiveness, *Cymbeline* is the most overtly Christian, and it is in this Christianity, with the doctrines of repentance and regeneration at its center, that I would place that "commanding significance, which penetrates the whole, ordering and informing everything," which Dr. Leavis has denied to the play. If I am correct in maintaining that *Cymbeline,* along with the other five plays under discussion here, is the literary descendant of one variety of the didactic Christian tales and drama of the Middle Ages, then that Christianity is a natural aspect of the form in which these plays are cast. The relationship of the comedies of forgiveness to the medieval miracle plays is most conveniently demonstrable in the case of *Cymbeline* because one of the surviving *Miracles de Nostre Dame par personnages* happens to be a dramatization of the story which Shakespeare tells of Posthumus and Imogen.

Ostes, Roy d'Espaigne[34] is, again, one of the late fourteenth-century miracle plays contained in the Cangé manuscripts. The resemblance of its plot to that of *Cymbeline* is remarkably close—closer in several aspects than the novella of Boccaccio which is usually thought to be, directly or indirectly, the ultimate "source" of the *Cymbeline* wager plot.[35] For one thing, the characters in the French play are royal and not—as in Boccaccio—members of the *haute bourgeoisie,* and the play, like *Cymbeline,* is concerned with a war between the emperor of Rome and his tributary kings. Denise, the miracle-play Imogen, is the daughter of Alphonse, who is king of Spain when the play opens. Ostes, the Posthumus figure, is the nephew of Lotaire, the Roman emperor. Ostes, aided by his uncle, gains both Spain and Denise by conquest. The love between hero and heroine is none the less intense for that, however, and, as a token of his affection, Ostes leaves with his wife a jewel made from one of his own toe bones when duty forces him to return to Rome. There he meets Berengier, the Iachimo of the miracle play. The wager is made. Berengier goes to Spain, where his attempts at seduction are unsuccessful. He bribes Denise's maid to obtain for him the previously agreed-upon "proof" of Denise's adultery—the knowledge of a secret mark on her body, and Ostes' jewel, the fatal toe bone. Berengier has no trouble in convincing Ostes that his wife has been unfaithful. Ostes rushes back to Spain to murder the supposed adulteress, but fortunately Denise is warned of his imminent arrival and intention. Her reaction is to pray to the Virgin, and she is right to do so. God, who is seated on-stage, as usual, hears her prayer and sends *Notre Dame* and three angels to comfort her. The Virgin tells Denise to disguise herself as a page and go to the palace of her uncle, the king of Granada, where her deposed father is living. She is not to despair, for all will turn to good:

> Et saches pour t'onnour accroistre,
> Combien que moult de paine aras,
> En la fin vengie seras

> De celui qui par fausseté
> T'a mis sus la desloiauté
> Pour quoy Oston a vers toy guerre.   (1113-118)

This resembles Jupiter's reassurance to the spirits in *Cymbeline*, though the happiness promised to Denise is the specific and unquestionably intense joy of seeing her enemy suffer.

There is nothing in the least mysterious about the power and presence of God in *Ostes*. God, the Virgin, and their attendant saints and angels were visible to the audience throughout the play. Divine power literally watched over the action of the miracles. Furthermore, that power is man's for the asking. There is less need for human good, in the form of a Pisanio, to assist and advise Denise. The Virgin will tell her what to do. Finally, the primarily important relationship in this play is not that of the lovers to one another, but that of each of them to God.

This becomes most strikingly clear in the sin of the *humanum genus* figure, Ostes himself. Posthumus sins by allowing his love for Imogen to turn to hate and by attempting to have her murdered. Ostes behaves in precisely the same way, but it is not this behavior that constitutes his most heinous offense. For one thing, the love between Ostes and Denise is never as vivid as its counterpart in *Cymbeline*. Furthermore, Ostes' crediting of Berengier's story is made to seem more natural by the fact that the proofs of Denise's guilt are agreed upon in advance. Finally, Ostes' attempt to kill his wife is overshadowed by a far more serious offense: he turns from God.

When he is unable to discover his wife's whereabouts, Ostes places the blame for her escape squarely where it belongs:

> Je croy que Diex a elle part:
> Ce fait mon, je la voy tresbien.
> Ha! mauvais Dieu, que ne te tien!
> Vraiement, se je te tenoie,
> De cops tout te desromperoie.   (1299-303)

This desire to give God a good drubbing must have gained in force from the fact that He was sitting, in His majesty, only a short distance from His enraged creature. But Ostes is to get still better and still worse:

> Egar! voiz: toy et ta creance
> Reni et toute ta puissance,
> Et si m'en vois droit oultre mer
> Conme Sarrazin demourer
> Et tenir la loy Mahommet;
> Car qui en toy s'entente met
>   Il fait folie.   (1304–10)

Posthumus loses his faith in human love; Ostes loses his faith in the Christian God. Like Posthumus, Ostes disappears (though much more briefly) from the action at this point, and, again like Posthumus, the next time we see him he is in a state of contrition, not for the treatment of his wife, but because he has denied "doulx Jhesus" and the Blessed Virgin. Ostes does not quite despair of God's forgiveness, however:

> Ha! sire, qui piteux et doulx
> Estes, ce dit sainte escripture,
> A toute humaine creature
> Qui se repent de son meffait,
> Pardon vous quier de ce qu'ay fait.
> Pardon! las! conment dire l'ose?
> Certes, je demande une chose
> Que vous m'avez bel escondire
> Et refuser par raison, sire:
> Pour ç'a terre cy m'asserray,
> Et mon pechié cy gemiray.
>   Amérement.   (1519–530)

This is the explicit equivalent of the implicit Christianity of Posthumus' soliloquies in Act Five of *Cymbeline,* and, as in Shakespeare, contrition is rewarded with epiphany. God again sends his mother to comfort suffering humanity and, indeed, condescends to address Ostes directly. This *deux ex machina,* unlike Shakespeare's, has a direct and essential effect upon the action of the play. God tells Ostes to go to Rome and make confession, and furthermore assures him of his wife's innocence. This theophany leaves *humanum genus,* not convinced that his life is incomprehensible, but assured that God will turn all to good.

The plot has not stood still while Ostes has been off serving Mahomet. Denise, unrecognized, has been serving her father and uncle and, in obedience to the Virgin, she retains her disguise even when news comes to her father that she is dead. Her uncle, meanwhile, is collecting allies for a war against Rome, but just before the battle is to be joined, Denise asks permission to negotiate a peace. On the way to the emperor's court she meets the repentant Ostes, who (not recognizing her) accompanies her into the emperor's presence. There both Denise and Ostes challenge Berengier to trial by combat. Ostes is chosen to do the fighting and, in the equivalent of the Shakespearean encounter in battle of Posthumus and Iachimo, soon defeats his wife's calumniator. Berengier confesses and, her honor vindicated, Denise reveals her true sex and self by the most direct method possible:

> Tenez, regardez ma poitrine:
> G'y ay mamelle conme fame;
> Du monstrer n'est point de diffame.
> Les autres membres secrez touz
> Femenins ay, ce savez vous,
> Ostes, plus parler n'en convient.   (1996–2001)

With the identification of the heroine and the reunion of husband and wife, we have reached the point in *Ostes* equivalent to that at which we left *Cymbeline.* The concluding passages of both plays are similar. Child is restored to father and the revelation of truth results in the reconciliation, not only of the characters, but of Rome with the nations warring against it. In both plays the conclusion is seen as the result of the working of divine power. "Diex a ceste assemblee fait" (2019) says the emperor in *Ostes,* and both plays conclude with a hymn of praise. In *Ostes* the emperor turns to his priests and says:

> Seigneurs, je vueil que sanz demeure
> Vous chantez, en nous conduisant,
> Un motet qui soit deduisant,
> > Plaisant et bel.
> > *Les Clers*
> Sire, nous le ferons ysnel.
> > Avant: chantons.   (2074–79)

Here, in spirit, is an equivalent of Cymbeline's famous final speech:

> Laud we the Gods,
> And let our crooked Smoakes climbe to their Nostrils
> From our blest Altars. . . .   (V.v.562–64)

That *Cymbeline* and *Ostes* are plays in the same dramatic tradition appears to me unmistakable. For works separated by two hundred and fifty years in time, they are remarkably alike and the superficial details of plot in which they resemble one another seem unimportant compared with their likenesses in emotional movement and final effect. It is hardly surprising that the later plays of Shakespeare have been characterized as, in the profoundest sense, Christian drama, for they surely descend, as artistic forms, from the religious drama of the Middle Ages.

However, once one has insisted that these plays of forgiveness are in the same Christian tradition, both philosophical and literary, one must redress the balance by insisting equally that, in the Shakespearean comedy of forgiveness, that tradition has been secularized. As a result of its secularization, the effect and significance of a play like *Cymbeline* has been importantly altered. The divinity that shapes the events of *Cymbeline* is far more mysterious than the constantly visible and available God of the miracles. Posthumus, when he prays to the gods, is answered with the riddling prophecy of Jupiter. Ostes, upon repenting, is told both the truth and what to do about it. Similarly, Denise's ordeal, unlike Imogen's, is lightened by the Virgin's assurance that she is the victim of a calumniator and that her sufferings will be rewarded in the end. In both *Ostes* and *Cymbeline* it is centrally important that man serve the purposes of God, but in Shakespeare those purposes are bewilderingly mysterious and man's power to serve them is far more limited.

The miracle plays primarily celebrate God's love for man and the mercy which God is constantly willing to extend to his repentant creatures. The human virtue which the medieval plays exalt is man's love for God. These varieties of love remain important in *Cymbeline*, but the primary emphasis is shifted to two kinds of human love: the romantic love of man and woman, and charity. The most powerful emotional moment of the last scene of *Cymbeline* comes in the lines that dramatize the reunion of Posthumus and Imogen:

> *Imo.*: Why did you throw your wedded Lady fro you?
> Thinke that you are vpon a Rocke, and now
> Throw me againe.
> *Post.*: Hang there like fruite, my soule,
> Till the Tree dye.   (V.v.306–10)

The emphasis in the equivalent moment of *Ostes* is quite different:

OSTON

> Ha! biau sire Diex, tost ou tart
> Rens tu des biens faiz les merites,
> Et de punir les maux t'aquittes.
> Aussi bien, ma tresdoulce suer,
> Baise moy; pour toy tout le cuer
>   En pleur me font.   (2010–15)

The speeches of Posthumus and Imogen ("among the tenderest lines in Shakespeare")[36] are an intense expression of their love for one another. Ostes' primary interest is in exalting the workings of divine providence.

The necessity for charity, the human equivalent of divine mercy, is little in evidence in *Ostes*. In *Cymbeline*, it is supremely important. As always in the romantic comedies of forgiveness, romantic love is seen to depend upon charity for its existence. Only the heroine's charitable capacity for forgiveness can preserve romantic love from destruction. But in *Cymbeline* charity becomes the preserver of the fabric of society itself as well as the preserver of romantic love. Posthumus' charity, whose source is in his newly acquired self-knowledge, is extended to the repentant villain. In *Ostes*, the Iachimo figure, Berengier, meets with no forgiveness. The emperor of Rome turns him over to Ostes and Denise for just but vengeful punishment. Posthumus' sparing of Iachimo, as we have seen, makes the happy ending of the play possible and his forgiveness of the man who has wronged him inspires Cymbeline's "Pardon's the word to all." From the regeneration of Posthumus through self-knowledge flows the charity that reconciles not only husband to wife and man to man, but ruler to subject and Britain to Rome.

The version of reality contained in the Empedoclean vision of the universe continues to be that which is presented in later Shakespearean comedy. The force of strife is omnipresent in these works and when it discovers, in the weakness of *humanum genus,* a means for establishing itself as the dominating force in the worlds of these plays, chaos threatens to destroy psychological and social order:

> If it were not thus, that the goodness of God were effectually in his creatures to rule them, how could it be that the main sea, so raging and labouring to overflow the earth, could be kept within his bonds and banks, as it is? . . . How could it be that the elements, so diverse and contrary as they be among themselves, should yet agree and abide together in a concord, without destruction one of another, to serve our use, if it came not only of God's goodness so to temper them? [37]

Cymbeline contains a demonstration of the means by which the goodness of God operates effectually in his human creatures to rule them. The process of regeneration results in charity, and that process has its ultimate origin in the grace of God. The forgiveness of man by man, on which psychological and social order depends, is the result of the forgiveness of man by God. A knowledge of this full pattern is essential to a complete understanding of *Cymbeline,* but the primary emphasis in Shakespeare is upon the necessity for man's recognition of God's purposes, and upon the difficulty of that recognition.

The late romances are often seen as hymns of optimism, and, to be sure, *Cymbeline, The Winter's Tale,* and *The Tempest* end with powerful affirmations of divine providence. Man is not seen, however, as able to repose comfortably in a knowledge of that providence. The reality of human evil and weakness are vividly presented and the mysterious workings of the gods entail the intense suffering of the innocent. A vision of man's world that insists as strongly as *Cymbeline* does upon these painful aspects of the human condition surely contains a large element of pessimism, and that pessimism deepens in *The Winter's Tale.*

The Winter's Tale

The Winter's Tale, unlike *Cymbeline,* has attracted a great deal of sympathetic consideration from recent critics. As we have seen, it is specifically by comparison with *The Winter's Tale* that Dr. Leavis finds *Cymbeline* an inferior work of art.[1] S. L. Bethell has written a fine monograph on the later play,[2] while, to name but three, E. M. W. Tillyard,[3] G. Wilson Knight,[4] and Derek Traversi[5] have each produced a lengthy and sensitive essay on it. There can be no doubt that *The Winter's Tale* is a more pleasing play than its immediate predecessor. Though, like *Cymbeline,* it contains strong elements of the grotesque and the deliberately archaic, the grotesquerie of the bear who dines upon Antigonus is less macabre and its dramatic purpose more apparent than the grotesquerie of the scene in which Imogen fondles the headless corpse of Cloten. The archaism of Father Time and the "ghost" of Hermione is more familiar and poetically less anomalous than the archaism of the descent of Jupiter in *Cymbeline.* Most importantly, the tormenting ordeal of Imogen is replaced by the gorgeous pastoralism of Perdita's Bohemia in Act Four of *The Winter's Tale.* Finally, Shakespeare has pursued a different and superior artistic strategy in the construction of his denouement. For the technical brilliance of the rapid-fire series of disclosures in the concluding scene of *Cymbeline,* he has substituted the gradual revelation of the three scenes of Act Five of *The Winter's Tale.* As a result, the emotional force of his culminating revelation is undiminished by the lesser revelations that surround it. The resurrection of Hermione is Shakespeare's most intensely moving "awakening from nightmare" and his most powerful evocation of the wonders of human forgiveness and divine providence. For all its beauty, however, *The Winter's*

Tale insists, even more strongly than *Cymbeline,* on the inherent weakness and evil of *humanum genus* and on the innocent suffering that is entailed in the workings of divine providence.

The Winter's Tale is a dramatization of Robert Greene's prose romance, *Pandosto; or, The Triumph of Time,*[6] but in transferring Greene's narrative to the stage, Shakespeare altered it fundamentally. *Pandosto,* like *The Winter's Tale,* is made up of two closely related stories. One of these, the romantic comedy of Dorastus and Fawnia, Shakespeare retained, almost unaltered, as the story of Florizel and Perdita. Greene's other action, which concerns Fawnia's father Pandosto, is grimly tragic, and it is this narrative which Shakespeare transforms into the comedy of Leontes' forgiveness. Pandosto, the king of Bohemia, sins, like Leontes, through a causeless jealousy which results in the deaths of his son and queen, and the loss of his infant daughter. In Greene, however, the queen is really dead, and when Fawnia is restored, unrecognized, to Pandosto, he conceives an incestuous passion for her. The subsequent revelation of the girl's identity causes her father to despair and the romance ends when, "to close vp the Comedie with a Tragicall stratageme," [7] Pandosto commits suicide.

Shakespeare's most obvious change in Greene's action consists of the elimination of this "Tragicall strategeme," and the substitution for it of the scene of forgiveness. Other, subtler alterations are made, however, and one of the most important of these comes in Shakespeare's dramatization of the sin of his *humanum genus* figure.

Pandosto's jealousy, like Leontes', is without any foundation in the actions or thoughts of his wife and friend, and yet Pandosto's emotion is not totally irrational. It takes its origin from appearances rather than from reality, but in Greene those appearances are presented as genuinely deceiving:

Bellaria (who in her time was the flower of curtesie), willing to show how vnfaynedly shee looued her husband by his friends intertainemēt, vsed him likewise so familiarly, that her countenance bewraied how her mind was affected towardes him: oftentimes comming her selfe into his bed chamber, to see that nothing should be amis to mislike him. This honest familiarity increased dayly more and more betwixt them; for *Bellaria*, noting in *Egistus* a princely and bountifull minde, adorned with sundrie and excellent qualities, and *Egistus*, finding in her a vertuous and curteous disposition, there grew such a secret vniting of their affections, that the one could not well be without the company of the other.[8]

It would be unnatural if "sundry and doubtfull thoughts" did not enter the mind of a husband in such a case. Pandosto's mistake lies in his allowing his suspicions to obsess him and finally to overwhelm his reason, but their conquest of his mind is a slow process which Greene describes for us:

These and such like doubtfull thoughtes a long time smoothering in his stomacke, beganne at last to kindle in his minde a secret mistrust, which increased by suspition, grewe at last to be a flaming Jealousie, that so tormented him as he could take no rest.[9]

This is the state of mind which Shakespeare must present dramatically at the beginning of *The Winter's Tale*. An ordinarily good man is unshakably but wrongly convinced that his best friend has committed adultery with his eminently virtuous and loving wife. For Greene, there is no problem. He simply tells us what has happened and what he describes is comprehensible to the point of being banal. In being transferred to the stage, however, the comprehensibility—and consequently the banality—of this jealousy disappear. Shakespeare accepts the jealousy of Leontes, as he had accepted the recalcitrance of Bertram, as the *sine qua non* of his action, and he reveals Leontes' state of mind in speeches of intense dramatic force.

The soliloquies (more properly "asides") in which Leontes presents his diseased psyche to us are among Shakespeare's most brilliant displays of his ability to dramatize the human mind. This brilliance is an artistic necessity, for Shakespeare, in convincing us of Leontes' state of mind, is substituting demonstration for explanation. In Leontes, Shakespeare is presenting us with a human mystery and he is presenting it *as* a mystery. His genius enables him to see and dramatize one of the most puzzling complexities of the mind: the presence of hate within love, and the constant danger that love will succumb to the desire to hate. Shakespeare does not attempt an explanation of this paradoxical coexistence. He presents us with a dramatic insight whose implications are uncomfortable, indeed.

That the presence of this discomfort is deliberate seems quite plain. The various methods by which Shakespeare could have "explained" and thus mitigated Leontes' crime are too numerous and too obvious to make Shakespeare's avoidance of them explicable as the result of carelessness or ineptitude. The appearances upon which Leontes' false suspicions are based could, for example, have been made more genuinely misleading—as Shakespeare made their equivalents in *Much Ado* and *Cymbeline*—but in *The Winter's Tale* it is clear that no excuse for the king can be discovered in Hermione's affection for Polixenes.[10] Shakespeare has dramatized that affection and its innocence is apparent to the audience. But he further emphasizes the complete irrationality of Leontes' suspicions through the reactions to them of the other characters. Not once do any of the Sicilian courtiers betray the slightest inclination to accept Leontes' version of his wife's conduct. It takes Leontes a good fifty lines simply to make his far from dim-witted councilor, Camillo, understand that he thinks Hermione has committed adultery. When Camillo finally comprehends, his reply to Leontes is completely uncourtierlike in its blunt contradiction of the king:

> *Cam.*: I would not be a stander-by, to heare
> My Soueraigne Mistresse clouded so, without
> My present vengeance taken; 'shrew my heart,
> You neuer spoke what did become you lesse
> Then this. . . .   (I.ii.324–28)

And he goes on to characterize Leontes' jealousy as a "diseased opinion."

Camillo's tone is echoed by all of the characters to whom Leontes accuses his queen, and their fearless and repeated defenses of Hermione give us a needed reassurance of the possibility of human decency. Indeed, their denunciations of Leontes redound oddly to his credit and we can only agree with him when he defends himself against the formidable Paulina:

> Were I a Tyrant,
> Where were her life? She durst not call me so,
> If she did know me one.   (II.iii.154–56)

Clearly, his subjects do not fear Leontes because he is not usually frightening. Their mode of addressing him makes it plain that they can ordinarily expect common sense and justice at his hands. The reaction of the Sicilian courtiers has the double effect of convincing us that the explanation for Leontes' conduct can be found neither in the appearance of the queen's affection for Polixenes nor in the fact that Leontes is by nature monstrous or inhumanly cruel. The courtiers' reactions in Greene's romance are quite different. There Pandosto does not even tell Franion (Camillo) why he wants Egistus (Polixenes) killed, so that the councilor has no opportunity to defend the queen.[11] Furthermore, Greene tells us that when Pandosto has the queen's supposed adultery announced to his subjects, "the suddaine & speedy pasage of *Egistus,* and the secret departure of *Franion,* induced them (the circumstances thoroughly considered) to thinke that both the proclamation was true, and the king greatly iniured." [12]

One of the mitigating factors which Greene provided for his hero —the genuinely suspicious appearance of the queen's affection for the visiting king—has been eliminated by Shakespeare. Another—the slow, "rational" growth of Pandosto's jealousy—has also been disregarded. Had he wished to, Shakespeare could have provided us with an equivalent, in an expository soliloquy, of Greene's tracing of the origin and development of Pandosto's suspicions. As S. L. Bethell has pointed out, "the lack of motivation cannot be ascribed to the exigencies of the Elizabethan drama; an address to the audience could have summarized Leontes' psychological history, like Gloucester's opening soliloquy in *Richard III*." [13]

Finally, Shakespeare has eschewed, in this play, what is perhaps the most obvious dramatic motivation for the murderous jealousy of Leontes: the handy figure of the calumniator. This solution must have occurred to the creator of Don John, Iago, and Iachimo, and been consciously rejected by him. Indeed, Shakespeare underlines the absence of this descendant of the old Vice by having Antigonus suspect his presence when he says to Leontes:

> You are abus'd, and by some putter on,
> That will be damn'd for 't: would I knew the Villaine,
> I would Land-damne him. . . .   (II.i.171–73)

But the villain is Leontes himself, and damned he will be, and his land to boot. Leontes is his own calumniator, the most completely unexcused of all Shakespeare's *humanum genus* figures. Bertram has the complaisance of Parolles to second his petulant self-absorption, and even Angelo and Antonio can be seen as tempted, the one by the beauty of Isabella, the other by the prospect of power. No one encourages or tempts Leontes, or lies to him. His sin is all his own work.

S. L. Bethell insists upon the significance of this lack of obvious motivation for Leontes' crimes:

> This is his sin, the sin of sexual jealousy, and it comes upon him with no warning, apparently from without. . . . Sin comes from without, as in the Christian scheme it comes from the temptation of the devil—we are concerned, I think, with the general origin of evil as well as with the particular sin of Leontes.[14]

I would agree as to the nature of our concern, but my own experience of the play would lead me to place the origin of its evil precisely *within* the mind of Leontes. By refusing to give evil any objective existence outside of *humanum genus,* Shakespeare, in *The Winter's*

Tale, insists that human nature is inherently evil—or rather, "of a mingled yarne, good and ill together," for the same human being may prove to be capable both of monstrous crime and subsequent regeneration.

Unjustifiable sexual jealousy is only the first of Leontes' sins. As always in the comedies of forgiveness, hatred's conquest of the mind of *humanum genus* sets off a chain reaction of consequent crimes which almost succeeds in permanently destroying an orderly, love-dominated world. Because Leontes is the ruler as well as the *humanum genus* figure of *The Winter's Tale,* the chaos in his mind threatens with a special effectiveness to replace the world of the play with an answering social and moral chaos. The kingdom of Sicily, as it is presented to us in the opening lines of the play, is a particularly happy one, and its happiness has for a foundation the varieties of love that center upon Leontes. There is the love of king for king, or friend for friend, a love whose source is the shared innocence of childhood and whose apparent strength leads its observers to conclude, overoptimistically, that "there is not in the World, either Malice or Matter, to alter it." (I.i.35–36) There is also the love of prince and king, or son and father, and the existence of Mamillius, "a Gentleman of the greatest Promise, that euer came into my note," (I.i.37–38) is what sets the seal upon the happiness of Sicily by appearing to guarantee its long continuance. Finally, and crowning all the rest, is the romantic, procreative love of queen and king, wife and husband. The love of Hermione is playful and fruitful and its contented sensuality betrays itself in her very manner of expression to her husband:

> You may ride's
> With one soft Kisse a thousand Furlongs, ere
> With Spur we heat an Acre.   (I.ii.117–19)

But Hermione's love is more, or represents more, than romantic love, for like Helena's and Imogen's, Hermione's love is a manifestation of God's love for *humanum genus.* As M. M. Mahood has put it,

Hermione "acts the role of regenerative grace to Leontes," [15] and, indeed, all the varieties of love that sustain the orderly, happy universe of the play's opening scenes have their ultimate source in divine grace. But, as always in Shakespeare, grace must be accepted if it is to continue and Leontes abruptly sets about to reject it and destroy its manifestations.

With hatred in control of his mind, Leontes attempts to destroy the innocent—to kill his best friend, his wife, and his own newborn child, and to suborn his virtuous councilor to murder an anointed and innocent king. Once turned tyrant, Leontes tries to out-Herod Herod by destroying the innocents upon whom his happiness depends. He succeeds, but never as he had intended. He does not kill Polixenes but he kills the friendship between them. He is not able to destroy the virtue of Camillo, but he does drive that virtue from his kingdom. His diseased mind is unable to make Hermione guilty of adultery, but he destroys their love as effectively as if she had indeed betrayed her husband. But the most horrible of these attempted sins is his exposure of Perdita, for this intended murder is "what Shakespeare makes the symbol for complete wickedness: the command to murder a child." [16] In *The Winter's Tale,* infanticide takes on an added horror from the fact that the child is Leontes' own.

The deadly sin into which Leontes falls as a result of his jealousy is wrath. His addled, hate-filled brain causes him to strike out in a blind, enraged effort to destroy all that is good around him. Yet his rage is defeated. It does not take its effect upon its intended objects and it finally awakens the answering wrath of the gods.

The communication of divine truth and will from the oracle at Delphi is an equivalent to the theophany in *Cymbeline.* But, unlike the mysterious prophecy of Jupiter, the oracle is bluntly comprehensible:

Hermione *is chast,* Polixenes *blamelesse,* Camillo *a true subject,* Leontes *a jealous Tyrant, his innocent Babe truly begotten, and the King shall liue without an Heire, if that which is lost, be not found.*

(III.ii.141–44)

For Leontes, this is the terrible truth about his own sinfulness and it should bring him, through self-knowledge, to contrition. But in his wrath, Leontes blasphemes by rejecting the word of the gods:

> There is no truth at all i'th'Oracle:
> The Sessions shall proceed: this is meere falsehood.
> (III.ii.149–50)

Punishment follows immediately:

> *Ser.:* . . . The Prince your Sonne, with meere conceit, and feare
> Of the Queenes speed, is gone.
> *Leo.:* How? gone?
> *Ser.:* Is dead.
> *Leo.:* Apollo's angry, and the Heauens themselues
> Doe strike at my Iniustice. (III.ii.154–59)

The death of Mamillius is one of the most painfully significant incidents in the play. It is seen as doubly caused. The naturalistic explanation is that Mamillius has died of sorrow as a result of Leontes' persecution of Hermione: Leontes has attempted to murder his daughter, Perdita. With horrible irony, he has succeeded in killing his son. On a supernatural level, the death of Mamillius is the gods' punishment for Leontes' sins, and particularly for his final sin of blasphemy. Leontes, in his wrath, has tried to destroy all the manifestations of the gods' grace except one—his son. He still loves this gift of the gods, so with terrible and inhuman justice, it is this gift which they take from him. Mamillius becomes an instrument of the gods for the punishment of Leontes. We have seen them employing their instruments before, in *Cymbeline*, but there it was the evil instruments, the queen and Cloten, who were "cast into the fire." Here it is the very symbol of innocence, the child, whom they destroy, or allow Leontes to destroy. And, of course, the punishment which that destruction entails does not fall upon Leontes alone. Mamillius is also the innocent Hermione's child and his death threatens to kill her as well. Indeed, all the deserved cruelty of the gods to Leontes is visited upon the undeserving Hermione as well, for she, too, must endure the ensuing sixteen years of unhappiness and the separation from her banished daughter.

Act Three of the play ends with one more demonstration of the mysterious working of divine power. Since it manages to contain both the seacoast of Bohemia and the stage direction "Exit, pursued by a bear," the scene in which Perdita is abandoned by Antigonus can stand for all that neoclassic taste finds most objectionable in Shakespeare. To what is fashionably called the "baroque sensibility," however, it represents the particular genius of Shakespeare at its most intense. It also represents an incident which Shakespeare deliberately devised for his own purposes, for there is no equivalent to it in Greene, where the newborn child is exposed by the time-honored romantic method—a method which Shakespeare was to use later in *The Tempest*—of being placed in a boat and abandoned to the winds and waves. Since Greene's procedure would have worked as well as Shakespeare's, we must conclude that Shakespeare wanted his bear and that he had his reasons for including it.

Antigonus' death makes its comment upon the complexity of the working of the gods and the means by which heaven brings about the fulfillment of its designs. The scene largely concerns the grotesque death of a good man who has had the ill luck to become the instrument both of Leontes and of the heavenly powers. Antigonus, whom Shakespeare has been at some pains to characterize as a decent and sympathetic figure, finds himself bound by oath to expose the infant Perdita. He has so bound himself, however, in an effort to save the child from certain death. Nonetheless, the deed itself is wrong, and the doers of it fear the consequences. The mariner who accompanies Antigonus to the shore says:

> In my conscience
> The heauens with that we haue in hand, are angry,
> And frowne vpon's.   (III.iii.8–10)

The moral problem of whether or not men are bound by oaths such as Antigonus has sworn is one on which the Anglican Church had taken a specific and careful stand. According to the *Homilies*:

> If a man at any time shall, either of ignorance or of malice, promise and swear to do anything which is either against the law of Almighty God or not in his power to perform, let him take it for an unlawful and ungodly oath.[17]

The example of such an oath given by the *Homilies* is that of Jephthah (Judges xi. 30–39), who promised to sacrifice to God the first person whom he should meet upon his successful return from battle, and who forced himself to kill "his own and only daughter." [18]

It is possible, then, to see Antigonus as a sinner deserving of punishment for failing to recognize that the oath he has given to Leontes is not binding since it requires him to commit a crime worse than oath-breaking. In context, however, the incident does not give the sense of having been designed to satisfy any nice calculation of just deserts. Rather, Antigonus is seen as the victim of the gods' unalterable design for Leontes. The false apparition of Hermione defines the moral position of "Good Antigonus" as follows:

> Fate (against thy better disposition)
> Hath made thy person for the Thrower-out
> Of my poor babe, according to thine oath,
>
> .   .   .   .   .   .
>
> For this vngentle businesse
> Put on thee, by my Lord, thou ne're shalt see
> Thy Wife *Paulina* more. . . .   (III.iii.35–43)

The gods will punish Leontes by keeping his daughter from him, and since he must have no clue as to where his child has been exposed, it is necessary that Antigonus and the entire crew of the ship on which he sailed should perish. Shakespeare, by deliberately altering the method of Perdita's exposure, has insisted on presenting us with this further example of the pitiless methods by which heaven achieves its purposes.

"Their sacred wills be done," Antigonus replies when the mariner fears the anger of the heavens. The heavens have chosen him to be their instrument in placing Perdita on the seacoast of Bohemia, and they have directed his choice of this shore through the false vision of Hermione. Now it is their sacred wills that their instrument, the good Antigonus, be pursued and eaten alive by a bear.

The sudden apparition of this animal, coming as it does after Antigonus's ornate description of his vision of Hermione, and his pathetic parting words to the infant he is abandoning, is a brilliantly grotesque Shakespearean moment. Its terrifying hilarity shatters at one blow and forever the mood of tragedy which has characterized the play so far. Much more than the formal dividing of the action by the chorus, the bear breaks the play into its two parts. As Nevill Coghill has put it, "the terrible and the grotesque come near to each other in a *frisson* of horror instantly succeeded by a shout of laughter; and so this bear, this unique and perfect link between the two halves of the play, slips into place and holds." [19] But the incident, in addition to its function as a shifting of dramatic gears, has (if I may so pervert the term) a symbolic logic of its own. Antigonus is the instrument and victim of Leontes' wrath and of heaven's answering wrath; and the wrathful bear, who pursues and dines upon him is, iconographically, wonderfully appropriate and one may suspect a macabre joke in his appearance. Theatrical illusion apart, Antigonus is destroyed by a man in a bear's skin, but he is also the victim of Leontes, whom jealousy and consequent fury have transformed into a wrathful animal—a bear in a man's skin.

The bear's exit is followed immediately by the entrance of a more obviously symbolic figure—the good shepherd. He is searching for his lost sheep, but he finds another innocent instead: the wronged Perdita. The shepherd is a type of god and an instrument of the gods, whose inexplicable ways are again presented to us. They have allowed the death of the innocent Mamillius. Now they preserve the equally innocent Perdita and their mercy takes place to the grotesque accompaniment of the bear who dines upon Antigonus and the natural fury of the storm which destroys the Sicilian ship and all its crew—both these events being comically described for us by a clown.

The most obviously symbolic figure of all enters last. The opening lines of Time, the Chorus, have, I think, been misinterpreted by some editors of the play in a way that reveals the pietistic approach which too many commentators on the late romances unconsciously assume:

> *Time:* I that please some, try all: both ioy and terror
> Of good, and bad . . .   (IV.i.3–4)

The Penguin editor tells us that Time is identifying himself here as one who brings "joy to good men and terror to bad."[20] But surely this is not what Time says or is. He says that he is "both joy and terror of good, and bad," and that is what he means. Time brings happiness and misery to both the good and the evil. We have seen him indifferently present both the good Hermione and the evil Leontes with terror. Now, after Leontes' regeneration, he will present them both with joy. The point may seem a minor one, but a pious "all is best" interpretation of these lines betrays a misunderstanding of the universe which *The Winter's Tale* presents. All is *not* best in a world where an innocent child dies for the sins of his father or a good servant dies for the sins of his master. The "moral" of Greene's *Pandosto* is, according to its title page:

> although by the meanes of sinister fortune, Truth may be concealed yet by Time in spight of fortune it is most manifestly reuealed.[21]

This is a comfortable thought and one that can be extracted from *The Winter's Tale,* just as the pious reassurances of the theophany find support in *Cymbeline.* But, again, the version of reality presented by *The Winter's Tale* is too complicated to lend itself to easy moralizing, and the function of Time in the play goes beyond that of serving as the father of Truth.

Time, as he tells us, is the process, the element, in which all men are subjected to their trials. These trials, both of happiness and misery, come to all sorts of men and the good are not restricted to the experience of joy, while the bad are not so consistently miserable as, no doubt, they should be. Indeed, since, as Leontes forcefully demonstrates, men are simultaneously good and bad, such simple justice is impossible. Nevertheless, the distribution of happiness and misery is not meaninglessly haphazard. The gods are above and their wills are done on earth, but the significance of the patterns they impose upon man is frequently beyond man's comprehension.

One of the most familiar of these temporal patterns is that of the changing seasons, and this pattern, with its analogue in the life of man, is symbolically central to *The Winter's Tale*. The whole story of Hermione and Perdita is analogous to the myth of Proserpina and Demeter[22]—a resemblance that is underlined by the reference in Perdita's flower speech:

> O *Proserpina*,
> For the Flowres now, that (frighted) thou let'st fall
> From *Dysses* Waggon . . . (IV.iv.136–38)

Throughout the scene, Perdita is costumed as a classical goddess of fertility:

> *Flo.*: These your vnvsuall weeds, to each part of you
> Do's giue a life: no Shepherdesse, but *Flora*
> Peering in Aprils front. (IV.iv.4–6)

Perdita's fruitfulness is still potential, however. It is not yet the actual fecundity of the pregnant Hermione of Act One. In *The Winter's Tale*, Shakespeare, by comparison with his earlier romantic comedies of forgiveness, has simplified his heroine by splitting her role into parts and assigning aspects of it to each of the resulting characters. Helena, in *All's Well*, was, as we have seen, forced to function as the sexually desirable maiden, the offended wife, the manipulator of the action, and the instrument of God's grace. Shakespeare simplified the role in *Cymbeline* by assigning the manipulative function to the gods and by having Imogen confine her actions almost completely to a passive suffering of the wrongs heaped upon her by father, step-mother, and husband. The process of simplification is carried even further in *The Winter's Tale*, where the gods again manipulate the action, while the role of the sexually desirable maiden is transferred from Hermione to Perdita. Hermione retains, however, her function as the primary symbol for God's grace and it is her return to Leontes that marks his achievement of forgiveness.

The long withdrawal of the visible signs of grace from Leontes is the result of the gods' insistence that he make satisfaction for his sin. Immediately upon the death of Mamillius, Leontes, suddenly over-come by a sense of his own sinfulness, experiences contrition, asks the gods' pardon, confesses what he now realizes are his sins, and ex-presses his desire to make satisfaction to those he has wronged:

> *Apollo* pardon
> My great prophanenesse 'gainst thine Oracle.
> Ile reconcile me to *Polixenes*,
> New woe my Queene, recall the good Camillo . . .
> (III.ii.166–69)

But with this the gods will not be satisfied. Through their instrument, Paulina, they conceal from Leontes the fact that Hermione is alive, and his ignorance, which is the source of his sixteen-year-long pen-ance, is his punishment. Like Claudio and Posthumus, Leontes must endure the false belief that he has killed the woman he loves, but his suffering is far lengthier and more intense than theirs. We see only the beginning and end of that suffering, but Paulina describes it for us metaphorically:

> betake thee
> To nothing but dispaire. A thousand knees,
> Ten thousand yeares together, naked, fasting,

Vpon a barren Mountaine, and still Winter
In storme perpetuall, could not moue the Gods
To looke that way thou wer't.   (III.ii.225–30)

Like Jehan le Paulu in the miracle play[13] Leontes imposes a terrible
penance on himself, and though his mental torment is less colorful
than Jehan's decision to go on all fours like a beast, what we see of
his suffering is no less intense.

When Act Five opens, we hear the voice of human reason, speaking through Cleomines and Dion, attempting to convince Leontes that
he has suffered enough and to persuade him, for the good of his
kingdom, to return to a normal mode of life:

Sir, you haue done enough, and haue perform'd
A Saint-like Sorrow: No fault could you make,
Which you haue not redeem'd; indeed pay'd downe
More penitence, then done trespas: At the last
Doe, as the Heauens haue done; forget your euill,
With them, forgiue your self.   (V.i.4–9)

Against these eminently reasonable arguments is opposed the voice
of Paulina. She has already served the gods by concealing Hermione
from her husband. Now she serves them further by exacerbating
Leontes' mental sufferings through her constant reminders of his
crimes. She is the personification of Leontes' conscience and she is
determined that his sufferings will continue until the pattern of the
gods has worked itself out. Cleomines and Dion want Leontes to
anticipate the purpose of the gods. Paulina remembers and insists
upon obeying the expressed will of Apollo:

the Gods
Will haue fulfill'd their secret purposes:
For ha's not the Diuine *Apollo* said?
Is't not the tenor of his Oracle,
That King *Leontes* shall not haue an Heire,
Till his lost Child be found? Which, that it shall,

Is all as monstrous to our humane reason,
As my *Antigonus* to breake his Graue,
And come againe to me: who, on my life,
Did perish with the Infant. 'Tis your counsell,
My Lord should to the Heauens be contrary,
Oppose against their wills. (V.i.45–56)

Cleomines and Dion are rational men and if Leontes were attempting to deal with the sort of purely human situation which reason can dominate, he would be mad to reject their advice. Paulina, however, realizes that Leontes is faced with the secret purposes of the gods and that these purposes are beyond the comprehension of reason. The design of the gods is "monstrous to our humane reason," but we are that design, or part of it, and human reason must accept the fact.

The force that keeps Leontes from violating the dictates of the gods is not his reason, but his sense of guilt. With Paulina to prompt him, he has fulfilled the will of the gods by subjecting himself to a nightmare existence of self-disgust and self-torment. Greene's Pandosto lives through the same trial, but to him suffering brings no forgiveness. Shakespeare and the gods take pity on the suffering Leontes and allow him to awaken from his nightmare. The scene in which the "statue" of Hermione comes to life is Shakespeare's most inspired moment of reconciliation and forgiveness. As in the case of Thaisa's resurrection, the sense of miracle is overwhelming despite the carefully provided naturalistic explanation. The wish to change the past, the most hopeless and thus the most intense of desires, is the one which Shakespeare here fulfills for Leontes. What's done *is* undone. Past crimes, though they were indeed committed, are discovered not to have had their apparent effect. The forgiveness of Leontes' sin, like that of Jehan le Paulu, is made perfect by the erasing of its consequence.

Almost perfect, but not quite. Hermione's seeming death was not the only one to result from Leontes' crime. Antigonus, too, perished and we are remainded of the fact by Paulina and by Leontes' insistence that she and Camillo be rewarded by marriage to one another.

But more important is the memory of Mamillius. The death of that innocent child appears to embarrass most critics of the play. Either they avoid discussion of it, or they assure us that somehow it doesn't count: "The loss of [Leontes'] son is more than made up for by the recovery of his wife and . . . daughter," [24] or, though "Paulina reminds us that her husband is gone; and we may remember Mamillius . . . the subsidiary persons are no longer, as persons, important." [25] I find such propositions dubious, indeed. If Shakespeare wants us to forget that death in Act Five of the play, why does he make the mistake of reminding us so forcefully of it? Only once in the last act does Leontes rebel against the torment that Paulina subjects him to. Upon the announcement of Florizel's arrival in Sicily, Paulina improves the occasion by remarking:

> Had our Prince
> (Iewell of Children) seene this houre, he had payr'd
> Well with this Lord; there was not a moneth
> Betweene their births.   (V.i.146–49)

To which Leontes replies:

> 'Prethee no more; cease: thou know'st
> He dyes to me againe, when talk'd-of: sure
> When I shall see this Gentleman, thy speeches
> Will bring me to consider that, which may
> Vnfurnish me of Reason.   (V.i.150–54)

One has the impression that critics of the play feel somewhat as Leontes does. They would rather not think about the implications of Mamillius' death. But the world which Shakespeare creates in *The Winter's Tale* includes that death, and any view of the play which fails to include it must be a partial view. Shakespeare could, after all, have revived Mamillius too. There was nothing, except artistic conscience, to prevent him from having the renowned Julio Romano create a mother-son group. Beaumont and Fletcher, I imagine, would have been strongly attracted by the possibility of such a denouement.

Shakespeare, in the late romances, never hesitates to use any of the more farfetched devices of romance that will serve his purpose, but he is a great artist and he does not, as lesser artists do, pander to us by telling us lies about the human condition. Evil is inherent in human nature and the innocent suffer as a result. The consequences of evil action are not entirely eradicable and Shakespeare does not pretend that they are. This is not a great, big, wide, wonderful world we live in, and he does not pretend that it is. On the other hand, he does not pander to that even odder human desire to see the world as worse than it is, and the universe as an engine devised entirely for our torment. Both happiness and misery, "both joy and terror" are human possibilities, and he insists upon the reality of both.

Measure for Measure

In the romantic comedies of forgiveness, *humanum genus*—Claudio, Bertram, Posthumus, Leontes—sins by rejecting romantic love. With a steadily increasing insistence, romantic love is presented in these plays as a manifestation of God's grace to man. The rejection of such love constitutes a rejection of grace. That rejection results in crimes which—though they do not occur in reality—appear to be serious threats to the existence of an orderly, love-dominated society. Especially in the late romances, the restoration of the saving ascendancy of love over hate is presented as the result of a divine providence which works through human instruments to achieve its purposes. In *Cymbeline* and *The Winter's Tale,* the reunion of the separated lovers and the denouement in forgiveness is recognized as the result of God's grace to man, and the happiness of the ending is attributed to the mysterious working of divine power:

> The fingers of the Powres aboue, do tune
> The harmony of this Peace. . . .   (V.v.551–52)

In *Measure for Measure* and *The Tempest*, the thematic concerns are similar, but the emphasis and the artistic strategy are different. In these plays the offense of *humanum genus* is against, not love, but law. Angelo and Alonso (tempted by Antonio) sin by directly threatening the social fabric. Angelo attempts to impose a cruelly unrealistic ethic upon his society and then proceeds to pervert the power of justice by trying to use it as an instrument for the satisfaction of his own evil propensities. Alonso deposes a good ruler and attempts to kill him and his innocent daughter. The happy endings of these two plays are the result, not so much of the workings of divine providence, as of the efforts of God's principal earthly instrument: the good ruler. The dukes of Vienna and Milan achieve their ends by effecting a partial regeneration of sinful humanity and by recognizing the necessity for charity. Harold S. Wilson has pointed out the fundamental relationship between these two plays:

> In each play, the action is set going and guided throughout by its duke; yet neither Duke Vincentio nor Prospero controls anyone else's choice; rather, they prepare the conditions in which others choose while taking precautions that no one shall give effect to a choice injurious to others. As Vincentio guides Claudio and Angelo to choose penitence and Isabel to prefer mercy to revenge or justice, so Prospero guides Alonso to choose penitence, Ferdinand to choose the love of Miranda, while he himself forgoes revenge or even justice in favor of mercy; and even Caliban shows signs of amendment at the end. As Barnardine and Lucio in *Measure for Measure* are given the chance to repent, though they remain unmoved, so with Antonio and Sebastian; but though all four are pardoned, they are also curbed of their evil propensities.
>
> The parallelism is not precise—nor should we expect it to be; Shakespeare does not repeat himself—but it is fundamental, arising as it does out of the identical ruling conception of the two plays: the virtue of forgiveness and the tempering of justice with mercy.[1]

In addition to their resemblance to one another, *Measure for Measure* and *The Tempest* are strongly linked to the other comedies of forgiveness. All six plays share, as one of their major concerns, an insistence upon the necessity of forgiveness as an essential condition of human happiness. Charity, born of self-knowledge and of a recognition of evil as inherent to human nature, is the virtue which they primarily exalt.

It is now over thirty years since G. Wilson Knight first published his brilliant essay, "*Measure for Measure* and the Gospels." [2] Since Knight's illumination of this play as a dramatic study in the meaning of Christ's "Judge not that ye be not judged," a great deal of scholarly work has been done on the theological implications of Shakespeare's play. This line of critical inquiry reaches its climax (though by no means its conclusion) in Roy Battenhouse's complex and fascinating "*Measure for Measure* and the Christian Doctrine of Atonement." [3] For Battenhouse and the other scholar-critics of his interests, *Measure for Measure* is primarily a work of Christian allegory, a dramatic revelation of man's relation to God and of the means by which humanity can attain its eternal salvation. Though I am equally indebted to Knight, and though I am far from denying the validity of many of the insights of the later theologizing critics, I should like to approach the play from a rather different point of view.

For me, *Measure for Measure* is primarily a secular work. The purpose of the play is—if we accept the opening lines as a statement of it—to unfold the properties of government, the interdependent government of self and of others. It presents us with the spectacle of man as an offender against the laws of government and asks (within the limits imposed by the comic form) how the problems raised by the misdeeds of a sinful humanity should be dealt with in this world. The dramatic investigation of such a problem immediately raises the question of the contradictory claims of two of the cardinal virtues: Justice and Mercy. We have already seen how their eternal opposition was dramatized in the Middle Ages, through the allegory of the Four Daughters of God.[4] In this earlier and forthrightly theological drama the playwright's problem was a different one from Shakespeare's. The mysteries and moralities tried, like *Paradise Lost,* to make the mysterious ways of God comprehensible to human reason. In *Measure for Measure* it is, I think, the perhaps equally mysterious ways of men to men that are in question. To be sure, the forms of medieval allegory are easily adaptable to secular purposes and the allegory of the Four Daughters of God had been so adapted some ten years before Shakespeare's birth in the pro-Marian propaganda play *Respublica. Measure for Measure,* particularly in its last scene, is strongly reminiscent of the medieval allegory and a consideration of the play in terms of the allegory can serve as a convenient means for determining the structure of the comedy.[5]

The allegory is made up of four distinct elements: the offender, *humanum genus*; his advocate, Mercy; his prosecutor, Justice; and his judge, God. In Shakespeare's comedy, God disappears from the scene, and though the duke can be said to stand, in some degree, for divine power in *Measure for Measure,* in fact, the quadrilateral structure of the allegory becomes triangular in the comedy. *Humanum genus* and Mercy preserve their previous functions, but Justice now combines the role of prosecutor and judge. It is possible to see *Measure for Measure* as a series of three such dramatic triangles, with different characters assigned to the various roles in each.

In the first of these triangles, Claudio is *humanum genus*. His judge and prosecutor is Angelo and his advocate is his sister, Isabella. In the second triangle, Angelo and Isabella shift their roles. With cruel irony, Angelo forces upon Isabella the power of life and death over Claudio. If she will commit the sin of fornication, Angelo will set Claudio free. Angelo thus becomes a perverse advocate for mercy —or for "foul redemption," as Isabella characterizes it. Isabella chooses to sacrifice her brother's life rather than her chastity, but an even more important judgment follows. Claudio reveals his very human weakness and begs his sister to save his life. Isabella's judgment on him at that moment is intensely harsh and bitter, and reminds us that the charity enjoined by Christ in the verses from which the play takes its title is even more difficult for the virtuous than for the ordinary sinner to attain. In the last act of the play, the third version of the triangle is constructed. Although the Duke appears to assume the role of Justice, Isabella, as we shall see, once again combines the functions of judge and prosecutor. Angelo must now play his true part—that of erring humanity, and Mariana, out of love for him, pleads the cause of mercy. By persuading Isabella to kneel and ask the duke to spare the life of the man who has wronged her, Mariana finally brings about the reconciliation of Mercy and Justice which traditionally concludes the medieval allegory.

But this play is not medieval allegory. It is Renaissance comedy, and to turn the characters into the abstractions of an earlier dramatic tradition, though it may help to clarify the play's structure, tends to falsify the significance of the comedy by oversimplifying it. Each of our triangles must be examined in detail and in context.

At the beginning of the play, *humanum genus*—Claudio—has offended against the law. He has committed fornication, and Justice, in the person of Angelo, has invoked against him an old law which makes the act of fornication punishable by death. There are grounds for mitigation of the sentence, however, as Claudio wishes to marry the girl who is with child by him. Indeed the couple is betrothed by a *de praesenti* contract—a state of affairs that, by Elizabethan custom, gave them the right to enjoy the pleasures of the marriage bed.[6] Technically, however, Claudio is guilty of the "crime" of which he stands accused, and Angelo's condemnation of him is attacked, within the play, on two grounds: the law is absurd, and the special circumstances of Claudio's case and character are grounds for mitigating the law's rigor.

It is not easy to determine the precise attitude toward Claudio's offense which the play would finally have us take. For the genuinely or seemingly virtuous characters, what Claudio has done is wrong and they are against it. It is repeatedly characterized as a sin, a fault, and a vice by Angelo, Isabella, and the duke. For Angelo, it is "a foul wrong" and "a filthy vice." Isabella begins her plea for mercy with the words:

> There is a vice that most I doe abhorre,
> And most desire should meet the blow of Iustice.
>
> (II.ii.39–40)

And the duke, when he plays the role of confessor to Juliet, tests her contrition for what he calls a sin and a "most offenseful act." Such orthodox attitudes are balanced by the reductive irony with which the less respectable characters treat the matter. The first description of the deed is Pompey's brilliantly bawdy reply to Mistress Overdone's question, "But what's his Offence?" "Groping for Trowts, in a peculiar Riuer." (I.ii.83–84) Lucio, though his metaphors never equal Pom-

pey's, does well enough with "a game of tick-tack," "the rebellion of
a cod-piece," and "filling a bottle with a tun-dish." The play would
seem to strike a balance between solemnity and flippancy and to arrive finally at a point of view not far from the admirable Provost's
common-sense description of Claudio as:

> a yong man,
> More fit to doe another such offence,
> Then dye for this.   (II.iii.13–15)

The point that, in and of itself, the sexual act is natural and that
its results are good is made in this play in much the same way as in
All's Well. Just as the disreputable Parolles becomes Nature's spokesman in the earlier play, so Lucio is given the job here, when he breaks
the news of Claudio's misfortune to Isabella:

> Your brother, and his louer haue embrac'd;
> As those that feed, grow full: as blossoming Time
> That from the seednes, the bare fallow brings
> To teeming foyson: euen so her plenteous wombe
> Expresseth his full Tilth, and husbandry.   (I.v.41–45)

Whether we regard it as a subject for moral outrage, jokes, common sense, or lyricism there can be no doubt that, despite the pre-
contract between the lovers, Christianity has always regarded Claudio's
offense as a sin against God, like gluttony, sloth, or pride. Angelo and
Vienna's old law propose to regard it as a crime as well, and a crime,
what is more, deserving of the death penalty. By doing so, Angelo
makes Claudio's sin serve as a stimulus for that unfolding of the
properties of government with which the play is so largely concerned.
Shakespeare thus has his controversy between Justice and Mercy take
as its subject one of the most complex and difficult of legal problems:
the regulation of sexual conduct.

It has always been a delicate matter for the law to indicate that
precise point at which the pursuit of sexual gratification becomes

criminal. The question was as much a subject for debate in the reigns of Elizabeth and James I as it is today. As we have seen, three sexual acts were defined as criminal by the civil law of Shakespeare's time. These were rape, "buggerie," and the carnal knowledge and abuse of "any woman child under the age of ten yeares." [7] These actions were felonies and were punishable by death. Other varieties of sexual activity were regarded as less seriously offensive, but were by no means allowed to go unpunished. It was the job of the ecclesiastical courts to punish the more ordinary offenses against the seventh commandment. According to number 109 of the *Constitutions and Canons Ecclesiastical* of 1603, those who "offend their brethren . . . by adultery, whoredom, incest" are to be certified into the ecclesiastical courts "to the intent that they . . . may be punished by the severity of the laws, according to their deserts." [8]

"The severity of the laws" in these cases appears to have resulted either in public penance or in the payment of a fine. Philip Stubbes, who is scornful of the lenity with which his fellow humans were treated by the law, describes the usual punishment as follows:

> The punishment appointed for whordom now is so light that they esteeme not of it; thei feare it not, they make but a iest of it. For what great thing is it to go ij or three dayes in a white sheete before the congregation, and that somtymes not past an howre or two in a day, hauing their vsuall garments underneth, as commonly they haue? . . . And yet as light and as easie as this punishment is, it may be, and is daiely dispensed with-all for monie. [9]

Such was the prospect faced by the adulterer or fornicator unfortunate enough to get caught at the time that Shakespeare was writing *Measure for Measure*. It would be wrong, however, to assume that the play's harsh old law punishing fornication with death was simply an invention of Whetstone taken over by Shakespeare. Shakespeare uses a nonexistent law to make his points about law and its relationship to Justice and Mercy, but, in fact, the necessity for passing extremely harsh statutes against adultery and fornication had been urged upon the English government for over half a century before the time of Shakespeare's play. Bishop Latimer, in a sermon preached before Edward VI in 1550, presented to his thirteen-year-old monarch the case for putting adulterers to death:

> I would therefore wish that there were a law provided in this behalf for adulterers, and that adultery should be punished with death; and that might be a remedy for all this matter. There would not be then so much adultery, whoredom, and lechery in England as there is. For the love of God take heed to it, and see a remedy provided for it.[10]

Latimer later justifies his demand by reference to Deuteronomy:

> I would wish that Moses's law were restored for punishment of lechery, and that the offenders therein might be punished according to the prescription of Moses's law.[11]

Alexander Nowell, preaching before Elizabeth and her Parliament in 1563 is less forthright and specific, urging only "some other sharper laws for adultery." [12] Stubbes is more zealous even than Latimer, however:

> I would wish that the Man or Woman, who are certenlye knowen, without all scruple or doubte, to haue committed the horryble fact of whordome, adulterie, incest, or fornication . . . should drinke a full draught of *Moyses* cuppe, that is, tast of present death as Gods word doth commaunde, and good pollicie allowe.[13]

Stubbes is aware of man's deplorable tendency to take pity on his fellow creatures, however, and is willing to moderate his demands a bit:

> Or els, if *that* be thought too seuere (for in euill, men will be more mercifull than the Author of mercie him selfe, but in goodnesse, fare well mercy) than wold GOD they might be cauterized and seared with a hote yron on the cheeke, forehead, or some other parte of their bodye that might be seene, to the end the honest and chast Christians might be discerned from the adulterous Children of Sathan.[14]

The intellectually more respectable Puritan polemicist, William Perkins, is calmer but as harsh, or harsher, in his demands:

> It was a iudiciall law among the Iewes that the adulterer & adulteresse should die the death . . . this law serves directly to maintaine necessary obedience to the seventh commandment: and the considerations upon which this law was giuen are perpetual and serue to uphold the common wealth.[15]

The dreams of these radical reformers were eventually to come true. In 1650, just one hundred years after Latimer's sermon to Edward VI, the Puritans, having finally attained power, enacted into law a statute providing that:

> In case any married woman shall . . . be carnally known by any man (other than her husband) (except in Case of Ravishment) and of such offence or offences shall be convicted as aforesaid by confession or otherwise, every such Offence and Offences shall be and is hereby adjudged Felony: and every person, as well the man as the woman, offending therin . . . shall suffer death as in case of Felony, without benefit of clergy.[16]

In proposing the situation that obtains at the beginning of *Measure for Measure*, therefore, Shakespeare was asking his audience to imagine a legal and political possibility that was anything but farfetched, and it is possible to see the play as, in part at least, a dramatic answer to Puritan polemics. Shakespeare is asking us to put the case that, first, a law exists that, by making fornication as well as adultery a capital crime, would more than satisfy the demands of the radical reformers, and that, in addition, the power to enforce such laws had been delegated to a certain sort of man—a "precise" man. The duke tells Friar Thomas that

> Lord *Angelo* is precise,
> Stands at a guard with Enuie: scarce confesses
> That his blood flowes: or that his appetite
> Is more to bread then stone. . . . (I.iv.50–53)

Though "precise" had its modern meaning in Shakespeare's time (Claudio "was euer precise in promise-keeping"), used as the duke uses it here, it is clearly meant to carry the connotation defined by the O.E.D. as "strict or scrupulous in religious observance; in 16th and 17th c., puritanical."

Shakespeare first casts in the role of Justice a contemporary type that his audience would have recognized—the Puritan. Furthermore, he gives his Justice figure a legal instrument—a law punishing offenses against the seventh commandment with death—which was precisely the weapon that the Puritans had been demanding for the reform of what appeared to them the excessive sexual immorality of the time. And he proceeds to demonstrate that a ruler who, like the duke, intrusts such power to such a figure would be allowing a man ignorant of human nature (including his own) to impose a dangerously unrealistic sexual ethic upon his fellow humans.

Duke Vincentio is fully aware of the risk he is taking by resigning his power to Angelo. He has two motives for doing so; one political, the other, so to speak, scientific. His political motive is straight out of Machiavelli.[17] Fearing that he has allowed his subjects too much license, he now decides to correct the abuses which have sprung up as a result. He knows that if he undertakes that correction himself, he will gain a reputation for tyranny, so he turns the job over to a substitute who can serve as a scapegoat for any ill will that develops. But his choice of Angelo, as he tells Friar Thomas, is also inspired by a species of scientific curiosity:

> hence shall we see
> If power change purpose: what our Seemers be.
> (I.iii.53–54)

The duke will add power to puritanism in order to observe the results, but the experiment will be controlled. The duke will be on the scene, disguised, ready to intervene when necessary.

So Angelo enters upon his role as Justice, his duty being to strike a balance between "Mortallitie and Mercie in *Vienna*." It is strongly

implied that his experience of government has been slight. He asks
the duke that "some more test" be made of his abilities before he is
given power, but the duke has already justified his choice on the
grounds that great abilities must not be allowed to waste themselves
in retirement:

> 　　　　　　　　　　　Thye selfe, and thy belongings
> Are not thine owne so proper, as to waste
> Thy selfe vpon thy vertues; they on thee:
> Heauen doth with vs, as we, with Torches doe,
> Not light them for themselues: For if our vertues
> Did not go forth of vs, 'twere all alike
> As if we had them not: Spirits are not finely touch'd,
> But to fine issues: nor nature neuer lends
> The smallest scruple of her excellence,
> But like a thrifty goddesse, she determines
> Her selfe the glory of a creditour,
> Both thanks, and vse. . . .　　　　　　　　　(I.i.30–41)

To the nonrecusants in Shakespeare's audience, these lines would
apply with even greater aptness to Isabella. Whatever the retirement
from which Angelo is called to assume the role of Justice, it is clearly
not the equal of the restraints imposed upon themselves by "the Sister-
hood, the Votarists of Saint *Clare*." Far more than Angelo's it is
Isabella's fugitive and cloistered virtue which must sally forth to seek
her adversary when she leaves her convent to plead the cause of
Mercy on her brother's behalf. Like Angelo, she is forced to subject
her untried ideals to the stresses of experience in the world.

As an advocate for Mercy, Isabella is profoundly impressive. Her
rhetoric reaches its climax when she cites to Angelo the example of
Christ's charity:

> 　Alas, alas:
> Why all the soules that were, were forfeit once,
> And he that might the vantage best haue tooke,
> Found out the remedie: how would you be,

> If he, which is the top of Iudgement, should
> But iudge you, as you are? Oh, thinke on that,
> And mercie then will breathe within your lips
> Like man new made. (II.ii.67–74)

That finding out of the remedy is the occasion allegorized by the Four Daughters of God, and one necessarily remembers these noble lines when, three scenes later, it is Isabella's turn to judge the erring Claudio.

Isabella now discovers that if she will consent to sleep with Angelo, he will pardon her brother. The proposal cruelly and cleverly forces upon her the role of judge over Claudio. She is forced to decide whether or not she should commit a mortal sin in order to save her brother's life. Her refusal is never in doubt. The theological niceties of her decision are, at least, arguable. She would, of course, place her soul in jeopardy by committing the sin of fornication—whatever her motives for doing so. Given, however, the knowledge of God's mercy which she has herself so eloquently stated, her assumption that surrendering to Angelo would automatically result in her eternal damnation strikes one as disingenuous.

> Better it were a brother dide at once,
> Then that a sister, by redeeming him
> Should die for euer. (II.iv.107–9)

It is humanly impossible to merit salvation by avoiding sin. It is also impossible to commit a sin which will not be forgiven if it is repented of. On the other hand, to commit a sin in the hope that it will be forgiven is to place one's soul in a perilous state indeed.

But if the theological implications of Isabella's decision are complex, so are the extratheological, the purely human ones. If Isabella's decision is admirable, it is admirable because it is the decision of a saint. But Shakespeare's audience (ourselves included) is not made up of saints, and it is at least problematical that we are expected to react to this particular example of saintliness with unalloyed admiration. Isabella's human justification for refusing to ransom her brother's life at the cost of her virginity is clearly stated. She is requiring no more of her brother than she would demand of herself. She is willing to do:

> As much for my poore Brother, as my selfe;
> That is: were I vnder the tearmes of death,
> Th'impression of keene whips, I'ld weare as Rubies,
> And strip my self to death, as to a bed,
> That longing have bin sicke for, ere I'ld yeeld
> My body vp to shame.   (II.iv.99–104)

There is not the slightest doubt that Isabella is speaking with absolute sincerity here. Under the circumstance she describes, she would undoubtedly behave with a heroism which the church does not demand of a woman faced with the choice of death or violation. But it is one thing to say, "Death before dishonor," and quite another to say, "*Your* death before *my* dishonor." In demanding that her brother subscribe to her own exalted ethic, Isabella is insisting that he behave like a hero or a saint. Claudio is neither. He is merely human.

When Claudio finally answers Isabella's explanation of their nightmarish situation with a tortured, "Sweet Sister, let me liue," she proceeds to pass judgment upon his human weakness with a vehemence that approaches hysteria:

> Oh you beast,
> Oh faithlesse Coward, oh dishonest wretch,
> Wilt thou be made a man, out of my vice?
> Is't not a kinde of Incest, to take life
> From thine owne sisters shame? What should I thinke,
> Heauen shield my Mother plaid my Father faire:
> For such a warped slip of wildernesse
> Nere issu'd from his blood. Take my defiance,
> Die, perish: Might but my bending downe
> Repreeue thee from thy fate, it should proceede.
> Ile pray a thousand praiers for thy death,
> No word to saue thee.   (III.i.135–46)

Let us juxtapose these sentiments against the verses from which the play takes its title:

> Judge not, that ye be not judged.
> For with what judgment ye judge, ye
> Shall be judged: and with what measure
> ye mete, it shall be measured to you
> again.
> And why beholdest thou the mote that
> is in thy brother's eye, but considerest
> not the beam that is in thine own
> eye?
> Or how wilt thou say to thy brother,
> Let me pull the mote out of thine eye;
> And, behold, a beam is in thine own
> eye? (Matt. 7. 1–4)

As the advocate of Mercy, Isabella has spoken with the tongue of men and of angels, but in the role of Justice she has proved notably lacking in charity. She has ruthlessly condemned her brother for falling short of her own heroic ideal. That ideal and the ethic from which it springs is certainly not being attacked in *Measure for Measure*, at least not so vehemently as the rigidly repressive Puritanical ethic of Angelo is being attacked. Isabella, I think, in some degree stands for the monastic ideal which predates Puritanism as an attempt to repress the human impulses with which *Measure for Measure* is concerned. It is an ideal of self-perfection which exalts chastity and achieves its ends through a withdrawal from the world. It does not ordinarily attempt, as Puritanism does, to impose its standards with harsh force upon an ordinary humanity that is incapable of the spiritual exaltation necessary to the achievement of saintliness. As a result, Shakespeare seems to find it more sympathetic and to handle it more gently. He by no means allows it to go uncriticized, however. His play demonstrates, through Isabella, that when forced to deal with the world of ordinary men, those who are devoted to the monastic ideal may respond to human perplexities with a notable lack of charity. And, in the comedies of forgiveness, a higher value is set on charity than on chastity.

In the world of ordinary men, the very sacrifice which Isabella heroically refuses to make can be seen as itself heroic. Montaigne so sees it:

> Some one that more esteemed her honestie then she loved her life, hath prostituted the same unto the lawlesse lust and raging sensuality of a mortall hatefull enemy, thereby to save her husbands life; and hath done that for him, which she could never have beene induced to do for her selfe. This is no place to extend these examples: they are too high and over-rich, to be presented in this luster: let us therefore reserve them for a nobler seat.[18]

Isabella is not capable of this variety of heroism. For that she should not be condemned, but neither should she be extravagantly praised (as she frequently has been). That she has admirable qualities is perfectly clear. "The hand that hath made you faire, hath made you good," the duke says to her immediately after her diatribe against Claudio. But that, at this point in the play, she lacks the essential quality of charity is, one would think, equally clear. She demonstrates her own variety of heroic goodness in her refusal to sacrifice her chastity to Angelo. She demonstrates her lack of charity in her harsh judgment of the human weakness of Claudio.

The duke now decides to continue his experiment by tricking Angelo into the belief that his rape of Isabella actually takes place. In arranging the substitution of Mariana for Isabella in Angelo's bed, the duke creates within Angelo's mind the illusion that he has committed a particularly heinous crime. Even the duke, however, is taken aback by the evil of which his deputy now proves himself capable. Despite his belief that Isabella has sacrificed her virginity to preserve her brother's life, Angelo orders the Provost to have Claudio executed and his head sent to his judge as a proof of his death. This treachery, though it takes him by surprise, provides the duke with an opportunity to transfer his experiments in human nature from Angelo, who has now proved that he is capable of any iniquity, to Isabella.

The duke will conceal from Isabella the fact that he has preserved Claudio's life. His stated motive for doing so is that he will thereby

> make her heauenly comforts of despaire,
> When it is least expected. (IV.iii.117–18)

But the effect of his decision goes beyond the treat provided for Isabella when she discovers that her brother is still alive. Her ignorance, along with the bed trick, makes possible the situation which, at the play's climax, enables Shakespeare to construct the third of his *humanum genus*-Justice-Mercy triangles.

In the opening scenes of the play, both Angelo and Isabella predict, with dramatic irony, the situation which will obtain at the conclusion of their drama. When Escalus suggests that, given the opportunity, even Angelo might have committed the crime for which he intends to execute Claudio, Angelo replies:

> You may not so extenuate his offence,
> For I haue had such faults; but rather tell me
> When I, that censure him, do so offend
> Let mine owne Iudgement patterne out my death,
> And nothing come in partiall. Sir, he must dye. (II.i.27–31)

And Isabella, in her plea for the mitigation of Claudio's sentence, says:

> I would to heauen I had your potencie,
> And you were *Isabell*: should it then be thus?
> No: I would tell what 'twere to be a Iudge,
> And what a prisoner. (II.ii.60–63)

In the play's last scene, the machinations of the duke have achieved this alteration of roles. The stern, complacent judge of the play's beginning has become the tormented figure of *humanum genus*—guiltier by far, he thinks, than the man he has condemned to death. He stands accused by Isabella, who identifies her role with her cry for ". . . Iustice, Iustice, Iustice, Iustice." Though the duke sits in the seat of judgment, it is not he whose sentence we are interested to see passed on Angelo. The duke knows that Angelo is, in fact, innocent of the crimes of which he believes himself guilty. Isabella, however, is convinced that Angelo has not only attempted to violate her, but has succeeded in murdering her brother. When the duke orders Angelo "to the very Blocke/ Where Claudio stoop'd to death," we know that no such block exists, and we concentrate less upon the fate of Angelo than upon the words and deeds of Isabella.

On hearing the duke's sentence, Mariana assumes the role of Mercy. Angelo is her husband and she is capable of loving him. At this point the purpose of Shakespeare's strategy in altering Whetstone's play to include the bed trick becomes clear. In *Promos and Cassandra,* it is the wronged heroine who must play the role of Mercy, for in righting her wrongs, the ruler has married her to her enemy and she feels constrained to plead for him as a wife should plead for her husband.[19] Isabella has no such motive for her forgiveness of Angelo. Her pardon of Angelo, if she is capable of it, must finally be inspired by the charity she did not demonstrate toward the human weakness of her brother. She must be able to continue in her role of Justice and yet be able to embrace the quality of Mercy without being influenced by any new relationship to the man who has wronged her.

Stage action makes (or should make) clear the central importance of Isabella's role in the final scene. When Mariana finds the duke adamant in his refusal to pardon Angelo, she turns to Isabella for mercy.

Isabell:

> Sweet *Isabel,* doe yet but kneele by me,
> Hold vp your hands, say nothing: I'll speake all.
> They say best men are moulded out of faults,
> And for the most, become much more the better

> For being a little bad: so may my husband.
> Oh *Isabel*: will you not lend a knee.   (V.i.446–52)

A long pause is clearly indicated at this point while we wait for Isabella to act. Finally we conclude that she is unyielding in her demand for retributive justice and the duke pronounces sentence: "He dies for *Claudio's* death." Then, for the first time in the play, Justice speaks with the voice of Mercy and of Charity:

> Most bounteous Sir.
> Looke if it please you, on this man condemn'd,
> As if my Brother liu'd. . . .   (V.i.454–56)

And now Justice can find reasons for the mitigation of the law's rigor:

> I partly thinke,
> A due sinceritie gouerned his deedes,
> Till he did looke on me: Since it is so,
> Let him not die: my Brother had but Iustice,
> In that he did the thing for which he dide.
> For *Angelo,* his Act did not ore-take his bad intent,
> And must be buried but as an intent
> That perish'd by the way: thoughts are no subiects
> Intents, but meerely thoughts.   (V.i.456–64)

So Isabella demonstrates what heretofore she has lacked: charity. As a result, "Mercy and truth are met together; righteousness and peace have kissed each other."

Both Angelo and Isabella entered the tawdry but very human world of Vienna encased in an armor of unyielding righteousness. Both of them have been impelled by the play's action to surrender an unrealistic ethic which they had thought to impose on themselves and others. Both have been forced to recognize their membership in the human race. Angelo's tormented acquisition of self-knowledge is obvious. Isabella's is far more subtle. The process which she undergoes is less one of regeneration than of fulfillment, but the fulfillment she attains is not that of the "thing en-skied and sainted" for which she was striving at the beginning of the play. She achieves, instead, a charitable humanity. Just as Angelo is forced to surrender his pharisaical Puritanism, Isabella is persuaded to leave behind the cloistered virtue of the votarists of St. Clare and become the wife of Vienna's ruler. *Measure for Measure* is, I think, a forceful rejection of the radical Protestantism of Shakespeare's day, but it is equally a refusal to accept the monastic ideal of Catholicism. In this connection, it is well to remember that this play alone was excised, in its entirety, from the Second Folio by the authorities of the Spanish Inquisition.[20]

The working out of Shakespeare's pattern in *Measure for Measure* is largely the function of the disguised duke. His role as manipulator of the action has led some critics to regard the duke as a type of God. And so he is, of course. All absolute earthly power is "like power divine," and all rulers are, in a special sense, the instruments of God. Finally, however, the duke, like the rest of the characters, is a man. As a ruler, he is a very special sort of man, but his problems, however special, remain recognizably human and his solutions depend upon his comprehension of humanity, which is the result, not of supernatural omniscience, but of his knowledge of himself as a human being.

The whole action of the play stems from the duke's decision to experiment with the properties of government. He subjects Angelo, Isabella, and the entire city of Vienna to a test whose purpose is to determine the best means of regulating man's sinful nature. The duke turns his power over to Angelo, a man whose solution to the problem of sin (and, for the purposes of the drama, sin is equated with sexual misbehavior) is simple: repression. Let man repress his sexual impulses. If he cannot, kill him. Let the final answer to sin be death. The duke has enjoined upon Angelo the necessity for being "Mortallitie and Mercie in *Vienna*." But Angelo has misinterpreted the duty to be both as an either/or choice, and he has chosen to be mortality.

Angelo's position has the usual delusive beauties of simplicity. It is all-encompassing and, as it turns out, rather too all-encompassing. For as we know by Christian precept and secular experience, sin is a condition of life. It is as unavoidable as breath and will not cease to exist until, as Lucio tells us, "eating and drinking be put down." To say "let the answer to sin be death" is to say "let the answer to life be death" and this is precisely what the leading characters of the play do say until experience has taught them better. For Isabella, the first solution to life's perplexities is an equivalent to Angelo's repression: withdrawal. Life becomes importunate, however, and she is forced to leave her convent. The complexity of life soon makes her long for death, and when faced with Angelo's cruel proposal, she states, with obvious sincerity, that she would rather strip herself to death "as to a bed,/ That longing have bin sick for." She is not given that alternative, however, and she must turn to her brother's heroism as a way out of her predicament. That, too, fails her and her solution to the problem of Claudio's sinful weakness is *his* death:

> Ile pray a thousand praiers for thy death,
> No word to saue thee.
>
> .   .   .   .   .
>
> Oh fie, fie, fie:
> Thy sinn's not accidentall, but a Trade;
> Mercy to thee would proue it selfe a Bawd,
> 'Tis best that thou diest quickly.   (III.i.145–51)

But perhaps the clearest revelation of Isabella's instinctive turning to death as a way out of life's difficulties comes in her casual reaction to the disguised duke's description of Mariana. When he has told her of the years of sorrow Mariana has suffered as a result of Angelo's desertion of her, Isabella replies, "What a merit were it in death to take this poore maid from the world?" (III.i.278–79)

Of all the defenders of death in this play, the most impressive and convincing is the duke himself. His "Be absolute for death" speech to Claudio (III.i.4ff.) is an almost unequaled hymn in praise of "the distinguished thing." For lyrical power it is comparable to Spenser's great verses from the *Faerie Queene*:

> What if some little pain the passage have
> That makes fraile flesh to fear the bitter waue?
> Is not short paine well borne, that brings long ease,
> And layes the soul to sleepe in quiet graue?
> Sleepe after toyle, port after stormie seas,
> Ease after warre, death after life doth greatly please. (I.ix.40)

In Spenser these lines are from the speech in which Despair tries to tempt the Red-Cross Knight to self-destruction. They are, in other words, a disingenuous dramatic utterance. To some extent, the same can be said of the duke's great speech. He is attempting, in his role of friar, to talk Claudio into that state of ripeness, or readiness for death, which is so important to the Shakespearean concept of the tragic hero. Claudio's fate is not finally to be tragic, however, and the problem arises of the duke's intentions with regard to him at this moment in the action. It is possible that he has already decided to intervene to save Claudio's life and that he plans, at this juncture, as he does later with Isabella, to make him "heauenly comforts of dispaire,/ When it is least expected." There is, however, no evidence to support this interpretation. It is not until the revelation of Angelo's wickedness that the duke demonstrates a desire to save Claudio's life. The duke moves to save Claudio only when he discovers that Angelo has forfeited the right to judge by sinning as Claudio has sinned. Before that discovery, it would seem, the duke has been willing to accept provisionally and to test Angelo's ethic of repression and/or death as a solution to the problems raised by man's sinful nature.

After the revelation of Angelo's weakness, the duke's rejection of that solution is complete. When he is confronted with Barnardine, whose "indifference to death . . . comes nearest to that preached by the Friar," [21] the duke is horrified and will not permit the execution to take place. And when he sits upon the seat of judgment in the last scene, and prepares to deal with the corruption which he has seen boil and bubble in Vienna, it is not to death that he turns for that corruption's cure. Like Angelo and Isabella, though far more deliberately, the duke has left shelter—the shelter of his position as ruler—in order to subject himself to the complexity of life. His confronting of the problem of man's sinful nature confirms the validity of his original solution: mercy. Isabella, too, has acquired enough confidence in life to be able to second Mariana's request that it be granted to Angelo. As for Angelo, like Iachimo and Posthumus, he at first desires only death:

> Immediate sentence then, and sequent death,
> Is all the grace I beg.   (V.i.373-74)
>
> .   .   .   .   .
>
> I am sorrie that such sorrow I procure,
> And so deepe sticks it in my penitent heart,
> That I craue death more willingly than mercy,
> 'Tis my deseruing, and I doe entreat it.   (V.i.487-90)

This is before his awakening from the nightmare which the experimenting duke has imposed upon him. When Angelo discovers that his crimes have not taken effect in reality, he, too, can turn to life:

> By this Lord *Angelo* perceiues he's safe,
> Methinkes I see a quickning in his eye:
> Well *Angelo,* your euill quits you well.
> Looke that you loue your wife: her worth, worth yours.
>   (V.i.508-11)

For the duke, the solution to the problem raised by the strong and swelling evil of our conception is neither extraordinary nor radical. He proposes marriage: marriage for himself with Isabella, for Angelo and Mariana, for Claudio and Juliet. Marriage even for Lucio and

Kate Keepdown. Marriage lacks the tidy finality of death, but the characters of *Measure for Measure* learn to prefer it as a solution to the complex problems of sexual morality.

The charity which makes possible the happy ending of *Measure for Measure* has as its source the knowledge and acceptance of our common humanity. Angelo's proposed harshness could succeed in governing only those who are less than human. Pompey Bum asks the pertinent question of Escalus:

> Do's your Worship meane to geld and splay all the youth of the City?
> *Esc.:* No, *Pompey.*
> *Clo.:* Truely Sir, in my poore opinion they will too't then. . . .
>
> (II.i.246–50)

"Which is the wiser here; *Justice* or *Iniquitie*?" Escalus has previously inquired. The answer would appear to be that Justice must learn from Iniquity—from the iniquity that is inevitably within every human striver for justice—the necessity for pardon. And surely each member of the audience is expected to recognize the iniquity of *humanum genus* as his own. As F. R. Leavis puts it, in the best of the many excellent essays on *Measure for Measure,* "If we don't see ourselves in Angelo, we have taken the play and the moral very imperfectly."[22]

The Tempest

> Come vnto these yellow sands,
>   and then take hands:
> Curtsied when you haue, and kist
>   the wild waues whist:
> Foote it featly heere, and there, and sweete Sprights
>   beare the burthen.   (I.ii.441–46)

Ariel is here issuing an invitation to the dance.[1] It is addressed to Ferdinand. Miranda, the partner whose hands he will take, is onstage, but, having been enchanted by her father, is as yet unseeing and unseen. They will enter upon the dance, whose symbolic implications for the Elizabethans have been fully presented by Sir John Davies—implications which move outward from the most basic activities of man and woman through the entire creation until they betoken that central force upon which an ordered universe depends:

> The Fire, Ayre, Earth, and water did agree
> By Loues perswasion, Nature's mighty King,
> To leaue their first disordred combating;
>   And in a daunce such measure to obserue,
>   As all the world their motion should preserue.[2]

The result of Ferdinand and Miranda's dance will be the stilling—the "whisting"—of the wild waves, for the ultimate source of the tempest of the play is the hatred and evil of the older generation, and the result of strife between the fathers has been a chaos which will be reduced to order by the love and marriage of the children.

Ariel's first song is followed immediately by another of a very different sort:

> Full fadom fiue thy Father lies,
> Of his bones are Corrall made:
> Those are pearles that were his eies,
> Nothing of him that doth fade,
> But doth suffer a Sea-change
> Into something rich, & strange:
> Sea Nimphs hourly ring his knell.
> Burthen: ding dong.
> Harke now I heare them, ding-dong bell.   (I.ii.460–68)

Ariel now passes to less festive matters and reminds Ferdinand of his supposedly drowned father in words of puzzling but significant beauty. Alonso's corpse, the dirge tells us, lies at the bottom of the sea, where it is undergoing a marvelous transformation.[3] Human flesh and bone fade and change from their mortal substance into the rich permanence of pearl and coral. A different but clearly analogous process does take place in the course of the play. Prospero will afflict his old enemy, Alonso, with a "heart-sorrow" so intense that it will drive him almost to suicide, yet it will result finally not in destruction, but in re-creation. Alonso will endure a psychological death of sorrow and remorse—a kind of sinking into the depths of his own mind. From this he will emerge regenerated, a new man, his psychological and spiritual substance transformed.

Ariel's two songs to Ferdinand serve, then, as thematic statements for the two plots of the play. Both of the processes—the falling in love of Ferdinand and Miranda, and the regeneration of Alonso— which the songs symbolically describe are essential to the full happiness of the play's ending. Since it combines the themes of romantic love and forgiveness, *The Tempest* is, in a sense, a romantic comedy of forgiveness. But unlike the four comedies I have already discussed under that rubric, *The Tempest* deals with the theme of forgiveness and the theme of romantic love in two separate actions. The erring *humanum genus* figure is not the romantic hero, his crimes do not include a rejection of romantic love, and romantic love is not the motive for his forgiveness.

Humanum genus in *The Tempest* is Alonso. His sin is the deposition of Prospero from his dukedom and the attempted murder both of Prospero and of his innocent child, Miranda. Because Shakespeare here chose to limit himself to what Tillyard has called "the regenerative phase of the tragic pattern," [4] and to make *The Tempest* an exercise in the observation of the neoclassic unities, Alonso's offense, unlike the crimes of the other *humanum genus* figures we have examined, cannot be presented to us on-stage. Through narration, re-enactment, and parody, however, Shakespeare makes certain that his audience is kept constantly aware of the guilt to be atoned for and forgiven.

Alonso's crime is the central subject of the long story of the past which Prospero tells Miranda for our benefit. He explains how, when rightful Duke of Milan, he had withdrawn from a direct concern with the affairs of state in order to devote himself to the bettering of his mind. This retirement provided a temptation and an opportunity for his evil-natured brother, Antonio, who proposed to subject Milan to Naples in return for Alonso's help in a *coup d'état* which would depose Prospero and put Antonio in power:

> This King of *Naples* being an Enemy
> To me inueterate, hearkens my Brothers suit,
> Which was, That he in lieu o' th' premises,
> Of homage, and I know not how much Tribute,
> Should presently extirpate me and mine
> Out of the Dukedome. . . .   (I.ii.143–48)

And Alonso and Antonio add an attempted slaughter of the innocents to their political treachery:

> In few, they hurried vs a-boord a Barke,
> Bore vs some Leagues to Sea, where they prepared
> A rotten carkasse of a Butt, not rigg'd,
> Nor tackle, sayle, nor mast, the very rats
> Instinctiuely haue quit it: There they hoyst vs
> To cry to th' Sea, that roar'd to vs. . . .   (I.ii.170–75)

Shakespeare is not satisfied, however, with such narration and verbal comment. In order to make as vivid as possible the original crime, he has it reenacted for us in the next scene, where we see Antonio and Sebastian attempt to murder the sleeping Alonso. Two of the actors in the original drama play parts in the reenactment, but their roles have altered. Alonso, who was tempted to villainy in the original plot, has become the intended victim of the second. Antonio, who previously combined the roles of tempter and treacherous brother, is now the tempter only, while Sebastian is tempted to destroy his brother and king.

The reenactment, the sight of Antonio and Sebastian standing with swords drawn over an innocent Gonzalo and an Alonso whose sleep is like the earlier naïve confidence of Prospero in his evil brother, has effects more important than the vivifying of Prospero's narrative, however. There is a sense, too, of the repetition of evil action which is the inevitable result of the inherent baseness of human nature. Given Antonio, murder and treachery will follow. He will prey instinctively upon those innocent enough to trust him or incautious enough to sleep in his presence. But Prospero's naïveté, which permitted the original crime, no longer exists. He now knows the inevitable consequences of the existence of Antonio, and he acts to prevent them. Ariel enters to Gonzalo with the words:

> My Master through his Art foresees the danger
> That you (his friend) are in. . . .   (II.i.329–30)

The intended victims awake, and the crime is prevented.

The manner of Prospero's frustration of the proposed murders is a reminder of the degree of control which he, as manipulator of the action, has exercised over the entire reenactment scene. Through Ariel, he has sent the king and courtiers to sleep, thus giving Antonio and Sebastian their opportunity. It is as if Prospero, like the duke in *Measure for Measure,* were deliberately setting up an experiment to test the nature and strength of human villainy. In any case, he discovers that Antonio is unchanged and probably incorrigible.

From reenactment, Shakespeare passes immediately to parody. The Caliban-Stefano-Trinculo plot to murder Prospero and seize the island is a comic analogue both to Alonso's original crime and to Antonio and Sebastian's frustrated attempt to repeat it. The effect of the analogue is principally a comic reduction of the pretensions of evil through a comparison of them to the deformed and drunken idiocies of the clowns. The most important equation in this analogue is that of Caliban to Antonio. Caliban tempts Stephano to kill the sleeping Prospero just as Antonio had tempted Sebastian to kill the sleeping Alonso:

> Ile yeeld him thee asleepe,
> Where thou maist knocke a naile into his head.
>
> (III.ii.63–64)

Like Antonio in the original and successful *coup d'état,* Caliban proposes to exchange his subjection to Prospero for a new subjection to a usurper whom he will help to power. Caliban's guilt parodies Antonio's but its source is slightly different. It proceeds from an unsophisticated, "innocent" but inherent corruption (for Caliban's "innocence" is a corrective comment on Miranda's). The source of Antonio's evil is a sophisticated but equally inherent corruption. Caliban, in his deformity, is a moral portrait (like the one in Dorian Gray's attic) of that "goodly person," Antonio. The Machiavellian cunning and sophisticated amorality of Antonio finally serve impulses which are as stupidly misguided as those of the "debosh'd fish" who takes a drunkard for a god and worships a dull fool. The brutish stupidity of evil, the fact that it is finally absurd—however dangerous —is the point of the parody of the two crimes.

Caliban's proposal to murder Prospero in the comic underplot is followed by the climax of the action which has Alonso at its center. Alonso is a remarkably quiet central figure. He addresses ten words to the boatswain in the opening scene. In Act Two, Scene One, his next appearance, he contributes exactly five words to the first one hundred lines: "Prithee, peace," and, "I prithee, spare." Yet the whole of this long scene revolves around his usually silent or sleeping figure.

So long as he remains awake, the speeches of the courtiers are designed to comfort or exasperate him. The effect of his silence is to intensify the agony expressed when he finally bursts out against the kind but clumsy attempt by Gonzalo to comfort him for the loss of his son by reminding him that he has a daughter who is still alive:

> You cram these words into mine eares, against
> the stomacke of my sense: would I had neuer
> Married my daughter there: For comming thence
> My sonne is lost, and (in my rate) she too,
> Who is so farre from *Italy* remoued,
> I ne're againe shall see her: O thou mine heire
> Of *Naples* and of *Millaine,* what strange fish
> Hath made his meale on thee?   (II.i.106–13)

Like Leontes, this erring king is punished for his sins with the loss of an only son. But, for Leontes, the death of the child revealed and confirmed the guilt of the father. For Alonso, the loss of Ferdinand seems to be a punishment without a crime, for the memory of his crime against Prospero has sunk to the bottom of his mind. The words of Ariel cause that guilt to rise to the surface—or, more accurately, force Alonso to descend to find it. Act III, Scene Three, opens with Alonso's announcement of his despair:

> Euen here I will put off my hope, and keepe it
> No longer for my Flatterer: he is droun'd
> Whom thus we stray to finde, and the Sea mocks
> Our frustrate search on land: well, let him goe.
>   (III.iii.11–14)

This speech demonstrates that the psychological condition of Alonso is now ready to receive with profit the arts which Prospero will practice on it. Alonso is in a state of "inward sorrow and grief." [5] It now remains for Prospero to force him to recognize the connection between his suffering and his "natural uncleanliness and the enormity of [his] sinful life." [6] By contrast to the wanhope of Alonso, however, Sebastian and Antonio are as far as possible from contrition:

> *Ant.:* I am right glad, that he's so out of hope:
> Doe not for one repulse forgoe the purpose
> That you resolu'd t'effect.
>   *Seb.:* The next aduantage will we take throughly.
>   *Ant.:* Let it be tonight . . .   (III.iii.15–19)

At this moment Prospero enters, unseen, to witness the discomfiture of his enemies. The "iconography" of the ensuing scene is fascinating in its implications. Strange spirits bring in a table with food upon it, but when the "men of sinne" attempt to "stand to, and feede," Ariel, in the form of a harpy, prevents them and causes the table and its contents to disappear. Shakespeare's contemporaries delighted in such visual or theatrical "metaphors" (perhaps a better term for them would be "emblems"). The older drama, with its frequent dumb shows, abounds in them, and they found a natural Jacobean habitat in the court masques. Nowadays we are likely to be puzzled by their significance and apt to dismiss them simply as opportunities for spectacular effect. They were meant, however, to invite interpretation and they need to be puzzled over.[7] Northrop Frye believes that "the vision of the disappearing banquet" is "symbolic of deceitful desires," [8] and the Arden editor suggests that this illusory banquet "is conceivably related to allegorical interpretations of scripture. Eve was tempted with an apple, and Christ with an illusory banquet; the former temptation successful, as with the 'men of sin,' the latter a failure, as with pure Gonzalo. . . . Banquets represent the voluptuous attractions of sense which (as in Marvell's *Dialogue*) the resolved soul must resist." [9]

There would seem to me to be a weakness in the interpretation of this "emblem" suggested by Mr. Frye and tentatively advanced by Mr. Kermode. The scriptural temptations which the latter cites as parallels are temptations of Good by Evil. The "temptation"—if it is that at all—here presented is of "men of sin" by the wise and good Prospero. Furthermore, the one good man in this group of sinners, "the pure Gonzalo," far from resisting the illusion, urges Alonso to trust in it. What occurs when the sinners approach the banquet is not the capitulation of weak men to the blandishments of sensuality, but the prevention of unworthy men from partaking of good things.

Prospero's banquet, I suggest, is a type, not of Satan's temptations, but of the commonest of all symbolic banquets: the Communion table. This is the supper from which notorious and unrepentant sinners are traditionally excluded:

> And if any of these [as do intend to be partakers of the Holy Communion] be an open and notorious evil liver, so that the congregation by him is offended, or have done any wrong to his neighbours by word or deed: The Curate having knowledge thereof, shall call him and advertise him, in any wise not to presume to the Lord's Table, until he have openly declared himself to have truly repented and amended his former naughty life, that the Congregation may thereby be satisfied, which afore were offended; and that he have recompensed the parties, whom he hath done wrong unto, or at the least declare himself to be in full purpose so to do, as soon he conveniently may.[10]

Ariel's disguise as a harpy is entirely appropriate to his minatory function here. Alonso and the rest are sinners like Phineus, "a kyng of Arcadie, who by the entysement of his second Wyfe, put out the eies of his sonnes, which he had by his first wyfe. But by the just vengeance of god, he was also made blind, and the foul ravenous byrds called Hapyiae [sic] defyled the meat that was prepared for him." [11]

The just vengeance of God is what Ariel invokes as the reason for his treatment of Prospero's enemies:

> You are three men of sinne, whom destiny
> That hath to instrument this lower world,
> And what is in't: the neuer surfeited Sea,
> Hath caus'd to belch vp you; and on this Island,

Where man doth not inhabit, you 'mongst men,
Being most vnfit to liue: I haue made you mad;
And euen with such like valour, men hang, and drowne
Their proper selues: you fooles, I and my fellowes
Are ministers of Fate, the Elements
Of whom your swords are temper'd, may as well
Wound the loud windes, or with bemockt-at-Stabs
Kill the still closing waters, as diminish
One dowle that's in my plumbe: My fellow ministers
Are like-invulnerable: if you could hurt,
Your swords are now too massie for your strengths,
And will not be vplifted: But remember
(For that's my businesse to you) that you three
From *Millaine* did supplant good *Prospero,*
Expos'd vnto the Sea (which hath requit it)
Him, and his innocent childe: for which foule deed,
The Powres, delaying (not forgetting) haue
Incens'd the Seas, and Shores; yea all the Creatures
Against your peace: Thee of thy Sonne, *Alonso*
They have bereft; and doe pronounce by me
Lingring perdition (worse then any death
Can be at once) shall step, by step attend
You, and your wayes, whose wraths to guard you from,
Which here, in this most desolate Isle, else fals
Vpon your heads, is nothing but hearts-sorrow,
And a cleere life ensuing.   (III.iii.74–103)

Ariel reveals to Alonso the real cause of his despair at the beginning
of the scene. The crime against Prospero has been revenged by the
seeming death of Ferdinand. The remainder of Alonso's life will be a
torment to him unless he can achieve "hearts-sorrow,/ And a cleere
life ensuing"—in other words, "contrition of the heart" and "an
amendment of life," [12] the first and last parts of repentance.

The first effect of Ariel's announcement upon Alonso is to drive
him not toward penance and salvation, but toward desperate self-
destruction. "The conscience of heinous offenses, and the force of

repentance, may be so great, that the mind of man, on each side com-
passed with fear, may be possessed with despair of salvation." [13] So it
is with Alonso:

> O, it is monstrous: monstrous:
> Me thought the billowes spoke, and told me of it,
> The windes did sing it to me: and the Thunder
> (That deepe and dreadfull Organ-Pipe) pronounc'd
> The name of *Prosper*: it did base my Trespasse,
> Therefore my Sonne i'th'Ooze is bedded; and
> I'le seeke him deeper then ere plummet sounded,
> And with him there lye mudded.   (III.iii.120–27)

Shakespeare differentiates Alonso's reaction to Ariel's accusation from
that of Antonio and Sebastian. As Gonzalo tells us:

> All three of them are desperate: their great guilt
> (Like poyson giuen to worke a great time after)
> Now gins to bite the spirits. . . .   (III.iii.131–33)

But the desperation of Alonso is directed at himself. His guilt im-
pels him to attempt suicide. Antonio and Sebastian defy the powers
that have justly accused them:

> *Seb.:* But one feend at a time,
> Ile fight their Legions ore.
> *Ant.:* Ile be thy Second.   (III.iii.128–30)

   Prospero prevents their desperation from having any physical
effect. Alonso will "lie mudded," not at the bottom of the sea, but at
the bottom of his mind, in the slime and ooze of his forgotten guilt.
It is there that the miraculous transformation predicted in Ariel's
"Dirge" must take place. There Alonso suffers, in a form which we
assume to be particularly intense as a result of his enchantment, the
"inward pinches" of contrition, the "again-bite" of conscience.

After allowing them to suffer for a brief period, Prospero releases his enemies:

> Thogh with their high wrongs I am strook to th' quick,
> Yet, with my nobler reason, gainst my furie
> Doe I take part: the rarer Action is
> In vertue, then in vengeance: they, being penitent,
> The sole drift of my purpose doth extend
> Not a frowne further: Goe, release them *Ariell*,
> My Charmes Ile breake, their sences Ile restore,
> And they shall be themselues. (V.i.31–38)

The process by which they recover their reason is described in the imagery which was introduced by Ariel's "Dirge":

> Their vnderstanding
> Begins to swell, and the approaching tide
> Will shortly fill the reasonable shore
> That now ly foule, and muddy. (V.i.91–94)

The return of reason enables Alonso to complete the process of repentance, which began with his contrition, by confessing his sin and making satisfaction to Prospero:

> Thy Dukedome I resigne, and doe entreat
> Thou pardon me my wrongs. (V.i.133–34)

Prospero rewards the regenerated Alonso with the resurrection of his son:

> My Dukedome since you haue giuen me againe,
> I will requite you with as good a thing,
> At least bring forth a wonder, to content ye
> As much, as me my Dukedome. (V.i.193–96)

The moment of Prospero's "discovery" of Ferdinand and Miranda "playing at Chesse" is the moment of "miracle" that we have seen to be the unvarying climax of the comedy of forgiveness. The resurrections of Hero, Helena, Imogen, Hermione, and Claudio have preceded this, Shakespeare's last "awakening from nightmare." Alonso discovers that the sin of which he has believed himself guilty—the deaths of Prospero and Miranda—has not occurred, and that his punishment—the death of Ferdinand—has been spared him in reality. The love of his son and Prospero's daughter will ratify the reconciliation of their fathers, though Alonso must first request the pardon of Miranda:

> But O, how odly will it sound, that I
> Must aske my childe forgiuenesse?   (V.i.232–33)

Prospero insists, however, that the time for the torments of conscience is past:

> There Sir stop,
> Let vs not burthen our remembrances, with
> A heauinesse that's gon.   (V.i.234–36)

And the good Gonzalo is ready to pronounce his benediction upon the play's events:

> *Gon.:* I haue inly wept,
> Or should haue spoke ere this: looke downe you gods
> And on this couple drop a blessed crowne;
> For it is you, that haue chalk'd forth the way
> Which brought vs hither.
>   *Alo.:* I say Amen, *Gonzallo.*
>   *Gon.:* Was *Millaine* thrust from *Millaine,* that his Issue
> Should become Kings of *Naples?* O reioyce
> Beyond a common ioy, and set it downe
> With gold on lasting Pillers: In one voyage

Did *Claribell* her husband finde at *Tunis*,
And *Ferdinand* her brother, found a wife,
Where he himself was lost: *Prospero,* his Dukedome
In a poor Isle: and all of vs, our selues,
When no man was his owne.   (V.i.237–51)

In this speech, so characteristic of the late romances, the sense of
the triumph of good and the attainment of happiness is complete
and, seemingly, only the gloomiest of specters at the comic feast would
insist upon its qualification. And yet it is Shakespeare himself who
so insists. We tend, upon the completion of our experience of *The
Tempest,* to remember Miranda's:

> O braue new world
> That has such people in't.   (V.i.215–16)

but to forget Prospero's reply:

> 'Tis new to thee.   (V.i.217)

We remember the regeneration of Alonso, but forget to wonder about
the spiritual condition of those other sinners, Antonio and Sebastian.

According to Gonzalo, the members of Alonso's party have, as a
result of their experiences on the island, found themselves. But what
a man finds when he finds himself clearly depends upon the man. For
Alonso, the "mortification of the old man" has resulted in the "quickening of the new man," [14] but regeneration is not an automatic process,
and there is no evidence that the old Antonio has altered as the result
of his mortification. Prospero, before he awakens the sinners from
their trance, apostrophizes the unhearing Antonio as follows:

> Flesh, and bloud,
> You, brother mine, that entertaine ambition,
> Expelld remorse, and nature, whom, with *Sebastian*
> (Whose inward pinches therefore are most strong)

> Would heere haue kill'd your King: I do forgiue thee,
> Vnnaturall though thou art. (V.i.86–91)

"Though thou *art.*" Antonio's evil nature has not changed and Prospero knows it, nor is Sebastian any more trustworthy. Prospero can only control them, as he has controlled Caliban, through the power of his knowledge of their evil:

> Wellcome, my friends all,
> But you my brace of Lords, were I so minded
> I heere could plucke his Highnesse frowne vpon you
> And iustifie you Traitors: at this time
> I will tell no tales. (V.i.143–47)

And yet, he forgives Antonio:

> For you (most wicked Sir) whom to call brother
> Would euen infect my mouth, I do forgiue
> Thy rankest fault; all of them: and require
> My Dukedome of thee, which, perforce I know
> Thou must restore. (V.i.150–54)

Here forgiveness is unjustified by contrition, confession, or satisfaction. If Antonio were to face the Last Judgment of the medieval mystery cycles in the spiritual state in which we find him at the end of *The Tempest,* he would take his place among the damned. To Prospero, however, he is forgivable precisely because Prospero is not the God of Judgment. As a man, Prospero forgives even the unregenerate, for the justice of man should be tempered with as much mercy as man would hope to find upon the Latter Day. Prospero's forgiveness springs, however, from no softness, either of heart or head. His emotional attitude toward a man "whom to call brother/ Would euen infect my mouth," is clearly lacking in tenderness. To forgive unregenerate evil is safe only when, as here and at the conclusion of *Measure for Measure,* the good are in firm and undeceived control.

More than any other of Shakespeare's plays, *The Tempest* insists strongly upon indestructibility of evil. Only a rigid and unceasing control of the sort that Prospero has exercised over Caliban and will, we assume, exercise over Antonio, can keep good in its natural ascendancy. The relaxation of such vigilance inevitably results in a spread of sin, hatred, and disorder. Evil cannot, however, be finally and completely destroyed. Antonio, in some form, will always exist and can only be forgiven for existing.

Conclusion

Shakespeare's last appeal to the complex of beliefs and attitudes which make up the Christian concept of forgiveness falls outside the purely dramatic context of *The Tempest*. The *Epilogue,* spoken by Prospero, is a traditional Elizabethan *plaudite*—an appeal for applause delivered by an actor who speaks simultaneously as actor and as the character he has represented. As Prospero, he speaks with reference to and on behalf of the play itself; as actor—let us call him "Burbage"—he is the spokesman for that group of artists, including Shakespeare, who have created the play. As "Burbage" he appeals to the audience, upon whose sensitivity and intelligence the success, though not the greatness, of even the greatest work of art must depend:

> Gentle breath of yours, my Sailes
> Must fill, or else my proiect failes,
> Which was to please. . . .   (Epilogue, 13–15)

The audience, he goes on to suggest, may, for the artist, be likened to the God of Judgment, and he asks that God to judge him, not according to his deserts, but mercifully:

> And my ending is despaire,
> Vnlesse I be relieu'd by praier
> Which pierces so, that it assaults
> Mercy it selfe, and frees all faults.
>   (Epilogue, 17–20)

It is clear, however, that he thinks of the natures to which he is appealing as far more human than divine, for he expects them to grant their charity in the hope that their own trespasses will be forgiven:

> As you from crimes would pardon'd be,
> Let your Indulgence set me free.   (Epilogue, 21–22)

As always, the source of human mercy is seen as the sense of common humanity, the knowledge of shared weakness. As "Burbage," the speaker of the Epilogue asks that the audience show mercy in passing aesthetic judgment; as Prospero, he reminds us that he deserves forgiveness because he has forgiven:

>   Let me not
> Since I have my Dukedome got,
> And pardon'd the deceiver, dwell
> In this barc Island, by your Spell. . . .
>   (Epilogue, 7–10)

As a work of art, *The Tempest* stands in no need of the charity requested by its Epilogue, for its artistic greatness is beyond challenge. As a comedy of forgiveness, however, its full *success* depends upon charity—depends, that is, upon the ability of its audience to participate in a celebration of the virtue of charity. Shakespeare's original audience, I would suggest, had been conditioned both by literary tradition and by religious belief to respond fully to such a demand. It is possible that a similar response is far less automatic in the case of a modern audience. Modern ethical systems, whether religious or secular, are certainly not behindhand in their exaltation of charity, but one may speculate that our sense of the sources and hence the nature of what is meant by charity have altered since Shakespeare's time. Medieval men and their Elizabethan descendants were taught to be charitable out of a sense of common humanity, which meant a sense of common evil. Original sin preceded the cradle and eternal damnation might follow the grave, and a man's trespasses were forgiven on the condition that he had forgiven those who trespassed against him. Modern charity—if I may be permitted a massive generalization—is more likely to be associated with making allowances, with pity and tolerance. We tend to forgive the man who does evil not because we recognize ourselves in him, but because we see him as a poor unfortunate, a victim of heredity and environment, the creature of an unhappy past—one who, through no fault of his own, is our inferior. We are likely, therefore, in our contemplation of the *humanum genus* figure to react rather as the pharisee reacted to the publican. This is not the reaction which the sinning mortals of Shakespeare's comedies and of the medieval plays which preceded them were intended to provoke. Such dramas invite us to forgive the sins of others not because we (unlike them) are good, but because we (like them) are not good.

The medieval narratives and plays which are the literary ancestors of Shakespeare's comedies of forgiveness were created for the specific purpose of teaching the glad tidings of God's mercy to the repentant sinner, and the success of the lesson depended upon the identification of the audience with the sinning protagonist. The religious beliefs which provided the attitudes and responses with which the medieval dramatist worked continued to be held by the audience Shakespeare wrote for. Though Luther had challenged the importance of penance with his assertion that faith alone brings salvation, the Anglican Church, as we have seen, managed to absorb his innovation without importantly disturbing traditional doctrine. The dramatic tradition, on the other hand, underwent the important change of secularization. The essential aspects of the medieval form survived the change, however, for the comedies of forgiveness continue to concern themselves with a central figure who sins and is forgiven, and an identification with this erring protagonist remains necessary to the complete success of the drama. As a result of secularization, however, one vitally important change does take place in the play of forgiveness: the primary emphasis necessarily shifts from the mercy of God to the emulation of that mercy by man. Men and societies are saved both by the grace of God, and as a result of contrition and forgiveness in the comedies of Shakespeare, but these Shakespearean salvations are of this world.

The world of Shakespeare's comedies of forgiveness is one where hate and love are opposed to one another in a precarious balance which only just permits the ascendancy of love and order. The sin or error of the *humanum genus* figures has the effect of threatening that balance and permitting the near-victory of strife and chaos. Only the erring protagonist's contrition and his forgiveness by those he has wronged saves the fabric of this world of comedy from destruction. The origin of contrition is self-knowledge, that is, a realization of one's own sinfulness, and the process by which the erring sinner is led to that moment of revelation is seen, with increasing insistence from play to play, to be the result of the guidance and grace of super-natural power. "The goodness of God" is "effectually in his creatures to rule them" [1] and the actions of the plays are thus guided to their happy conclusions. But frequently the rule of goodness fails within individual characters, for in the comedies of forgiveness, evil is seen as a strong, omnipresent, and inevitable threat to the rule of good, of love, and of concord. Because it has its roots in all human creatures, evil is ineradicable. It can only be recognized, controlled, and for-given.

According to Northrop Frye, at the end of comedy "an act of com-munion with the audience is in order. . . . The resolution of comedy comes, so to speak, from the audience's side of the stage." [2] In the version of the world presented by Shakespeare's later comedies, charity, born of self-knowledge, is not simply a commendable virtue. It is an absolute essential, and the audience's sympathetic recognition of its necessity is essential to the act of communion Frye speaks of, and consequently to the full artistic success of these plays.

Notes

I: INTRODUCTION

1. Dowden, *Shakspere*, pp. 58–60.
2. G. K. Hunter, ed., *All's Well That Ends Well*, introd., p. lv.
3. The quoted definitions are from the Oxford English Dictionary.
4. Frye, *Anatomy of Criticism*, p. 162. I am much indebted to Frye's work for the view of comic structure that follows.
5. Baldwin, *Shakspere's Five Act Structure*, p. 33. Baldwin is quoting the *Evanthius De Fabula* of Donatus.
6. Johnson, ed., *The Plays of William Shakespeare*, III, 399.
7. Coleridge, *Coleridge's Shakespearean Criticism*, ed. Raysor, II, 356–57.
8. *Ibid.*, I. 113–14.
9. Three excellent books which define Shakespeare's attitude toward forgiveness and such related concepts as justice, charity, mercy, etc., and which place these attitudes in their historical and philosophical context are: Sehrt, *Vergebung Und Gnade Bei Shakespeare*; Parker, *The Slave of Life*; and Matthews, *Character and Symbol in Shakespeare's Plays*. The last of these appeared after the substantial completion of my own book.

2: FORGIVENESS OF SINS IN THE MEDIEVAL DRAMA

1. Deimling and Matthews, eds., *The Chester Plays*, II, 427ff.
2. Lucy Smith, ed., *York Plays*, pp. 497ff.
3. Thomas Preston, *Cambises, King of Percia*, in Adams, ed., *Chief Pre-Shakespearean Dramas*, p. 638. The story (originally from Herodotus) was a medieval favorite and is one of the *exempla* of the *Gesta Romanorum* and of *An Alphabet of Tales*.
4. This engraving is reproduced as number 135 in Bastelaer, *Les Estampes de Peter Bruegel L'Ancien*.
5. Ninane, "Un Chef-d'oeuvre de Thierry Bouts au Musées Roy-

aux," *Bulletin des Musées Royaux des Beaux-Arts de Bruxelles,* VI
(1957), 23.

6. Traver, *The Four Daughters of God.* See also, Chew, *The Virtues
Reconciled; An Iconographic Study.*

7. Traver, pp. 16–17.

8. Block, ed., *Ludus Coventriae,* pp. 97ff.

9. *The Castell of Perseverance,* in Furnivall and Pollard, eds., *The
Macro Plays,* pp. 75–186.

10. Aquinas, *The "Summa Theologica,"* trans. Fathers of the English
Dominican Province, Part I, Fourth Number.

11. Aquinas, p. 99.

12. *Ibid.,* p. 101.

13. *Ibid.,* p. 130.

14. *Ibid.*

15. *Ibid.*

16. *Ibid.,* p. 93.

17. Luther, *What Luther Says: An Anthology,* ed. Plass, I, 517.

18. See Chambers, *The Medieval Stage,* I, 104.

19. *English Drama from Early Times to the Elizabethane,* p. 51.

20. "The Miracle Plays in Mediaeval England," in *Essays by Divers
Hands, Being the Transactions of the Royal Society of Literature of the
United Kingdom,* ed. Woods, New Series, VII (1927), 153. See also,
Gayley, ed., *Representative English Comedies,* I, introd., p. xxxviii.

21. Manley, p. 137.

22. These are *The Croxton Play of the Sacrament,* the *Duk Moraud*
fragment, and the latter half of the *Play of Mary Magdalene.* The two
former are discussed in this chapter, the latter in chap. 6, pp. 200ff.

23. For the influence of the didactic methods of medieval preachers on
the drama, I am indebted to Owst, *Literature and Pulpit in Medieval
England.*

24. No medieval example of a martyr play has survived in English,
though there are later plays related to the tradition, e.g. W. Rowley's
A Shoemaker a Gentleman.

25. *Histoire Générale du Théâtre en France,* I, 259.

26. Frank, *The Medieval French Drama,* p. 200.

27. Paris and Robert, eds., *Miracles de Nostre Dame par Personnages,*
Tome V.

28. Frank, p. 114.

29. Paris and Robert, Tome V.

30. *Ibid.,* Tome I.

31. Heuser, "*Dux Moraud,* einzelrolle aus einem verlorenen drama des 14. jahrhunderts," *Anglia,* XXX (1907), 180ff.

32. Chambers, *English Literature at the Close of the Middle Ages,* p. 65.

33. Horstmann, "A Tale of an Incestuous Daughter (ms. Rawlinson 118)," *Archiv für das Studium der Neueren Sprachen und Litteraturen,* 79 (1887), 421–24.

34. Herrtage, ed., *Gesta Romanorum,* pp. 390–92 and Banks, ed., *An Alphabet of Tales,* I, 145–46.

35. Herrtage, p. 392.

36. *The Play of the Sacrament,* in Adams, pp. 243ff.

37. Gayley, I, introd. xxxix.

38. See Chambers, *The Medieval Stage,* Vol. I, chaps. XIII and XIV, and Rossiter, *English Drama from Early Times to the Elizabethans,* chap. III and pp. 69–70.

39. Petit de Juleville, *Histoire du Théâtre en France,* I, 127.

40. Johnson, I, introd. xix–xx.

41. Coleridge, I, 113–14.

42. Aquinas, p. 42.

43. The collectors of *exempla* sometimes classified their stories according to the points they were meant to illustrate. Thus a reader of *An Alphabet of Tales* would find fifteen stories listed or cross-referenced under "contrition." Among them is the tale of the incestuous daughter.

44. See below, pp. 177ff.

3: PRE-SHAKESPEAREAN COMEDIES OF FORGIVENESS

1. Greg, ed., *The Interlude of Calisto and Melebea.*

2. de Rojas, *Celestina, or the Tragi-Comedy of Calisto and Melebea,* ed. Allen, trans. Mabbe.

3. Reed, *Early Tudor Drama,* p. 17.

4. I have used the "act" divisions given in Allen's edition.

5. H. Warner Allen includes as an appendix to his edition of de Rojas a reprint of the English interlude together with an essay on it which meticulously analyzes the indebtedness of the English dramatist to his source.

6. Gayley, I, introd., p. lxviii.

7. Reed, p. 113.

8. Garter, *The Most Virtuous and Godly Susanna,* ed. Evans and Greg.

9. The stage direction is taken from the *Book of Susannah*: "the Lorde raysed up the sprete of a yōge chylde, whose name was Daniel." Garter used *The Byble in Englyshe* (London: Rychard Grafton and Edward Whitchurch, 1539). This is the translation commonly known as the "Great Bible."

10. *Ibid.*

11. George Whetstone, *Promos and Cassandra* in Bullough, ed., *Narrative and Dramatic Sources of Shakespeare, II: The Comedies, 1597–1603,* 442–513.

12. Izard, *George Whetstone,* p. 52.

13. That honor would appear to go, among the dramatists whose works have survived, to John Phillip, author of *The Commodye of pacient and meeke Grissill.*

14. Giraldi Cinthio, *Gli Hecatommithi,* II, 415–30. I have also used the translation which appears in Bullough, II, pp. 420ff.

15. Mary Lascelles in her book-length study *Shakespeare's "Measure for Measure,"* p. 17, refers to Andrugio's crime as "rape"—a description which Whetstone softens "by suggesting that it might be regarded as mutual consent between impatient lovers to anticipate marriage." To this she adds in a footnote, p. 44, "He is not very clear or consistent in his references to it." I am not very clear as to what Miss Lascelles means by these statements. In the Argument to the play Whetstone calls Andrugio's offense "incontinency" and refers to Polina as Andrugio's "minion." In the first mention of the crime in the play, Rosko says that Andrugio must die "for loving too kindlie." (p. 448) Cassandra, in addition to the statement quoted, defends Andrugio on the grounds that "He hath defilde no nuptial bed, nor forced rape hath mov'd." (p. 452) This seems clear enough, but there may be inconsistencies in the text which I have overlooked. It would, however, be rather odd to punish Polina for having been the victim of a violent attack.

16. Giraldi Cinthio, II, 418.

17. Bullough, II, 403.

18. Rape was the only sexual offense which was a felony before 1533. In that year "the detestable and abominable vice of buggery committed with mankind or beast" was made a capital crime. In the first year of her reign, Mary passed a statute which struck from the books all felonies which had not been felonies before her father's time. Elizabeth re-

established capital punishment for "buggery" in 1562, and added "unlawful and carnal knowledge" of "any woman-child under the age of ten years" in 1576. The applicable statutes are: for rape, 13 Edward I, cap. 34; for "buggery," 25 Henry VIII, cap. 6, and 5 Elizabeth I, cap. 17; for carnal knowledge, 18 Elizabeth I, cap. 7. I have used Pickering, *The Statutes at Large,* Vols. I, IV, and VI.

19. Whetstone in Bullough, II, 451. This comment appears as a shoulder note in the original.

20. Giraldi Cinthio, *Epitia,* summarized in Bullough, II, 430–42.

21. Cinthio also arranged for the survival of the brother when he dramatized the story. There seems no point in summarizing yet again the complex question of the relationship of the various narrative and dramatic versions of Cinthio's novella. The problems are well treated by Bullough, Lascelles, and Izard. I have confined myself to the basic and universally admitted proposition that Whetstone used Cinthio's novella and that Shakespeare used *Promos and Cassandra.*

22. The phrase is Ben Jonson's: "Prologue" to *Every Man In His Humour,* ed. Carter, p. 21, l. 29.

23. *Anatomy of Criticism,* p. 179.

24. *Endeavors of Art,* p. 291.

25. Greg, ed., *The Rare Triumphs of Love and Fortune.*

26. Chambers, *The Elizabethan Stage,* II, 118.

27. *Cymbeline,* introd., p. xxxi.

28. Pettet, *Shakespeare and the Romance Tradition,* p. 24.

29. Lyly delighted in this sort of arbitrary motivation. His most thoroughgoing use of it is in *The Woman in the Moon,* a play whose indebtedness to *Love and Fortune* has been noted by Bond in his edition of *The Complete Works of John Lyly,* III, 236.

30. Greene, *Orlando Furioso,* in *The Plays and Poems of Robert Greene,* ed. Collins, I, 223ff.

31. *Ibid.,* I, 217.

32. Ariosto, *Orlando Furioso,* trans. Harington, p. 147.

33. Jordan, *Robert Greene,* pp. 197–99.

34. Frank, *The Medieval French Drama,* p. 157. It is probable, but not certain, that de Mézières was the author of the dramatic version.

35. Greene, I, 236.

36. *Ibid.,* II, 87ff.

37. Boccaccio, *Il Decameron,* ed. Fanfani and Camerini, I, 366.

38. See above, p. 25. Another mother-in-law analogue among the *Miracles de Notre Dame* is *La Fille du Roy de Hongrie*.

39. See Clouston, "The Innocent and Persecuted Wife: Asiatic and European Versions of Chaucer's 'Man of Law's Tale,' " in Furnivall, Brock, and Clouston, eds., *Originals and Analogues of Some of Chaucer's "Canterbury Tales*," pp. 365–414.

40. Clouston gives the following analogues in which the husband believes the calumny and persecutes the wife: "The Vazier's Pious Daughter" (Persian), p. 390; "De la bonne Imperatrice qui guarda loyalement la foi du mariage," p. 497; Vincent de Beauvais *Speculum Historiale*: cap. xc & cap. xci, p. 399; *Rappresentazione di Santa Guglielma* (particularly interesting as a dramatic version), p. 403. Dramatic versions not noted by Clouston are the *Miracles de Nostre Dame par Personnages*; *L'Empereris de Romme*; *La Marquise de la Gaudine*; and (closest of all to *Cymbeline*) *Ostes, roy d'Espaigne*.

41. Cinthio's novella is translated in Collins' edition of Greene, II, 80ff. Cinthio also dramatized this story as *Arrenopia*. According to Collins, Greene made no use of the play.

42. The subject of the relationship of the old Vice to Shakespeare's villains is exhaustively discussed by Spivack, *Shakespeare and the Allegory of Evil*. Spivack is more interested in the Vice as the amoral, jesting, motiveless malignant than in his manifestations as an evil councilor like Ateukin, however.

43. See Barber, *Shakespeare's Festive Comedy*, chaps. II, III, and IV.

4: MUCH ADO ABOUT NOTHING

1. Bullough, I, 210.

2. *Shakespearian Comedy*, p. 37.

3. Cited by Johnson, I, 255.

4. *Vergebung Und Gnade Bei Shakespeare*, p. 82.

5. In addition to Shylock, there is another barrier to the felicity of the lovers in this play: the last will and testament of Portia's father.

6. Spenser, "An Hymne in Honovr of Loue" in *The Poetical Works of Edmund Spenser*, ed. J. C. Smith and de Selincourt, p. 587.

7. "The Celebration of Charis," in *Poems*, ed. G. B. Johnson, p. 115.

8. "A Medieval Commonplace in Spenser's Cosmology," *Studies in Philology*, XXX (April, 1933), 133–147.

9. Charles G. Smith, *Spenser's Theory of Friendship*, pp. 3–13.

10. Spenser, *The Faerie Qveene,* in *The Poetical Works of Edmund Spenser,* ed. J. C. Smith and de Selincourt, pp. 263–64.

11. See *Macbeth:*

> Nay, had I powre, I should
> Poure the sweet Milke of Concord, into Hell,
> Vprore the vniuersall peace, confound
> All vnity on earth.   (V.iii.97–100)

12. See Watkins, *Shakespeare and Spenser,* pp. 19, 208.

13. Dunn, "The Storm in *King Lear,*" *Shakespeare Quarterly,* III (October, 1952), 329–33.

14. Bradbrook, *Shakespeare and Elizabethan Poetry,* p. 184.

15. For the homonymic pun or "noting" and "nothing" see Hockey, "Notes Notes, Forsooth . . . ," *Shakespeare Quarterly,* VIII (Winter, 1957), 353–58.

16. Lang, *"Much Ado About Nothing,"* *Harper's Magazine,* LXXXIII (September, 1891), 502.

17. *"Much Ado About Nothing,"* *Scrutiny,* XIX (October, 1953), 314.

18. Page, "The Public Repudiation of Hero," *PMLA,* L (September, 1935), 743.

19. *The Sources of "Much Ado About Nothing,"* p. 62.

20. Neill, "More Ado About Claudio: An Acquittal for the Slandered Groom," *Shakespeare Quarterly,* III (April, 1952), 97.

21. See Frye, *The Anatomy of Criticism,* p. 174.

22. Bradbrook, p. 187.

23. *Ibid.*

5: ALL'S WELL THAT ENDS WELL

1. Quiller-Couch and Wilson, eds., *All's Well That Ends Well,* introd. (by Quiller-Couch), p. xxv.

2. *All's Well That Ends Well,* introd., p. xlii.

3. *"All's Well That Ends Well,"* *Harper's Magazine,* LXXXV (July, 1892), 216.

4. *Shakespeare's Problem Comedies.*

5. *Ibid.,* p. 60.

6. *Ibid.,* p. 62.

7. *Ibid.,* p. 61.

8. *Shakespeare,* p. 215.

9. *From Ritual to Romance.*

10. Holinshed, *Chronicles of England, Scotland and Ireland,* I, 527ff.

Holinshed is very cautious about the historicity of Helena: "I leaue that to be decided of the learned." He is careful, however, to give a detailed account of her legendary achievements.

11. Chambers, *William Shakespeare*, I, 76.

12. "Stone" (l.69) = testicle (cf. *Merry Wives*, I.iv.118); "arayse King Pippen" (l.72) ". . . a pen in's hand" (l.73); pen = the penis. (See Partridge, *Dictionary of Slang and Unconventional English*, p. 616.) For further bawdy in this scene see Halio, "'Traitor' in *All's Well* and *Troilus and Cressida*," *Modern Language Notes*, LXXII (June, 1957), 408–9.

13. It is perhaps worth noting that the Dauphin in *I Henry VI* compares Joan to "Helen the mother of great Constantine" (I.iii.142).

14. See the reviews of Tyrone Guthrie's 1959 production; for example, Brown, "Three Adaptations," *Shakespeare Survey*, XIII (1960), 141.

15. Legouis, "La Comtesse de Roussillon," *English*, I (1937), 399–404.

16. Hurstfield, *The Queen's Wards*, pp. 139ff.

17. See Bradbrook, pp. 162–70.

18. I am thinking of Sir John Harington, *Nugae Antiquae*, II, 101, 130–31.

19. Rossiter, *Angel with Horns*, ed. Storey, p. 96.

20. Griffiths, ed., *Certain Sermons or Homilies Appointed to Be Read In Churches In The Time of Queen Elizabeth of Famous Memory*, p. 19.

21. "The Theme of Ambition in *All's Well That Ends Well*," *ELH*, XXI (March, 1954), p. 20.

22. Griffiths, *Homilies*, p. 571.

23. *Ibid.*, p. 516.

24. Hunter, p. 82.

25. Johnson, III, 399.

26. Quiller-Couch and Wilson, *All's Well That Ends Well*, introd. (by Quiller-Couch) p. xxxiv.

27. "Dramatic Conventions in *All's Well That Ends Well*," *PMLA*, LXXV (December, 1960), 502.

28. Griffiths, *Homilies*, p. 584.

29. *Ibid.*, p. 580.

6: THE ROMANCE AND THE COMEDY OF FORGIVENESS

1. *Shakespeare's Last Plays*, p. 20.

2. *Ibid.*, p. 25.

3. Muir, *Shakespeare as Collaborator*, p. 77.

4. Chambers, *The Elizabethan Stage,* IV, 36.

5. Renwick and Greg, eds., *John of Bordeaux,* ll. 764–80.

6. *The Trial of Chivalry,* Old English Drama; Students' Facsimile Edition, 1912, H₂ recto. For the statue motif see Lancaster, "Hermione's Statue," *Studies in Philology,* XXIX (April, 1932), 233–38.

7. Edwards, "Shakespeare's Romances: 1900–1957," *Shakespeare Survey,* XI (1958), 4. It must be emphasized that Mr. Edwards is here summarizing a scholarly position of which he does not approve.

8. Original: "preserd." I have used the collotype facsimile of the 1609 Quarto, ed. Greg.

9. Frye, *The Anatomy of Criticism,* p. 33.

10. *Syr Clyomon . . . and [Syr] Clamydes,* Old English Drama: Students' Facsimile Edition, 1913, F₄ verso.

11. Ships were a common feature of medieval *décor simultanée* staging, and *Mary Magdalene* appears to have been written for such a production. See Penn, *The Staging of the "Miracles de Nostre Dame par Personnages" of Ms. Cangé,* pp. 19–22. Miss Penn believes that the "sea" of the miracle plays was a tank of real water. In any case, Chambers' statement in *English Literature at the Close of the Middle Ages,* p. 45, that "perhaps [the author of *Mary Magdalene*] hardly expected the play to be performed" cannot be justified on the basis of our knowledge of medieval stagecraft. See also, Cohen, *Histoire de la Mise en Scène dans le Théâtre Religieux Français du Moyen-Age,* pp. 100–2, and Loomis, "Secular Dramatics in the Royal Palace, Paris, 1378, 1389, and Chaucer's 'Tregetoures,'" *Speculum,* XXXIII (1958), pp. 242–55.

12. *Mary Magdalene,* in Furnivall, ed., *The Digby Mysteries,* ll. 1888–899.

13. It is the longest of the stories in the *Gesta Romanorum.* See Swann and Hooper, pp. 259–99.

7: CYMBELINE

1. Johnson, VII, 403.

2. Leavis, "The Criticism of Shakespeare's Late Plays: A Caveat," *Scrutiny,* X (April, 1942), 340.

3. *Shakespeare's Workmanship,* p. 217.

4. See Stephenson, "The Significance of *Cymbeline,*" *Scrutiny,* X (April, 1942), 329–38. Fr. Stephenson holds that "the pervading idea [of the imagery] is that of worth, value." (p. 331)

5. The notes on these passages in the Variorum edition contain several comments to the effect that the term is here used in its Calvinistic sense.

Furness is quite right in being dubious of such an interpretation (p. 35). Shakespeare's use of the term is the opposite of the Calvinist. The Calvinist doctrine of unconditional election has as its main point that God's grace cannot be merited, even by faith. Shakespeare is here supposing that election is the result of merit. The controversy over the doctrine has, however, had the effect of giving the term a strong theological tone.

6. *Cymbeline*, p. 18.

7. Granville-Barker, *Prefaces to Shakespeare: Second Series*, p. 310.

8. *Shakespeare's Comedies*, pp. 261–62.

9. Kökeritz, *Shakespeare's Pronunciation*, p. 113.

10. Evans, p. 277.

11. *A Catechism Written in Latin*, ed. Corrie, trans. Norton, p. 177.

12. *Ibid.*

13. *What Luther Says: An Anthology*, ed. Plass, I, 524.

14. Luther, I, 527.

15. Nowell, p. 200.

16. Nosworthy, p. 152.

17. Griffiths, p. 68.

18. *Cymbeline*, p. 354.

19. Granville-Barker, p. 259.

20. Evans, p. 281.

21. Original: "constrain'd . . ." but the sense demands a definite pause at this point.

22. Griffiths, pp. 561–62.

23. *Ibid.*, pp. 573ff.

24. *The "Summa Theologica,"* Part III, Fourth Number, trans. Fathers of the English Dominican Province, pp. 210–11.

25. Wilson, "Prefatory Note" to *Cymbeline*, ed. Maxwell, ix–x. Maxwell himself is of the opinion that the theophany is Shakespearean.

26. *The Crown of Life*, pp. 168ff.

27. See Bryant, *Hippolyta's View*, p. 201.

28. Knight, p. 189.

29. Bryant, p. 200.

30. Jonson, *Every Man In His Hvmovr*, ed. Carter, Prologue, l. 21.

31. *The Tempest*, III.iii.83.

32. Griffiths, p. 516.

33. *Ibid.*, p. 517.

34. In Paris and Robert, Tome IV.

35. The resemblance of *Ostes* to *Cymbeline* was first noted by J. P. Collier. See Furness, p. 474.

36. According to Tennyson. See Nosworthy, p. 185.
37. Griffiths, p. 509.

8: THE WINTER'S TALE

1. See above, p. 143.
2. *The Winter's Tale: A Study.*
3. *Shakespeare's Last Plays.*
4. *The Crown of Life,* pp. 76–128.
5. *Shakespeare: The Last Phase,* pp. 105–92.
6. In Greene, *Life and Works of Robert Greene,* ed. Grosart, IV, 227–317.
7. *Ibid.,* IV, 317.
8. *Ibid.,* IV, 237.
9. *Ibid.,* IV, 238.
10. One should mention at this point J. Dover Wilson's ingenious theory, in his edition of the play (Cambridge, 1931), p. 131, that Leontes overhears and misinterprets Hermione's lines:

> Th'offences we haue made you doe, wee'le answere,
> If you first sinn'd with vs: and that with vs
> You did continue fault; and that you slipt not
> With any, but with vs.   (I.ii.102–5)

S. L. Bethell's objections to Wilson's proposed staging (see Bethell, pp. 121–22) are cogent, but he does not sufficiently emphasize the theatrical impracticability of such "business." The objection to Leontes' eavesdropping is the same as that to Wilson's equally ingenious theory about Hamlet's overhearing of Polonius's "I'll loose my daughter to him . . ." (*Hamlet,* II.iii.162ff). Such ingenuities will not work on-stage—and for a very good reason. If an actor is to convey to us the fact that he is spying, he must distract our attention from what he is spying upon. But if he so distracts us, we do not overhear what he overhears, so the significance of his overhearing is entirely lost. If such business is to work, the actor must tell us what he has overheard and what he makes of it.

11. By changing his source in order to emphasize the Queen's innocence, Shakespeare created for himself a minor dramatic problem which he does not attempt to solve. In *Pandosto,* Egistus knows only that his life is in danger when he flees the country. No matter how we interpret Polixenes' parting lines (I.ii.458–60) we cannot help feeling that he is leaving the unfortunate Hermione in a perilous situation, and exacerbating Leontes' suspicions by his flight.

12. Greene, IV, 247.

13. Bethell, p. 78.

14. *Ibid.*

15. *Shakespeare's Wordplay,* p. 151; see also Traversi, pp. 119–21.

16. Siegel, "Leontes A Jealous Tyrant," *Review of English Studies,* I, n.s. (October, 1950), 307.

17. Griffiths, p. 78.

18. *Ibid.,* p. 77.

19. "Six Points of Stage-craft in *The Winter's Tale,*" *Shakespeare Survey,* XI (1958), 35.

20. Baldwin Maxwell, ed., *The Winter's Tale,* p. 80.

21. Greene, IV, 227.

22. See Knight, p. 106, and B. Maxwell, pp. 20–21.

23. See above, pp. 27ff.

24. Siegel, "Leontes A Jealous Tyrant," *Review of English Studies,* I, n.s. (October, 1950), 306.

25. Knight, p. 126.

9: MEASURE FOR MEASURE

1. "Action and Symbol in *Measure for Measure* and *The Tempest,*" *Shakespeare Quarterly,* IV (October, 1953), 383.

2. In *The Wheel of Fire,* pp. 80–106.

3. Battenhouse, "*Measure for Measure* and the Christian Doctrine of the Atonement," *PMLA,* LXI (December, 1946), 1029–59.

4. See above, pp. 13ff.

5. For the resemblance of *Measure for Measure* to the Four Daughters of God allegory, see Battenhouse, "*Measure for Measure* and the Christian Doctrine of the Atonement," *PMLA,* LXI (December, 1946), 1034.

6. See Schanzer, "The Marriage Contracts in *Measure for Measure,*" *Shakespeare Survey,* XIII (1960), 81–89.

7. See Chapter III, n. 18.

8. *Constitutions and Canons Ecclesiastical of the Church of England,* pp. 59–60.

9. *The Anatomy of Abuses,* ed. Furnivall, Part I, p. 98.

10. *Sermons,* ed. Corrie, p. 244.

11. *Ibid.,* p. 258.

12. *A Catechism Written in Latin,* ed. Corrie, trans. Norton, Appendix, p. 226.

13. Stubbes, Part I, p. 99.

14. *Ibid.*

15. *A Discourse of Conscience*, p. 17.

16. Firth and Rait, eds., *Acts and Ordinances of the Interregnum*, II, 388.

17. Holland, "*Measure for Measure*: The Duke and the Prince," *Comparative Literature*, XI (Winter, 1959), 16–20.

18. *Essayes,* ed. Rhys, trans. Florio, III, 94.

19. See above, p. 58.

20. Lee, "Shakespeare and the Spanish Inquisition," *Living Age,* XXVI (May 13, 1922), 460–66.

21. Leavis, "The Greatness of *Measure for Measure*," *Scrutiny,* X (January, 1942), 238.

22. *Ibid.,* p. 246.

10: THE TEMPEST

1. The usual interpretation of these lines assumes that the entire invitation is addressed to the "sweete Sprights." I believe that they are asked only to "beare the burthen." See the excellent article by Cutts, "Music and the Supernatural in *The Tempest*: A Study in Interpretation," *Music and Letters,* XXXIX (October, 1958), 347–58.

2. "Orchestra or A Poem of Dauncing," in *The Poems of Sir John Davies,* ed. Howard, p. 70. See also above, p. 129.

3. See Brower, pp. 114ff.

4. Tillyard, p. 21.

5. Griffiths, p. 573.

6. *Ibid.*

7. One of the few scraps of Shakespearean biographical information we possess indicates that he was regarded as skilled in the creation of visual metaphors of this kind. On March 31, 1613, he was paid 44 shillings for devising an *impresa* for the Earl of Rutland. Burbage was paid a like sum for "paynting and makyng yt." An *impresa* was a paper shield carried by knights prior to tilting. These were emblazoned with symbolic figures. Of the *imprese* carried by the knights on the occasion for which Shakespeare designed Rutland's (King's Accession day, March 24, 1613) it is recorded that "some were so dark that their meaning is not yet understood, unless perchance that were their meaning, not to be understood." See Chambers, *William Shakespeare,* II, 153.

8. *The Tempest,* p. 15.

9. Kermode, ed., *The Tempest,* p. 85.

10. *The Book of Common Prayer and Administration of the Sacra-*

ments, and Other Rites and Ceremonies in the Church of England (1559) reprinted in Clay, ed., *Liturgies And Occasional Forms of Prayer Set Forth in the Reign of Queen Elizabeth*, p. 180.

11. Cooper, *Thesaurus linguae Romanae et Brittaniae.*
12. Griffiths, pp. 573, 579.
13. Nowell, p. 177.
14. *Ibid.*

11: CONCLUSION

1. See above, p. 183.
2. *The Anatomy of Criticism*, p. 164.

Bibliography

Adams, Joseph Quincy, ed. Chief Pre-Shakespearean Dramas. Cambridge, Mass., 1924.

Aquinas, St. Thomas. The "Summa Theologica." Translated by Fathers of the English Dominican Province. 21 vols. London, 1912–17.

Ariosto, Lodovico. Orlando Furioso. Translated by Sir John Harington. London, 1634.

Baldwin, T. W. Shakspere's Five Act Structure. Urbana, 1947.

Banks, Mary MacLeod, ed. An Alphabet of Tales. 2 vols. London, 1904–05, Early English Text Society.

Barber, C. L. Shakespeare's Festive Comedy. Princeton, 1959.

Bastelaer, René van. Les Estampes de Peter Bruegel L'Ancien. Brussels, 1908.

Battenhouse, Roy. "Measure for Measure and the Christian Doctrine of the Atonement." PMLA, LXI (1946), 1029–59.

Bethell, S. L. The Winter's Tale: A Study. London, 1947.

Block, K. S., ed. Ludus Coventriae. London, 1922, Early English Text Society.

Boccaccio, Giovanni. Il Decameron. Edited by P. Fanfani and E. Camerini. 2 vols. Milan, 1910.

Bradbrook, M. C. Shakespeare and Elizabethan Poetry. New York, 1957.

Brower, Reuben. The Fields of Light. New York, 1951.

Brown, John Russell. "Three Adaptations," Shakespeare Survey, XIII (1960), 137–45.

Bryant, J. A. Hippolyta's View. Lexington, 1961.

Bullough, Geoffrey, ed. Narrative and Dramatic Sources of Shakespeare. 4 vols. New York, 1957–61.

Chambers, E. K. The Elizabethan Stage. 4 vols. Oxford, 1923.

————— English Literature at the Close of the Middle Ages. Oxford, 1945.

————— The Medieval Stage. 2 vols. Oxford, 1903.

————— William Shakespeare. 2 vols. Oxford, 1930.

Charlton, H. B. Shakespearian Comedy. London, 1938.

Chew, Samuel. The Virtues Reconciled: an Iconographic Study. Toronto, 1947.

Clay, William Keatinge, ed. Liturgies and Occasional Forms of Prayer Set Forth in the Reign of Queen Elizabeth. London, 1847. The Parker Society.

Coghill, Nevill. "Six Points of Stagecraft in *The Winter's Tale*," *Shakespeare Survey*, XI (1958), 31–41.

Cohen, Gustav. Histoire de la Mise-en-scène dans le Théâtre Religieux Français du Moyen-Age. Paris, 1926.

Coleridge, Samuel. Coleridge's Shakespearean Criticism. Edited by Thomas M. Raysor. 2 vols. New York, 1930.

Cooper, Thomas. Thesaurus linguae Romanae et Brittaniae. London, 1565.

Craik, T. W., "*Much Ado About Nothing*," *Scrutiny*, XIX (1953), 297–316.

Cutts, John P. "Music and the Supernatural in *The Tempest*," *Music and Letters*, XXXIX (1958), 347–58.

Davies, Sir John. The Poems of Sir John Davies. Edited by Clare Howard. New York, 1941.

Deimling, Hermann and Dr. Matthews, eds. The Chester Plays. 2 vols. London, 1916. Early English Text Society.

Doran, Madeleine. Endeavors of Art. Madison, 1954.

Dowden, Edward. Shakespere. New York, 1918.

Dunn, E. Catherine. "The Storm in *King Lear*," *Shakespeare Quarterly*, III (1952), 329–34.

Edwards, Philip. "Shakespeare's Romances: 1900–1957," *Shakespeare Survey*, XI (1958), 1–18.

Evans, Bertrand. Shakespeare's Comedies. Oxford, 1960.

Farmer, John, ed. Sir Clyomon and Sir Clamydes. Amersham, 1913. Students' Facsimile Edition.

—— The Trial of Chivalry. Amersham, 1913. Students' Facsimile Edition.

Firth, C. H. and R. S. Rait, eds. Acts and Ordinances of the Interregnum.

Frank, Grace. The Medieval French Drama. Oxford, 1954.

3 vols. London, 1911.

Frye, Northrop. Anatomy of Criticism. Princeton, 1957.

——, ed. The Penguin Shakespeare: The Tempest. Baltimore, 1959.

Furness, H. H. The Variorum Shakespeare: Cymbeline. Philadelphia, 1913.

———— The Variorum Shakespeare: The Tempest. Philadelphia, 1892.

———— The Variorum Shakespeare: The Winter's Tale. Philadelphia, 1898.

Furnivall, F. J., ed. The Digby Mysteries. London, 1882. The New Shakespeare Society.

———— and Alfred W. Pollard, eds. The Macro Plays. London, 1904. Early English Text Society.

————, Edmund Brock, and W. A. Clouston, eds. Originals and Analogues of Some of Chaucer's "Canterbury Tales." London, 1888. The Chaucer Society.

Garter, Thomas. The Most Virtuous and Godly Susanna. Edited by B. Ifor Evans and W. W. Greg. London, 1937. Malone Society Reprints.

Gayley, C. M., ed. Representative English Comedies. 3 vols. New York, 1903–14.

Giraldi Cinthio, Giovanbattista. Gli Hecatommithi. 2 vols. Monte Regale, 1565.

Granville-Barker, Harley. Prefaces to Shakespeare: Second Series. London, 1930.

Greene, Robert. The Life and Works of Robert Greene. Edited by Alexander B. Grosart. 15 vols. London, 1881–86.

———— The Plays and Poems of Robert Greene. Edited by J. Churton Collins. 2 vols. Oxford, 1905.

Greg, W. W., ed. The Interlude of Calisto and Melebea. London, 1908. Malone Society Reprints.

———— Pericles (1609). London, 1940.

———— The Rare Triumphs of Love and Fortune. London, 1930. Malone Society Reprints.

Griffiths, John, ed. Certain Sermons or Homilies Appointed to be Read in Churches in the Times of Queen Elizabeth. London, 1908.

Halio, Jay Leon. " 'Traitor' in *All's Well* and *Troilus and Cressida*." *Modern Language Notes*, LXXII (1957), 408–9.

Harington, Sir John. Nugae Antiquae. London, 1775.

Herrtage, Sidney J. H., ed. The Early English Versions of the Gesta Romanorum. London, 1879. Early English Text Society.

Heuser, W. *"Dux Moraud*, einzelrolle aus einem verlorenen drama des 14. jahrhunderts." *Anglia*. XXX (1907), 180–208.

Hockey, Dorothy C. "Notes, Notes, Forsooth . . ." *Shakespeare Quarterly*, VIII (1957), 353–58.

Holinshed, Raphael. Chronicles of England, Scotland and Ireland. 6 vols. London, 1807–08.

Holland, Norman N. "*Measure for Measure*: The Duke and the Prince," *Comparative Literature*, XI (1959), 16–20.

Horstmann, C. "A Tale of an Incestuous Daughter (Rawlinson ms. 118)" *Archiv für das Studium der Neueren Sprachen und Litteraturen*, Band 79 (1887), 421–24.

Hunter, G. K., ed. The Arden Shakespeare: All's Well That Ends Well. Cambridge, 1959.

Hurstfield, Joel. The Queen's Wards. New York, 1960.

Izard, Thomas C. George Whetstone. New York, 1942.

Johnson, Samuel, ed. The Plays of William Shakespeare. 8 vols. London, 1765.

Jonson, Ben. Every Man In His Humour. Edited by Henry Holland Carter. New Haven, 1921.

——— Poems. Edited by George Burke Johnson. Cambridge, Mass., 1955.

Jordan, John Clark. Robert Greene. New York, 1915.

Kermode, Frank, ed. The Arden Shakespeare: The Tempest. London, 1954.

Knight, G. Wilson. The Crown of Life. London, 1947.

——— The Wheel of Fire. London, 1930.

Kökeritz, Helge and C. T. Prouty, eds. Shakespeare's Comedies, Histories and Tragedies: A Facsimile Edition. New Haven, 1954.

——— Shakespeare's Pronunciation. New Haven, 1953.

Lang, Andrew. "*All's Well That Ends Well*," *Harper's Magazine*, LXXXIV (1892), 213–27.

——— "*Much Ado About Nothing*," *Harper's Magazine*, LXXXIII (1891), 489–502.

Lancaster, H. Carrington. "Hermione's Statue," *Studies in Philology*, XXIX (1932), 233–38.

Lascelles, Mary. Shakespeare's "Measure for Measure." London, 1953.

Latimer, Hugh. Sermons. Edited by Rev. George Elwes Corrie. Cambridge, 1844. Parker Society.

Lawrence, W. W. Shakespeare's Problem Comedies. New York, 1931.

Leavis, F. R. "The Criticism of Shakespeare's Later Plays: A Caveat." *Scrutiny*, X (1942), 339–45.

——— "The Greatness of *Measure for Measure*." *Scrutiny*, X (1942), 234–47.

Lee, Sidney. "Shakespeare and the Spanish Inquisition," *Living Age*, xxvi (1922), 460–66.

Leech, Clifford. "The Theme of Ambition in *All's Well That Ends Well*," *ELH*, XXI (1954), 17–29.

Legouis, E. "La Comtesse de Rousillon," *English,* I (1937), 399–404.

Lintilhac, Eugène. Histoire Générale du Théâtre en France. 5 vols. Paris, 1904–11.

Loomis, Laura Hibbard. "Secular Dramatics in the Royal Palace, Paris, 1378, 1389, and Chaucer's 'Tregetoures'," *Speculum,* XXXIII (1958), 242–55.

Luther, Martin. What Luther Says: An Anthology. Edited by Ewald M. Plass. 3 vols. St. Louis, 1959.

Lyly, John. The Complete Works of John Lyly. Edited by R. W. Bond. 3 vols. Oxford, 1902.

Mahood, M. M. Shakespeare's Wordplay. London, 1957.

Manly, J. M. "The Miracle Play in Mediaeval England," *Essays by Divers Hands, Being the Transactions of the Royal Society of Literature of the United Kingdom,* New Series, VII (1927), 133–53. Edited by Margaret L. Woods.

Matthews, Honor. Character and Symbol in Shakespeare's Plays. Cambridge, 1962.

Maxwell, Baldwin. The Penguin Shakespeare: The Winter's Tale. Baltimore, 1956.

Maxwell, J. C., ed. The New Cambridge Shakespeare: Cymbeline. Cambridge, 1960.

Montaigne, Michael de. Essayes. Edited by Ernest Rhys. Translated by John Florio. 3 vols. London, 1933.

Moorman, F. W., ed. The Arden Shakespeare: The Winter's Tale. London, 1912.

Muir, Kenneth. Shakespeare as Collaborator. London, 1960.

Neill, J. K. "More Ado About Claudio: An Acquittal for the Slandered Bridegroom," *Shakespeare Quarterly,* III (1952), 91–107.

Ninane, Lucie. "Un Chef-d'oeuvre de Thierry Bouts Aux Musees Royaux," *Bulletin des Musees Royaux des Beaux-Arts de Bruxelles,* VI (1957).

Nosworthy, J. M., ed. The Arden Shakespeare: Cymbeline. Cambridge, Mass., 1955.

Nowell, Alexander. A Catechism Written in Latin (1570). Edited by G. E. Corrie. Translated by Thomas Norton. Cambridge, 1853. Parker Society.

Owst, G. R. Literature and Pulpit in Medieval England. Cambridge, 1933.

Page, Nadine, "The Public Repudiation of Hero," *PMLA,* L (1935), 739–44.

Paris, Gaston and Ulysse Robert, eds. Miracles de Nostre Dame par Person-nages. 8 vols. Paris, 1876–93.

Parker, M. D. H. The Slave of Life. London, 1955.

Partridge, Eric. Dictionary of Slang and Unconventional English. New York, 1961.

Penn, Dorothy. The Staging of the "Miracles de Nostre Dame par Person-nages" of Ms. Cangé. New York, 1933.

Perkins, William. A Discourse of Conscience. London, 1596.

Petit de Juleville, L. Histoire du Théâtre en France. 2 vols. Paris, 1880.

Pettet, E. C. Shakespeare and the Romance Tradition. London, 1949.

Pickering, Danby, ed. The Statutes at Large. 6 vols. Cambridge, 1762.

Prouty, C. T. The Sources of "Much Ado About Nothing." New Haven, 1950.

Quiller-Couch, Sir Arthur and John Dover Wilson, eds. The New Cam-bridge Shakespeare: All's Well That Ends Well. Cambridge, 1929.

———— and John Dover Wilson, eds. The New Cambridge Shakespeare: The Winter's Tale. Cambridge, 1931.

———— Shakespeare's Workmanship. Cambridge, 1937.

Reed, Arthur W. Early Tudor Drama. London, 1926.

Renwick, William Lindsay and W. W. Greg, eds. John of Bordeaux. London, 1936.

de Rojas, Fernando. Celestina, or the Tragicke-Comedy of Calisto and Melibea. Edited by H. Warner Allen. Translated by James Mabbe. London, 1894.

Rossiter, A. P. Angel with Horns. Edited by Graham Storey. New York, 1961.

———— English Drama from Early Times to the Elizabethans. London, 1950.

Schanzer, Ernest. "The Marriage Contracts in *Measure for Measure*," *Shakespeare Survey*, XIII (1960), 81–89.

Sehrt, Ernst Theodor. Vergebung Und Gnade Bei Shakespeare. Stuttgart, 1952.

Siegel, Paul N. "Leontes A Jealous Tyrant," *Review of English Studies*, n. s. I (1950), 302–7.

Smith, Charles G. Spenser's Theory of Friendship. Baltimore, 1935.

Smith, Lucy Toulmin, ed. The York Plays. Oxford, 1885.

Spenser, Edmund. The Poetical Works of Edmund Spenser. Edited by J. C. Smith and E. de Selincourt. Oxford, 1912.

Spivack, Bernard. Shakespeare and the Allegory of Evil. New York, 1958.

Stephenson, A. A. "The Significance of *Cymbeline*," *Scrutiny*, X (1942), 329–38.

Stubbes, Phillip. The Anatomy of Abuses. Edited by Frederick J. Furnivall. London, 1876. New Shakespeare Society.

Swan, Charles and Wynnard Hooper, eds. Gesta Romanorum. New York, 1959.

Tillyard, E. M. W. Shakespeare's Last Plays. London, 1938.

Traver, Hope. The Four Daughters of God. Philadelphia, 1907.

Traversi, Derek. Shakespeare: The Last Phase. New York, 1955.

Turner, Robert Y. "Dramatic Conventions in *All's Well That Ends Well*," *PMLA*, LXXV (1960), 497–502.

Tuve, Rosemond. "A Medieval Commonplace in Spenser's Cosmology," *Studies in Philology*, XXX (1933), 133–47.

van Doren, Mark. Shakespeare. New York, 1939.

Watkins, W. B. C. Shakespeare and Spenser. Princeton, 1950.

Weston, Jessie L. From Ritual to Romance. Cambridge, 1920.

Wilson, Harold S. "Action and Symbol in *Measure for Measure* and *The Tempest*," *Shakespeare Quarterly*, IV (1953), 375–84.

Index